WHEN MEN DON'T CRY AND OTHER PLAYS FOR TEENS

Hearing the Voices of Today's Youths

Book Four

SAMUEL WILLIAMS

PARTRIDGE
A Penguin Random House Company

To order additional copies of this book, contact
Toll Free 800 101 2657 (Singapore)
Toll Free 1 800 81 7340 (Malaysia)
orders.singapore@partridgepublishing.com

www.partridgepublishing.com/singapore

TABLE OF CONTENTS

A Note from the Author

These plays have been written as much for teaching as for enjoyment. While many may relate and relegate them to a specific group or location, as the author of them all, I would readily confront this mischaracterization of their collective contents, reach and intent. Their messages are universal and their applications are timeless. There is much more to them than meets the eye. I sincerely hope that you will enjoy them yet take from them their true intent, purpose and power.

SPECIAL ACKNOWLEDGEMENTS

Any time a book such as this is written, without question there are many people to whom special recognition is due. As such I would like to recognize:

God: For your motivation, inspiration, insight and gifting to complete this task.

Sharleen (My wife): For being that constant support system and for granting me the time and space required to accomplish this task.

Samuel and Shundalynn (Our children): For your inspiration, motivation, support and faith in me.

Ruby Williams (My mother): For your constant love, support and listening ear.

Geraldine, Bevelyn, Joanne, Patricia and Sonya (My sisters): For all the prayers, support, confidence and love each of you shows me every day of my life.

Rev (Dr.) Christopher Lowe (Friend and mentor): For being that spiritual brother and advisor that I definitely needed.

I would like to also recognize the individuals whose lives inspired me to write the plays which appear in this four volume series. Thank you for sharing a deeply private and protected part of yourselves with me. I pray that I have done your experiences justice.

BLENDING
COLORS

CAST OF CHARACTERS

Mother (Bipsey)
Terror
Stripes
Bonz
Max
Simp
Blockers
Freeze
Ice
Scratch
Policeman
Father (Zeeke)
Terrance (Bipsey's and Zeeke's son)
Grandma
Doctor
MK
OG (Blood)
OG (Crips)
Slasher
Blade
Caper

*Some gang members' names are changed in the final house scene. The characters are the same, however, they are referred to by their given and not their street names in the final scene.

(The action opens in the bedroom of the grandmother who is the proud and wise matriarch of the family. She is in a jolly mood and insists upon giving the family's physician a difficult time as he desperately tries to conclude an exam on her. The family's home is rather mundane and it displays many visual indicators of the long years the family has lived there.)

GRANDMA

Can't think of no reason in the world why it ought to take you so long just to put that thing (pointing to the doctor's stethoscope) on my chest, your finger on my wrist, and a thermostat in my mouth . . .

DOCTOR

Sh-h-h-h!! (Checking her pulse and heart rate. Finishes and makes a notation.) And besides, it's thermometer.

GRANDMA

What you say?

DOCTOR

I said it's *thermometer,* Maxine. Not *thermostat.* Thermostats regulate the temperature in your house, or a building, or in your car. On the other hand a "ther-mon-e-ter" lets us know how hot or how cold the inside of your body is. OK?

GRANDMA

You look a here, Mr. Fancy pants . . . .

DOCTOR

Alright. Don't you go there on me, girl. Now you know I've known you all of your life . . . and I don't care one bit if I am your doctor either. Now if you go around here calling me Mr. Fancy Pants, I bet I'll take off old Roscoe (Tugging on his belt beneath his jacket) and . . .

GRANDMA

Aw-w-w shut up! You ain't gonna do no more than you use to do when we were little and I use to beat you up every day.

DOCTOR

Max! I know you didn't just lay right there in front of my face and tell that wonderful sounding lie. Why I use to whip you three times a day before breakfast, young lady. And twice more before noon. (Grandma begins sitting up as if she is trying to get out of bed. The doctor looks at her quizzically and earnestly.) Max . . . where you going? (Family members come over to assist her.)

BIPSEY

(Taking her by the arm but unsure just what to do.) What are you trying to do, Mama? Where are you trying to go?

GRANDMA

Just trying to move away from him a little bit so when the good Lord sends down his lightning, won't none of it hit me. (Laughter) 'Cause when we were kids we use to say "Liar! Liar! Pants on fire!" And I for one sure don't want to be on fire today. (More laughter) Oh no. Too hot for that!

BIPSEY

Oh, Ma!

ZEEKE

Good one, Ma! You got him that time!

DOCTOR

Yeah she did. You got me that time, Max. I owe you one.

GRANDMA

One? Don't you fool yourself! I been getting you all your life. You can't ever count how many you owe me. What your thermostat say anyway?

ZEEKE

Now Mama, he told you it's a thermometer and not a thermostat!

GRANDMA

Hush your mouth up, Zeeke. I'm talking to Mr. Fancy Pants now. (Doctor looks over his glasses and faints at his belt.)

DOCTOR

The (accenting) thermometer says your body temperature is well within normal range.

GRANDMA

How well?

DOCTOR

An even ninety-nine.

GRANDMA

Ninety-nine? Then why I'm sweating like a sow at a fourth of July bar-b-que? (No answer from the doctor who is busy writing a prescription.) And how my heart sound on that telescope thing you got 'round your neck?

BIPSEY

*Steth*oscope, Ma.

GRANDMA

Once again. I was attempting to engage in a confidential dialogue with my personal physician regarding the current status of my *personal* and immediate health. Ha! Ha! Ha! See y'all didn't even know I could talk like that did you? See. Grandma full of tricks, ain't I? Ha! Ha! Whew!

DOCTOR

Tricks or not, Max. I want you in bed and resting for another 10 to 14 days. (She prepares to say something. He raises his finger and stops her.) I mean it, Max. This has nothing to do with our friendship. Nothing. But it does have everything in the world to do with your health. Now I need you to obey me. For once in your life anyway. Alright?

GRANDMA

Author . . . You've been a friend for as long as I can remember. And I appreciate that. And you're a good doctor too. Not to mention you never charge me a penny for nothing, no matter how many times you have to come out here and pay me visit after visit. And I appreciate that too. But I ain't crazy, Author. I ain't no doctor . . . but I'm not a fool either.

BIPSEY

Now, Grandma . . .

GRANDMA

No, baby. Now y'all listen to me while I got most the mind . . . and the strength . . . and the will to tell you this. I'm okay. I mean with . . . with leaving . . . when my time comes. (Grandson Terrance enters the room and stands by his mother. She puts her arms around his shoulder.)

ZEEKE

Cut it out, Ma! Cut it. Cut it. Cut it. We're not hearing any of that kind of talk today.

GRANDMA

Zeeke, some things you don't have to tell people. Nobody has to tell them. Their families don't have to tell them. Their friends don't have to tell them. Their doctors don't have to tell them. They just know. And when you know . . . you just know. Angels. (They all look to each other quizzically.) Angels. Y'all do know what those are, don't you? They tell you. That's their job you know. They're messengers . . . sent from God . . . to tell us stuff. Angels. You did your best, Author. And if you could have done more, I know in my heart you would have . . . and you wouldn't have charged me one penny for that either. But some things lie beyond the understanding of the doctor and their stethoscopes, you know. Yeah, they do. But, you, Author, you've been the best friend and doctor anybody could have ever been and any sick person could have ever hoped to have had looking after them. You're something special. How y'all young people say it? Come over here and give me some love boy! (He goes over and gives her a hug and kisses her on the cheek.) Thank you, Arthur.

DOCTOR

This is your . . . (stops and clears his throat as he tries to fight back tears) . . . your prescri . . . (sniffle. sniffle.)

GRANDMA

And I thank you. Bipsey, take this and go call it in to the local pharmacy for Mama, baby. (She does. Wipes tears from her eyes and gives Grandma a hug and kiss.) Thank you, baby. You go with her, Zeeke. (Trying not to show her rising emotions.) She might need you to help her dial that fancy cell phone of hers or something. Can't ever tell now-a-days you know. (He hugs her and kisses her on the cheek then leaves.) You're a doctor, Arthur. That means that you probably got an office full of sick people complaining right now about how long they've been waiting to see you. Now get on out of here and go take care of them. Go ahead. (He never looks back at her. He grabs his bags and begins walking briskly toward the door.) Author! (He stops.) You've been just like a brother to me . . . *ALL* my life . . . and I just want you to know that I really do appreciate that.

DOCTOR

What do you mean I *have* been?

GRANDMA

Angels, Author. Angels. They never lie . . . and they're never wrong. I always did say if anybody had either a lying or ignorant angel that would be the biggest mess they'd ever have to deal with in this life or the next one. (Laughs at her own joke. Then becomes serious again) Thank you, Author. Now go on and get out of here and take care of the ones you were put on this earth to help. Believe me, I'm just fine. (Author exits.) (To her young grandson, JT who is standing near.) Now why is Grandma's little man crying? No need to. None a bit. Hey! Grandma's got a special task for you. You up to it? (Zeeke and Bipsey are re-entering the room.)

BIPSEY

What you got for him to do, Ma?

GRANDMA

I want him to take this letter I wrote to your brother.

ZEEKE

Albert?!?

GRANDMA

He's still your brother, Zeeke . . . and he's still my son. Bone of my bone and flesh of me and your daddy's flesh. I just want to see him. That's all.

ZEEKE

Mama, word on the streets is that Albert's hooked up with some of those gang members . . . and everybody else he shouldn't be having dealings with.

BIPSEY

It's not like you didn't teach him better, Ma.

GRANDMA

Whether I taught Albert or not, or what I taught him isn't the issue any more. I just need him to get here . . . and quick. Now I don't care what kind of gang that boy has hooked up with, I'm still his mama. And my angel has told me . . . I need to see him real soon.

ZEEKE

Give it to me, Ma. I'll go. This is no job for a little kid like him. That area where Albert hangs out is a pretty rough side of town.

GRANDMA

Don't want him to do a single thing except deliver this letter to Albert for me, son, then come straight back home. There's plenty daylight left. If he leaves now, he'll be able to do that for his grandma and get back here before the sun sets and the street lights come on. I imagine he'll be alright doing that, don't you?

ZEEKE

Sounds like he ought to be. Can't imagine much happening to him in broad daylight on public streets. I believe he can handle it, Ma. (To his son) Just deliver the letter, JT, then get your butt from over there just as quickly as you can. And if you need to, you stop someplace and just give me or your mom a call and let us know exactly where you are and one or both or us will be there in no time flat to get you. Got me? (JT nods approvingly).

GRANDMA

To my knowledge, Albert's a pretty popular character around the area where he hangs out. But if you don't see him anywhere within a block or two either way of 4th Avenue and Vineyard Road, don't wander off around in that area looking for him. You can just bring Grandma her letter back and she'll send you back out there to deliver it on another day. You don't have to worry yourself about it.

We'll be sure to get this letter to Albert before it's too late. After that, he has to make a decision whether he ever wants to see his mama alive again or not. (They look at each other as if surprised to hear her say that.) I guess now I'll know which family is *really* the most important one in his life. (Hands the letter to her grandson.) Here you go, JT. Go ahead and be safe out there, boy!

BIPSEY

Ma, from what I've heard Albert doesn't hang out around 4th and Vineyard anymore.

GRANDMA

No? Then where does he hand out these days?

BIPSEY

The last I heard is that he and his (gesturing) "boys" now hang out on the corners of Brown Avenue and 13th Street. Right down the street from the Blue Door Club. JT shouldn't have any problem finding that area, after all everybody knows exactly where the Blue Door is.

ZEEKE

(To his son) You still think you can handle this, son? (shakes his head) You up to this? Like I said before, it tends to get a little rough in that area sometimes, but that's mostly after the sun sets and the streets get dark. But by that time you're be back here safe and sound with us. Unless you want me to deliver that for your grandma. I can do it if you want me to.

TERRANCE

It's only a few blocks over, Dad. Nothing to it. I got it. I'll go and do a good job, Grandma . . . and I won't come back until I get this in Uncle Albert's very own hands . . . just for you. Love you, Grandma! Love you, Ma! Love you, Dad! Be back soon! (Starts to exit)

ZEEKE

Terrance!!

TERRANCE

Yeah, Dad?

ZEEKE

Your uncle may or may not be known by his real name, Albert, on the streets. When they join up with those street gangs they try to take on a new imagine, a new identity, a new façade. So they call themselves something new as well. Your uncle's street name is Bonz. So if you have to ask anybody about him, be sure you ask for Bonz and not Uncle Albert. OK?

TERRANCE

Should I ask for Uncle Bonz or just Bonz?

ZEEKE

Bonz, son. Just Bonz.

TERRANCE

Bonz! Got it, Dad. (exits)

GRANDMA

That's a good child there. Not many like that left in the world today. I'll tell y'all the truth. I don't know of anything in the whole wide world that could ever separate this doting Grandma from that little boy there! He's just a down right good child.

ZEEKE

Yeah, you're right about that, Ma. I still say he's destined to be the first medical doctor in this family.

BIPSEY

That's my baby! Mama, we'll be back soon, okay? We're going to pay a couple of bills and pick up your prescription that I just phoned in.

GRANDMA

Good! Now that the house is going to be quiet for a little while, maybe I can finally get some sleep.

BIPSEY

You ready to go, Babe?

ZEEKE

Ready as I'll ever be.

BIPSEY

Let's go then. See you I a little bit, Ma.

GRANDMA

Take your time, baby. Like I said, I'm gonna take advantage of the quite and get me a few minutes of much needed shut eye. Y'all go ahead now. And don't worry about rushing back here just to wake me out of my nap. I've been trying to get me some shut eye for the last hour or two. Pull the door up tight and lock it on your way out. (Yawning) My Lord, I can hear my bed calling my name.

LIGHTS

ACT II

Music is blaring. Drinking and drugging are evident. Terrance wanders onto the stage [Cressions' territory]. Their OG is alerted to his approach by members of the gang. He immediately directs two of his members to apprehend the trespasser. Two Cressionss accost the young boy and rough house him back over to the OG.)

TERRANCE

Hey dog!! What's up with that man? Hey man chill out!! What's up with y'all, dog? (The gang members release him. He is gathering himself when he notices the OG has risen and is giving him a not so friendly once over.) Yeah? So who you s'pose to be?

CRESSION OG

(Slaps Terrance hard across his face) SHUT UP, FOOL!!! (Terrance collects himself and starts after OG. The gang members quickly step between them.) Ha, ha, ha, ha. So this FOOL wants to play hard ball with OG. (Nods. Terrance is kneed in the stomach and beaten about the face. OG goes over and stabs him in the stomach. He falls to the ground.) Fool just don't know. Nobody plays hard ball with OG. Get this hunk of trash off Cressions' turf!! (Terrence's body is dragged from the Cressions' territory by two lower ranking gang members. Bloodied and badly beaten, Terrance is spotted by Exterminators as he painfully and unknowingly staggers into their territory. He is holding the stab wound and obviously has no idea where he is. Exterminators are jamming, drinking and generally "chilling" in their own area.)

STRIPES

(Pointing across stage to the staggering and collapsing Terrance.) OG, we got company.

EXTERMINATORS OG

Get the brother and bring him here. (Terrance collapses before the bloods reach him. As Max tries to help him back to his feet, he notices the blood on his hand. He quickly rolls Terrance onto his back and gives him a visual once over inspection.)

MAX

Somebody done knifed this fool real good man.

STRIPES

Ain't nothing to do but just leave the brother here to die.

EXTERMINATORS OG

(Pensively) Can't do that. Everybody knows whose territory this is. We leave him here and no doubt about it, we'll get blamed for this knifing just as sure as we're alive.

BLOCKERS

Yeah, you right, OG. We can't just leave the brother like this—not here anyway. But if we 911 for help and they come and pick him up from here, we still gonna get named for this knifing just the same, OG.

SIMP

Alright already. I keep hearing the problem, but I ain't heard nobody come up with the solution. All I need to know is what do we need to do to get out of this situation clean 'cause we don't need no face time with no cops. So what's our out, brother? How we gonna get outta this one? Yo! Check him out, man! The brother's trying to talk. Hey, man, y'all chill. I'm trying to hear the brother. Could be saying something important, man. (Places his head near Terrance's mouth. MK enters while Simp is trying to talk with Terrance. He sees his relative and runs over to him. He pushes Simp out of the way and begins to talk to Terrance.)

MK

TERRANCE! TERRANCE!! Who did this, man? Who did this to you? TERRANCE ANSWER ME! Who did this, man?

TERRANCE

(Weak.) I heard'em say Cressions. They said I was in their area . . . and that I wasn't one of them. So they knifed me and threw me off their turf.

MK

C'mon, TERRENCE!! You know them boys, cuz!! Why'd you even go out like that man? You know if you ain't one of them you can't be caught in their area.

TERRANCE

(Removing a bloody letter from his pocket and handing it to his relative.) I wasn't doing anything wrong, MK. I just promised my Grandma Max I'd get this to Uncle Albert for her. I didn't do nothing, man. I swear.

MK

I know you didn't, Lil' Cuz. I know you didn't. 'Cause I know you, Cuz and I know you too smart to just go walking up in them boys' areas and to do anything stupid enough to cause them to do this kind of damage to you. (Looks at the letter. Seems confused.) Bonz? Bonz? That's who trying to get this to?

TERRANCE

Yeah. I think he belongs to the Cressians. You know. The ones who operate over there not far from the Blue Door Club. My Dad said he's with them now.

MK

Yeah. They use to go by . . . 1 . . . 8 . . . 7 Street Gang. But the cops and the authorities got so hot on their trail that they had to take on another name. So now they go by the name of Cressions. I don't get this, man. How come your old man let you over here if he knows gangs operate in this area?

TERRANCE

He said he thought I'd be safe because it was daylight outside. I was suppose to get this to Uncle Albert, er, Bonz, and then head straight back home before the street lights came on.

MK

Word. I can feel your pops on that one except you can't bank on nothing operating normal out here dog. Normal is for normal people. These are gang-controlled street, lil bro! They decide what's normal out here. Hey, man, you sure it was the Cressions who did this to you?

TERRANCE

Yeah.

MK

You sure, Lil' Cuz?

TERRANCE

Yeah. I'm sure. They're the ones who did this to me. I remember seeing on a jacket one of them had on. (cough, cough) It's important, MK. Please get it to Uncle Al . . . Bonz . . . for my grandma. Please. Grandma's sick and she wants to see you *and* Bonz . . . before . . . well, you know . . . before something bad happens to her. Just get this to him. I promised Grandma that I would get it to him myself, but now (cough) don't look like I'll be able to. (Frowns and groans) It hurts, MK. It hurts so bad.

MK

You hang in there, lil' cuz. I'll get you some help. (Yells to his brothers.) Don't just stand there!! Somebody call 911. Don't you see the brother needs help. (No one moves.) NINE ONE ONE SOMEBODY!!!

EXTERMINATORS OG

(Goes over and places his hand on MK's shoulder) MK we can't 911 this scene, brother. Yo' boy rolled up in the Crissons' area and got himself knifed for his efforts—ever how innocent they may have been. Still you know the rules out here, man. Nobody who ain't with the group can roll up on the real estate. So they took care of business and threw him out for dead. Now he's here in on our turf . . . Exterminators' turf, brother. And if any one of us calls for help for your cousin, the authorities will say we did this anyway and will try to pend an attempted murder on one of us. And from that point on we're gonna have problems with the cops and every other official in this city. And you know that too, brother.

MK

You think I care about trouble—with the cops— OG? Do you? If I cared about cop trouble I never would have joined a gang in the first place. Now this is my *family*, OG. And he's DYING. And I need somebody to call 911 so I can get my lil' cuz here to the hospital and save his life.

EXTERMINATORS OG

Don't raise up on me, MK. I don't care nothing about your cousin being hurt; this is still my empire and I still run it like I see fit. And I already said, we ain't calling no help for this brother. Sorry.

STRIPES

(Kneeling over Terrance with his ear near his chest.) Hey!! This guy is hardly breathing anymore! We gotta do something quick or he's won't make, brothers.

MK

(Rushes over to Terrance and shoves Stripes out of the way) Get out of the way! (Kneels down and listens for signs of respiration. Visually distraught. OG signals for two of his members.)

EXTERMINATORS OG

Put him somewhere safe (hands one of them his cellular phone) then call for an ambulance. Then get the heck out of there quick and get back here. Watch your back and make sure there ain't no tail on you. Like I said, we don't need no beef with the authorities, especially over something we didn't do. (Two members exit carrying the Terrance. MK starts to exit . . .) Going somewhere, MK?

MK

You darn right I am. I got a special delivery to make, OG.

EXTERMINATORS OG

OG didn't give you no delivery to make and no permission to make no delivery for nobody else either. So where you going, MK?

MK

I respect you as my leader, OG, but what you got to understand is that my very own flesh and blood cousin just got knifed trying to deliver this letter to Bonz, OG. Now if it's the last thang I do, I'm gonna finish making this delivery for him. That's where I'm going, OG, and I'm making this delivery . . . with or without your permission. (OG pulls a handgun and points it at MK.)

EXTERMINATORS OG

You still one of my boys, MK, and you know for sure that I ain't got nothing but big love for you. But I'm the man up in here, MK. Me . . . not you . . . and not your cousin . . . not his grandma . . . . and not Bonz. I'm the Exterminator OG and I ain't going to be disrespected on my own turf by one of my own members. Clear? So you best SIT DOWN and just chill out or against my will, and my love for you, Old OG won't have no other choice but to make your family two members smaller.

MK

A man's gotta do what a man's gotta do, OG. I ain't going against your authority, OG. I ain't got nothing but mad love for you and all the Exterminators, and you know that, but this is something I got to do no matter what. All I can do is hope you can understand where I'm coming from, OG. Now you got a gun and all I've got is a bloody letter. OG, either you go on and use your gun on me or watch me walk out of here to deliver this letter. But we both gotta do what we gotta do. And either it way it goes down, OG, I just want you to know I understand. (Pauses and gives OG time to act.) I 'preciate that, OG. On the real I do. And I promise, I'll make it up to you somehow, someday. But right now, well, you know what I gotta do. Later, OG. (Starts to exit)

EXTERMINATORS OG

HEY!! (MK stops but never turns around. OG nods to the group to follow MK) Now you can walk. Exterminators got your back. (Just as the gang starts off Cappers and MK are returning from "dishing" Terrence.)

MK

My cousin . . . where did y'all put him, Cappers?

CAPPERS

We dropped him on the corners of 2nd and Truesland, right around the corner from Augusta General. Good news though. We saw this beat cop and told him we scoped some young boys fighting on the corner of 2nd and Truesland. Told him we thought it might be some gang activity about to go down. So he phoned in for backup and zoomed to the scene. Soon as he got there, he found Terrence. Within two minutes the ambulance from Angelico General was there and rushed him off to the ER. So I'm sure your lil' man's gonna be good to go in a day or so. You know Angelico General, don't you?

MK

Yeah, I know the place. It's the same one where my old man spent the last three months of his life. He died there six months ago. Gunshot wound. OG, can I see your phone? (OG visually examines him then thoughtfully hands him the phone. He dials and talks briefly) Hello. Hello. Yeah. Uh . . . uh . . . Like . . . uh . . . I'm the brother of Terrence Johnson. He was just brought in with stab wounds to the stomach. Yeah, thanks. I'll hold. (Pause) Er, er, uh, Rodney. Yeah Rodney Johnson. Older brother of Terrance Johnson. Y'all just wheeled him in minutes ago. Just trying to cop a status on my little brother. (Pause) Look lady,

I swear Terrence is my kid brother, but I just can't get to the hospital right now. That's all. I just want to know how he is. (Pause) Yes . . . yes . . . yes ma'am. I'm his older brother . . . er . . . and . . . er . . . I'm out of town and I can't be there right now. (Pause. Visually shocked.) I see. Thank you. Good bye. (Hands the phone back and drops his head) Dead on arrival. Cause of death was prolonged controllable bleeding. In other words, the nurse said, if he'd gotten there five minutes earlier, they probably could have saved him. Lil' Cuz. (Gives the phone back to OG. The gang proceeds.)

(The Crissons continue to party in their own territory when two of their members enter quickly and address the OG excitedly.)

SLASHER

OG! OG! We were just on the corners of 7th Ave and Martin Luther King, Jr. Blvd . . . .

TERROR

(Interrupting his friend.) Yeah, when we saw the Exterminators headed this way.

CRIP OG

What?!? Exterminators!! What are they doing in my area?

TERROR

Don't know, OG, but it sure was a lot of 'em though.

CRISSONS OG

(Announcing to the gang) Exterminators in our area. Let's go check this out.

(As the CRISSONS prepare to leave, they encounter the Exterminators in their area. The two groups are face to face. Each OG steps forward and faces the other. His "boys" are closely behind him "guarding his back.")

CRISSIONS OG

This is Crissons' territory, OG. You know that! And you know that you don't come in my world unless I invite you in, and I don't go in yours unless you do the same. So why you here with your boys, OG? And I sure do hope you got a real good reason too. Otherwise some of us just might not leave here today.

EXTERMINATORS OG

When a man's right, I give him credit for being right, OG. This *is* your territory. And I *am* trespassing. But I'm not here to fight or kill. I came here in peace. Understand?

CRESSIONS OG

Just say what you here for, OG. I don't need no nice words from you. You know me. I'm all about doing business and not so much about talking. Now what you want over here?

EXTERMINATORS OG

A young boy was knifed to death by someone in your gang today, OG.

CRISSONS OG

Knife to death? Well, if the boy's dead how you know who knifed him?

EXTERMINATORS OG

He told us before he died. His name was Jonathan Terrence Johnson.

BONZ

JT? (Coming forward) JT? *Knifed*? To *death*? JT?? Where is he? Where's his body? I've got to go! J . . . J . . . JT??

EXTERMINATOR OG

Bonz? (As if he hardly recognizes him.)

ICE

Yeah, he's Bonz? What's it to you?

BONZ

(To the CRISSONS' OG) Hey, brother, I've got to get to JT, man. Gotta find him. Oh-h-h man!! Not JT!

EXTERMINATOR OG

(MK passes the bloodied letter to his OG who then offers it to Bonze) This is yours. (Takes it carefully) JT was on his way to give this to you when your "brothers" (pointing to the rival gang members) roughed him up and knifed him to death earlier today.

BONZ

(Confused that his boys would do such a thing to his little cousin.) JT? JT? Y'all knifed little JT? Today? JT?

CRISSONS OG

Hey, he came on the turf, brother, and we didn't know who he was, Bonz! So just chill out, alright. It's all cool. It was an accident, ok?

BONZ

An accident? How the heck do you knife an innocent kid like that to death on an accident, OG. How??

BLADE

Hey, Bonz, you got to understand. We didn't know who he was. He could have been the heat for all we know.

BONZ

We? So you were in on it too, Blade? My closest friend? You helped to knife my innocent nephew to death too?

BLADE

Hey, dude, it wasn't like you're making it out to me, brother. Like I said before, we didn't know who that dude was, man. He could have been the heat for all we know.

BONZ

THE HEAT?? YOU FOOL!! JT WAS ONLY 14 YEARS OLD!! HOW DID YOU MISTAKE HIM FOR THE HEAT? (EMOTIONS WANING. Now becoming more reflective in nature and speech.) He was just trying to get this letter to me, that's all. Just get me this letter . . . and y'all killed him for that? Lil' JT. My flesh and blood nephew. My own family. Truth is since we grew up in the same house, and ate from the same table, and shared a bike, a bedroom, and even memories together—really he was more like the younger brother I never really had. And you—my so-called brothers—killed him—just because . . . .

CRISSONS OG

THEY SAID THEY DIDN'T KNOW WHO THE KID WAS, BONZ! YOU HEARD THEM!! So get rid of all the sentimental talk—now!! You heard what they said. So just take the apology and just let it ride, huh?

BONZ

(In total disbelief) I heard what they said? I heard what they said?? Is that what you just said to me, OG. I heard what they said? Yeah, yeah, OG. Your're right man. You're right. I did hear what they said. I really did.

CRISSONS OG

Good. Then let it go and let's get back to the business of getting some more trash out of our area.

BONZ

Not so fast, OG. 'Cause unlike you, I been listening real close to everything that's been said and even that that ain't been said since these boys showed up here on "our turf."

CRISSONS OG

What the hell are you talking about, Bonz. What's up with you, homie? You loosing it or something?

BONZ

Oh no, OG. I ain't loosing it. Matter of fact, you might say, I just found it, OG. See, I was listening *real* close to what's been said and what ain't been said, but it's been thought and felt and finally realized.

CRISSONS OG

Bonz, don't make me turn yo' pit bull brothers on you and mop up this street with what's left of you. And I hope you heard that.

BONZ

Yeah, OG, I heard it. But you know what else I heard, OG? You wanna know what else I heard? Listen real close now 'cause I think you seriously missed it. I heard that my fourteen year old nephew died today because he was stabbed TO DEATH over nothing! Nothing, OG!! Just trying to deliver a letter—a piece of paper—a note— to me from my mama—that's all. DELIVERING A NOTE, OG!!! And for that y'all took his whole life away from him! And all you can tell me is you didn't know who he was? Get over it? It was a mistake?

CRISSONS OG

You heard me loud and clear, Bonz and that's exactly what I said. Your cousin, nephew, son or whatever got knifed because he came walking up here on our turn and we DIDN'T KNOW WHO THE HECK HE WAS!!! He rose up on me in this camp, Bonz! On me!! OG!! Your boy rose up on me, and so me and the boys had to go on and take care of business the way I teach y'all to do it up in here. Yeah, we took yo' boy out! You know the rules up in here. I couldn't let him front on me in front of the boys and walk out of here like he hadn't done nothing!

BONZ

And so you and my so-called brothers killed a 14 year old innocent kid because he . . . um, how do you say it, boss man . . . he fronted on you in front of your boys. Why? I'm sorry but I must have missed it or misunderstood you when you explained that part of this fairy tale. You, a grown behind man gave orders to two other near grown young men to kill an innocent adolescent, why? What was that reason you gave again? Because he walked up on a piece of sidewalk that none of us owns—but we lay claim to it and try to control it as if it's ours personally—and *fronted* on you? And for THAT his whole life is gone? I can't believe I heard that fool say that this fourteen year old *child* could have been mistaken as the police. Come on, man! Which one of us up in here don't know what the po-po looks like, even when they come around here all dressed up in their undercover outfits. You asked me if I heard what that fool said. I did, but

31

you know what else I just heard? Until today I'd never heard it, because we were always the ones causing the pain and grief to others, but today I finally got a chance to feel for myself and to understand for myself just what we've been doing to other families and just how they feel when we do what we've been doing much too long to them. See, OG, while I was standing there *listening*, what I heard was that an innocent kid violated some make believe street laws that have been written, codified, ratified and activated by some out of control, authority hating, rebellious minded, loosers who try real hard at any cost to convince the whole world that though they have failed at everything they've ever attempted, they are still the man . . . the woman . . . the bomb . . . . the power . . . to respect. I heard that this gang of young people killed an innocent child, only an hour or so ago, and with no conscious or remorse for the innocent life they so casually took or the pain of the family, they all came right back here and laughed and drank and chilled as usual. I heard—and I now can see how you—a complete looser in life—have convinced our innocent and unsuspecting young minds to serve and honor you (staring into the Crissons' OG's eyes) more than we serve and honor our own souls, futures and families. And I heard young men and women confess to taking a part in an unnecessary and senseless killing of another bright and promising life in our community. And you know what, OG. Look around. All y'all. Look around. What 'cha see? Bin Laden? No Terrorists? No. A race war? No. A natural disaster? No. Just us. Once again—it's us doing what we seem to do best—destroying ourselves, our people, and our dreamers. Well, there went another dream up in smoke today ladies and gentlemen. Courtesy of you local neighborhood street gangs! Oh yeah, WE did it. We successfully robbed ourselves one more time. Yeah we did! So please, don't just stand there. Why don't you give yourselves a rousing round of applause. Aren't you proud of your work? Your efforts? Yourselves?

BLADE

Ease up, dog and just let it, go man. It's over. It's history. We did it. And we're sorry. But it's done. So get with the program and stop your whining. What else you want to hear from us, man? I know he was your flesh and blood, but for real, dog, this ain't the end of the world, you know. Just hear me out, man. Listen. We didn't do nothing wrong, man. Nothing! Your nephew stepped up on our territory and fronted on OG like he was the regulator up in this camp or something; so we did what we had to do. We dusted him. Plain and simple. Take it or leave it, but you know how this camp roll up in here.

BONZ

A fourteen year old boy accidently walked up on a piece of public property that nobody owns . . . but we try to control . . . and all he was trying to do was to deliver a letter to his uncle. Not take over our (gesturing) turf . . . not play some undercover role for the cops . . . not try to spy on us or turn anybody in to the police . . . but all he wanted to do was to give me a piece of paper from my mama, and y'all killed him. And now after you kill my nephew, you want to stand here in my face and tell me that one fourteen year old innocent boy walks up into this camp, and all y'all together killed him because all y'all thought that that was what y'all had to do. Brothers against brothers. Blacks against blacks. Poor against poor. Poverty against poverty. Inner city against inner city. Housing project against housing project. And you know the saddest part of this whole thing.? Check it out. When we get done "defending" our corners—our territory—our turf . . . guess what? We don't own jack! NOTHING. We still in poverty. We still live in the government's projects. We still have the highest crime, teen pregnancy, infant death, and high school drop out rates—not to mention the highest crime rate against each other. And, by the way, we can't look outside of ourselves to blame nobody else. 'Cause it ain't the white man. It ain't the Indian. It ain't the Jews. It ain't Bin Laden and it ain't the Taliban. It ain't the republicans or the democrats. It's just *us* doing this to ourselves. And the scary thing is that now we've gotten so comfortable doing this, that it don't even bother us no more. We don't even give a thought or a care about whether it's right or wrong. We just did it because somebody else told us to . . . because somebody said it was cool. Somebody else said it would make us look like tough guys. What a sad thang we've turned out to be.

CRISSONS OG

(Making his way quickly to Bonz. Grabbing him by the collar and jerking him face to face.) Shut up your whining, Bonz! Shut it up! It was a freaking mistake! Can't you see that? Can't you?!? Hey!! I'm sorry about your fourteen year old nephew man! I really am. I'm sorry. But right now ain't nothing I can do about it. Nothing! That's just the way it is. Just gotta live with what happened and just get over it. So let it go, man . . . and get on with your life. Accidents happen in this business all the time, dude, and you know that. (Extends his fist to give him dap?) So don't go playing dumb on me now.

BONZ

What *accident*? Call it what it really was, OG! This was no *accident*. What *accident* are *you* talking about, OG? This was a straight out *murder*. Which one of us here don't already know that? Even you know that's what it was, OG. But you want to pass it off to me as an accident? You gave the word to do it, OG! So why don't you act like a real man and stand up and go ahead and call it what it is? Murder, OG. Cold blooded murder. Of an innocent 14 year old boy. Trying to do nothing more than to deliver a note to his uncle. This was no accident, OG. No even. This was an authorized murder. And it was authorized by you.

CRIP OG

(Highly emotional. He senses he's losing the battle.) I said it was an accident, Bonz, and damn it that what it was! So as far as we're concerned this kid's death was an accident. You understand? Now, I told you to shut your mouth, Bonz. So maybe you had better just shut up right now before um forced to . . . .

BONZ

To what? To what? To pull out your blade? To put it to my throat? To say some intimidating words to me, then turn me into the same kind of *accident* y'all turned my nephew into earlier today? Is that what you'll be forced to do if I don't shut up, OG? Is it? (Snatches away. Walks to center stage. Slowly opens then begins reading the bloodied letter.) Dear Son, How is mama's favorite child doing? Well, I know you're doing better than mama because I've been diagnosed (the voice of the mother is slowly fading in) with cancer. Naw, the doctor didn't tell me, but my angel did. You know my angel always did keep me up on things. My doctor doesn't know that I already know this, but my angel told me that the cancer is already in the advance stages and that there really ain't much nobody can do now except to just try to keep me as comfortable as my old body will allow them to. I ain't got but one fear in this whole thing though, and that is that you won't decide to come home to see me in time. The angel says I'll be around for a few more days, but not as many as the children and the doctor may think. That is why I wrote you this letter. I don't want to leave without telling you face to face how much I still love you. So I sent this letter to you by Terrence, just hoping that after you'd read it, you would come off those streets long enough to spend some precious time with me before I go on home. You be sure to take extra good care of Terrance while he's out there. I know the only reason he volunteered to deliver this letter is because he knows how sick I am and everybody knows how much he loves his only uncle and wants to see him come home off the streets—and out of the gang. Terrance will do anything in the world to get you back with your real flesh and blood family, Bonz. You mean that much to him. Please do the right thing by him . . . and by me. He saw me when I started writing this letter a few days ago, and he told me then that he'd find you and get it to you even if it cost him his very life. But we all know it won't come to down to that. I love you, Bonz and I hope to see you and Terrance walk back through my bedroom door any minute now. And Bonz, whatever you do, don't let anything—NOTHING—happen to my grandchild. He's such a wonderful young man. God gave this family and this community a pure miracle when He gave us that boy. (Voice is now fading back from Grandma's to Bonz) Well I won't keep you, Son, but I will hope to see you real soon. Truth be told, Bonz, Terrence loves and misses you a whole lot too. And he desperately wants his favorite uncle in his life. I pray to God that we can all sit down around the table this weekend and enjoy a good old fashion Sunday family dinner like we use to. It'll do my heart and soul more good than you'll ever know. We'll let you make the potato salad. I always said you made the best potato salad in town every since you were eleven years old. God bless you, baby, and see you soon.

Ma and the family.

CRISSONS OG

Hey!! Where you going? I said where you going, Bonz?

SCRATCH

It's okay, OG; give him a little space.

TERROR

Yeah, cut him some slack, OG.

CRISSONS OG

SLACK?!! HE'S A CRISSON!! AND CRISSONS DON'T NEED SPACE! CRISSONS DON'T NEED SLACK!! CRISSONS NEED CRISSONS AND NOTHING OR NOBODY ELSE!!!

EXTERMINATORS OG

He's lost a close blood relative, OG. Let him grieve.

CRISSONS OG

You stay out of Crissons' business, Exterminator!!!

EXTERMINATORS OG

This is more than Crissons business, OG!! This is my business too!!

CRISSONS OG

How you figure?

EXTERMINATORS OG

'Cause he was my cousin too! His grandmother is my father's aunt. We both need some time with our family—and to grieve over our parts in this.

CRISSONS OG

You listen to me, OG. You can run your Exterminators like you want to, but I run these Crissons, and I say Crissons don't need no family other than other Crissons.

EXTERMINATORS OG

We're talking about this brother's dead nephew and his dying mother, OG! His mother!! Have you come to love this façade so much that you have totally lost contact with reality? His mother, OG. Yo' boy's *mother*. Now maybe that don't mean a lot to you. Maybe if someone brought you a note from your dying mama, it wouldn't move you to be human again. But that don't mean that's the way it is with him.

CRISSONS OG

You shut up!!!

ICE

OG, listen, Blade, Bonz, Blocker, Freeze, Simp . . . they're all my cousins too. And so is the Exterminators' OG . . . and so was JT. I just never said it to nobody. I know I should'da, but I wanted to be my own man and stand on my own two feet. See, I recognized JT when he came up in this camp. But I had to turn my back on my own blood relative just to be accepted in the group that killed him. I didn't know how to say, "Hey! Don't lay hands on that brother. That's my blood. My real flesh and blood. I had a golden opportunity to stand up on my own feet and be a man, but I didn't do it. Instead I punked out. Yeah. That's what I did. I punkout out. When the real test of true manhood came and stared me squared in the face, I failed miserably . . . again . . . inspite of being a member of this (emphasing) GANG that was suppose to give me so much courage and make me into such a big and tough man. I punked out. I didn't do what I thought the gang was would make me tough enough to do . . . and that was to be a real man in tough situations . . . in tough times. I didn't do it. With all of my so-called brothers around me, I still punked out when push came to shove. I betrayed my own flesh and blood. Yeah, that's what I did. I punked out when it counted the most. And it cost my little cousin his life. My cousin died because I showed more love to the gang than I showed to him. And so from that, I've learned one thing. And that is that right now is best time for me to be my own man and to make a decision to stand on my own two feet. And, OG, the truth is the more I look at this (gesturing to the opposing gang members) the more I ask myself why am I *really* here. I mean, I was one of the ones who helped to rough up my own blood kin. And I watched you jab your blade in the stomach of my own blood kin. And now you have me here ready to fight and kill another of my own blood kin. And I see you denying my own blood kin the right to go home and grieve properly with his family over the loss of his own nephew and his dying mother.

CRISSONS OG

'Cause we're CRISSONS!!! CRISSONS!! We don't need nobody else!

EXTERMINATORS OG

No, OG, you don't need nobody else. But right now he does—he needs his family!!

CRISSON OG

The Crissons *are* his family!!

EXTERMINATORS OG

And so are his sisters and brothers and aunts and uncles and grandparents and cousins.

CRISSONS OG

Don't you come up on my turf and boost up this kind of confusion in my Crissons, you slime! (Goes after him. The gang members restrain him.) Let me go!! Let me go!! Take your hands off of me!!

EXTERMINATORS OG

So that you can do what, OG? Do more killing? Bring about more grief. Divide our young people more? Don't you see what's happening here? We're killing each other every single day . . . and for no good reason.

ICE

Brother's right. These brothers took a chance and came all the way over here and onto our turf just to tell one of us that his nephew was dead . . . and just because they don't have the same gang name as we do . . . . or because they don't wear the same colors as us . . . . or because they come from another street . . . we were ready to kill them too. When does it all stop, brothers? When? (Unties and drops his colors and weapon) It's got to stop sometime and somewhere . . . I guess it may as well begin right now and right here with me.

CRISSONS OG

Don't be no fool, Ice!! You know the only way out of this gang is by blood or death. Ain't no other way you gonna walk out on this gang. And that's the law brother.

FREEZE

Law, huh? Whose law, OG? Whose?

CRISSONS OG

MY LAW!! CRISSONS' LAW!! AND YO' LAW TOO IF YOU'RE A REAL CRISSON, BROTHER!!

FREEZE

So that's the law, huh?

CRISSONS OG

You heard it. We live by it. And when necessary . . . we die by it.

FREEZE

Then do what you got to do—*Sherrif* OG— 'cause I got to do what I gotta to do. And the way I'm feeling right now is like I just got to leave all this gang stuff along and go somewhere and get myself together. Hey, man. Love to all y'all but I'm outta here dog. I just can't do this no more. It just ain't me. I just can't take part in killing an innocent kid and then writing it off to "gang law."

Come on dog! That couldda been my own kid brother or my own nephew. I just can't do this no more man. I may not be much, but I know I'm better than this.

ICE

I'm with you on that one dog. I can feel you all the way on that one. I mean, um just standing here thinking how I would feel if that had been my little brother or sister and they (pointing to the Exterminators) had done the same thing to either one of them. Tell you the truth, I don't even know that I could have walked up here as peacefully as they did. Much props to y'all for doing the right thang . . . the right way. (To the Exterminators' OG.) And that's for real brother. Mad props man! (He steps forward and offers a fist bump to the Exterminators' OG who returns the gesture.)

FREEZE

Yo man. Like I said. I gotta go somewhere and get my head and my life back together man. I'll never snitch. Never talk. Never turn coat on y'all. You got my word on that. That's real and it's from the heart. But it's just come a time when I got to be a real man—my own man—and make a hard decision to do what's right for me for once in my life. Kindda like old folks use to say when I was a kid. It's time for me to finally decide to be true to myself. Like I said (to the OG), I won't turn on ya, I won't talk and I won't snitch, but I gotta go; so I'm walking up outta here right now, OG. Now if you don't want me to do that, then you're gonna have to kill me to stop me. Otherwise, (offers a fist bump to the very stoic and visually angered OG. He receives no response at all. The OG continues to look as if he's frozen in time.) It's been real, OG. Peace brother. That's all I want . . . is peace. (Starts to exit)

TERROR

Hey! Where you going when you leave here, brother?

FREEZE

I'm going to walk with Bonz to his crib, and I'm going to stand up like the human being and man that I really am, and I'm going to look Cousin Bipsey and Cousin Zeeke straight in their eyes, and I'm going to apologize to them and Auntie Maxie for what happened here today and for my part in it. I know I could be setting myself up for the slammer, but I just don't wanna live like this no more. I need my life back. I need my sanity back. I need my family back. Peace y'all. (Starts to exit.)

MAX

Hold up!! (Freeze stops and looks back.) I'm coming with you. Terrance was my little cousin's good friend man. I can't just let this go down like ain't nothing happened. I mean if I do that what am I? I'm not only less than a man, but I'm less than a decent human being. You spoke some good words a minute ago brother. You made me think. And what I thought about was if I was thinking at all, how could I ever let myself get caught up in something like this. I had to ask myself, was my life really that bad *that* I would trade it for this? I'm glad you spoke brother. You made me see somethings I wish I'd seen a long time ago. I'm with y'all, man. Let's roll up out of here, home. We should have done this a long time ago. (One after the other and without words members of both gangs toss off their gang colors and paraphernalia into a pile on the stage and exit behind Bonz, Freeze, and Max. The trend continues no one remains on stage except the two OG's.)

EXTERMINATORS OG

You can come with us, you know.

CRISSONS OG

You are going to pay for this one, OG.

EXTERMINAOTRS OG

(Ignoring his remark.) We don't have to say anything about you actually doing the knifing. You can just start life all over again . . . as a real person. You can help kids instead of killing them.

CRISSONS OG

Nobody comes into my territory and does this (pointing to the discarded colors)—and lives!!

EXTERMINATORS OG

You've missed it all, haven't you? You're still talking about killing more of your own kind. And for what? Exterminators killing Crissons. Crissons killing Exterminators. Exterminators and Crissons being killed by the cops. Lives being destroyed. Futures being taken away. Babies dying in their mothers' wombs. And you're still talking about adding more killing to that. You're not a Crisson— you're a creep. (Starts off.) Who knows? Maybe God sent JT this way just for this purpose. Too bad you're not smart enough to heed His warning. Peace, OG. But trust me. Your day is coming . . . and real soon too. (Exits)

CRIP OG

(Calling off stage to the exiting OG. His voice pulls him off stage.) We ain't done with this, OG! It ain't over! I promise you, OG! This ain't over! I'll raise me up another army of warriors. You're see. We'll make you pay for this, OG. OG, do you hear me??? OG . . . You'll see . . . OG . . . . OG . . . OG (His words are pulling him off stage in the direction of the others. Cops enter from the opposite side. He does not notice them until he turns around.)

COP #1

(Examining the mound of gang paraphernalia.) Gang paraphernalia. This yours?

COP #2

Whose else? Look like traces of fresh blood. Is it?

CRISSONS OG

What do you think? (Tries to exit. Stopped by the cops.)

COP #1

Who-a-a! Who-a-a, there tough guy. Not so fast. In a hurry aren't you? You just stand there for a minute while we go through this stuff. Just for safety purposes, I'm going to have to frisk you too. (Pulling the knife from Crissons OG's trousers. A trace of blood still remains on it. Cops goes over to the pile of paraphernalia and picks up a Crisson bandana. Notices blood on it as well.) Well, well big boy. I wonder if this is leading us somewhere. This may be enough to put somebody like you away for good. Turn around. Hands behind you. Feet apart.

You have the right to remain silent. You have the right to a lawyer. Anything that you say can and will be used against you in a court of law.

CRISSONS OG

Hey man, I ain't done no crime. You can't do nothing to me.

COP #2

Thirston Harris, III. Better known as Big T. OG type. Three times looser to the system. Come on, brother. Every cop out here knows you and your rep. Don't give me that crap. You're always doing something that could get you some time because that's just the way you operate. Now ain't it? What's this in your pocket? Marijuana. Bloody knife and gang paraphernalia. Oh I think you did enough at least to get yourself fifteen to twenty. (To his partner) Maybe twenty to thirty, with him being a perpetual. What you think?

COP #1

Twenty to thirty at least. Say, where'd that blood on the knife come from?

CRISSONS OG

Whadda I look like? A detective?

COP #2

Hang tight, Jim. Let me check something right quick. Just a minute.

COP #1

Do yourself a big favor and come clean, with us Big T. I'm going to ask you once more and once more only. What's the story behind this? (Points to the pile of colors)

CRISSONS OG

Don't know what you talking 'bout—COP!!

COP #1

You don't know. I guess you don't know nothing about a teenage boy who was stabbed to death earlier today either, huh?

CRISSONS OG

Sure don't.

COP #1

That's funny. He described you and your boys to a T to the ambulance attendant in route to the hospital just before he died. Even told us how he happened to get caught up on "you turf". Oh yeah. He had no problem remembering and describing you to a T. So now do you want to tell me here or at the precinct?

CRISSONS OG

Tell you what?

COP #1

What's the story behind the bloody knife and the gang paraphernalia?

CRISSONS OG

Hey!! I already told you one time, didn't I? I ain't no surgeon and I ain't no dectective? You want answers? Go get'em yourself. Besides that, ain't my attorney s'pose to be present befo' you pigs start interrogating me?

COP #2

Okay, Big T, have it your way. Hard ball you want. Hard ball you'll get. Let's go. It's slammer time for you again.

COP #1

What did you find out?

COP #2

Man, this dude's records grows every time we look him up in the system. I swear. His record has to be a country mile long *to include* THREE outstanding warrants. This boy's wanted everywhere east of Pluto. A born loser who just couldn't help but try to make losers out of everybody else he met too.

COP #1

Our lucky day, huh? I mean this wasn't even our regular beat. But like I told you, I just had a feeling that we were suppose to come down this street today. Good thing we did, huh? (Points to the pile of paraphernalia). Looks like somebody had enough sense to let go of this so called gang foolishness though.

COP #2

Yeah. And I'm glad they did. That's fewer kids we'll have to arrest or escort their parents down to the morgue to make identifications. Good choice. Darn good choice.

CRISSONS OG

You might think it's a good choice now, but when I'm done with them you'll know it was the worst thing they ever did.

COP #1

Yeah, yeah, yeah, bad guy. I know. Get moving. There's a welcoming committee just waiting to sign you into your new home down town.

CRISSONS OG

(Yelling back over his shoulder.) It ain't over baby! You can bet on that! That's for real. Don't nobody come on my turf and cause this kind of confusion and live! It ain't over! I'll be back! I swear! I'll be back! If it's the last thing I do.

COP #2

And it probably will be too.

CRIP OG

I'll be back, OG!!! You hear me OG!! You hear me?? (Being forcibly led off by the cops) I'll be back. I'll be back!!

(LIGHTS)

ACT III

(Zeeke and Bipsey are returning from the pharmacy. They are in an unusually jovial mood. Grandma is asleep on the couch.)

BIPSEY

Come on, Zeeke, baby. Now even you have to admit it. There ain't no denying it. Those boots were absolutely beautiful, and they won't ever look as good on anybody else's feet as they do on mine. Man! Those boots were just made for me(to her husband)—just me and my feet and nobody else's.

ZEEKE

Awww-l-l man! Am I going to have to have to put up with a never ending tongue lashing about the boots you didn't buy?

BIPSEY

You better know it for sure. I can't believe I let you talk me out of a bargain like that! Forty percent off too! Man!

ZEEKE

What I can't believe is how I let you sucker me into stopping by the mall in the first place. How did that happen anyway? We were suppose to be running to the pharmacy to pick up Mom's medicine and coming right back home. The next thing I know, I'm standing between two rude, loud, and obnoxious screaming women going, "No, it's mine. I spotted it first. It's mine. It's mine." My gosh! I don't know how you women can do it.

BIPSEY

Hey! Don't hate on us just because we're the stronger gender.

ZEEKE

Yeah. I have to admit you are pretty strong, 'cause it took all of my strength for me to hold my wallet in my pocket when you were trying to pull it out to pay for those boots.

BIPSEY

OK, honey, all jokes aside. Don't front now. Be honest. Didn't you like them? Come on now! Tell the truth. Be honest. Be a man about it. Admit that those boots look absolutely gorgeous on my feet, and that they will never ever do anyone else nearly the justice they do me. Go ahead. You can say it now. Go ahead. I'm listening. Tell the truth and shame the devil up in this house . . . Deacon. Make the Lord proud now.

ZEEKE

Now why you got to church on me, Bipsey? Why you got to leave the earth and go all the way to heaven and try to pull the Lord in this boot thing? And why I got to be DEACON Zeeke Johnson instead of just Zeeke Johnson when it comes to answering questions about those boots?

BIPSEY

Stay in the spirit, with me now baby. Stay in the spirit. See, I know if you're in the spirit then you can't lie about how cute those shoes were. That's all. No harm intended—DEACON. Just trying to help a brother out, that's all!

ZEEKE

None taken—Missionary. But if you really want to help a brother stay righteous all day, quit finding your way by that mall every time you go outside to get the mail out of the box.

BIPSEY

Come on now, Zeeke. I'm not that bad. (Thoughtfully) Am I? Zeeke? Am I?

ZEEKE

Naw. You're not bad at all. As a matter of fact . . . (starts toward her slowly . . .) You're a good woman, Bipsey . . .

BIPSEY

(Slowly approaching him from the opposite side of the stage.) And good women deserve to be pampered.

ZEEKE

A really good woman.

BIPSEY

Who deserves to be catered to . . . every now and then.

ZEEKE

An extraordinarily good woman.

BIPSEY

Who still has time to run back to the mall and get that pair of boots that she pulled off the shelf and hid inside a large pot in the cookware section. (They are now face to face and begin a slow romantic embrace, when suddenly . . .)

GRANDMA

(Aware that the couple has not yet spotted her entering the room.) Well, I guess I might'a had to leave the room if you had been trying to get him to buy you a whole outfit with a matching bag and hat. But since it's just a pair of boots ya' after, I guess it's reasonably safe for me to stay in here.

ZEEKE

Mama!

BIPSEY

We thought you were asleep.

GRANDMA

Uh-hum! I know you did. Y'all always think I'm sleep when I ain't. Sometimes I just be sitting or lying down with my eyes closed so I can see.

ZEEKE

You close your eyes so you can see, Mama?

GRANDMA

Yeah. I found out I can see my angels a lot easier with my eyes closed than I can with'em open. Don't know why, but it just works better that way.

BIPSEY

Are we back with this angel thing again, Ma?

GRANDMA

What you mean by back? I ain't never left this angel thing, as you call it. Y'all picked up my medicine . . . or did you just buy boots while you were gone? (Laughs)

BIPSEY

Yes and no, Ma. Yes we picked up your medicine from the pharmacy (holding up the filled prescription) and no we did not buy any boots.

GRANDMA

Well, I can sho' see it wasn't do to a lack of persuasive effort on your part. You still think they in that pot or you suppose somebody done found them and bought'em by now?

BIPSEY

MAMA!! (Laughter)

GRANDMA

A-a-h! That's not important. But I've got to talk to y'all about some that is.

ZEEKE

Now, Ma?

GRANDMA

Yeah. I think you might want to hear what I've got to say. Come on. (Patting the couch to indicate she wishes them to come and sit near her.) This is mighty important, but I promise it won't take me long to tell you. (They sit and listen.)

BIPSEY

Alright, Ma. We're listening. What is this about?

ZEEKE

You feel ok, Ma?

BIPSEY

We don't need to call the doctor or anything, do we?

ZEEKE

How's your blood pressure? You need something to eat? Take your medicine?

GRANDMA

Hey! Hey! Hey! You said (to Bipsey) y'all were ready to listen to what I called you over here for, didn't you? Well, that means both of you are going to have to starting resting your lips a little bit and puttin' your ears to work a whole lot.

BIPSEY

Yes ma'am.

GRANDMA

Well how in all God's creation are you going to hear me if you won't stop talking yourself? (Pause) Now I appreciate both of y'all concern over me, but I'm fine . . . at least for the moment any way. You needn't worry. I can't go nowhere until it's my time. And worrying about it ain't gonna lengthen or shorten it by one second. So just enjoy it and be thankful for it. Alright? Because dying is like a bridge. If you drive along any road long enough, sooner or later you're going to have to drive across a bridge. No matter how you feel about bridges, there will still come a time when you will have to cross at least one in your life time. And that's the way dying is. No matter how you feel about it, if you keep living long enough, the road of life will inevitably bring you to the bridge called death. But the bridge is not the end of your journey. It's just your passage to the other side. And then the journey starts all over again. Never be afraid of bridges baby. They're just there to help you cross over. (Pause) Now to what I called you over here for in the first place. (She takes one of each of their hands in her hands) Now listen. When they come here today . . . and they will . . . you still have to love them no matter what. Love is the only thing that's gonna change them. The lack of it is what pushed them out there in the first place, and it's only an abundance of it that's gonna heal their pains.

BIPSEY

They who, Mama? I'm lost. I'm not following you. I don't even know who you're talking about. Who are the "they" you keep mentioning?

GRANDMA

Won't be long now, and you're see. I ain't suppose to tell you no more than that. That's all they told me to tell you. That's it.

ZEEKE

They?

GRANDMA

My angels, baby. They been given charge over me. They watch over me. They see after me. And they don't leave me in the dark about nothing. (Zeeke and Bipsey glance at one another through very confused eyes.) Nothing. You hear me. You love'em when God brings them in this house and in your path—Deacon and Missionary! You love'em. That's the only thing that's strong enough to erase their hurt or yours.

ZEEKE

Our hurt? What hurt?

GRANDMA

I told you before. I already told you everything they told me to tell you. Alrigh-dy! I'm going in my room and relax for a while. And remember, sometimes somethings just have to be. Just because they do. But you? Just love'em. That's your duty. Just love'em. (Exit. A knock is heard at the front door.)

ZEEKE

I'll get it, baby. (A policeman enters and speak quietly to Zeeke.)

BIPSEY

Is there something wrong, Honey? Why is there a cop here? (Zeeke says nothing to her. In a daze, crosses and seats himself. He drops his tearful head in his hands and begins to sob loudly. Bipsey goes over to console him.) Zeeke . . . what . . . is . . . it, baby? Zeeke? (Zeeke says nothing but reaches up and draws her into a tender embrace. He strokes her hair gently, then carefully and privately reveals the heartbreaking news to his wife by whispering it in her ear. In shock and disbelief . . .) Ze-e-ek? Ze-e-ek? Honey, T-T-Terrance is what? (Zeeke does not reply. He simply hangs his head in sorrow.) Ze-e-k? Honey, I asked you a question? Y-y-you said Terrance is what? (To the officer) Officer? Did my husband (Grandma is now standing in the doorway observing her child, but saying nothing at all.) just say . . . that you came over here . . . to inform us that our son, Terrance was killed? He's dead?

OFFICER

I'm sorry, Ms. Johnson. Truly, I am. It's the toughest part of our duty to have to tell such a wonderful set of parents as yourselves that their child has been killed. But it *is* part of the job.

BIPSEY

Job! (Very emotional) The toughest part of your job should have been to keep my innocent baby alive! Why couldn't you do that? Isn't that what you're paid to do?

ZEEKE

You can't blame him, baby. He didn't do it. The gang members did?

BIPSEY

Zeeke, you know good and well my baby wasn't in any gang.

ZEEKE

I know. But . . .

BIPSEY

But what, Zeeke? But what? My baby is dead because he left this house two hours ago to deliver a note from his grandmother to her son? And now you (to the cop) waltz up in here to bring us this horrible news, and you (to Zeeke) say to me, you can't blame him, baby, it's not his fault. Well who do I blame, Zeeke? My boy is dead and by God I'm going to blame somebody for his death.

GRANDMA

(Crossing to Bipsey) Don't do it, Bipsey. Don't do it. Right now the worse thing in the world you can do is to try to set blame. It'll be counterproductive and stop you from doing the right thing . . . and that is to be able to show them love from a pure heart when they get here in a few minutes. There ain't no blame, baby. There ain't no fault. It's just the route the map of life is taking us, that's all. And even though we're traveling on this highway, we ain't the one that mapped out the route. Sometimes we must go through the valley in order to get to the mountain top. But we still make it to the top just the same.

BIPSEY

I don't understand, Ma.

GRANDMA

I know. But you will.

BIPSEY

Mama, that boy was your heart. How can you be so calm at a time like this?

GRANDMA

Because I understand, Bipsey. I do. Angels. They're kind of like little tattle tales. They tell you everything, so that you will never be surprised by anything.

BIPSEY

Ma, are you telling me that your angel . . . (a knock is heard at the door.)

GRANDMA

Love from a pure heart now y'all. It'll do y'all as much good or more as it does them. Love from a pure heart . . . that's the only answer to this situation.

(Bonz, Freeze, and two other gang members enter the house.)

GRANDMA

Albert!! Son!! (Opens her arms for him to come over and hug her.)

BONZ

(Hesitates. Grandma beckons him over to her. Then timidly . . .) Mama . . .

GRANDMA

Now don't you stand wa-a-ay back over there and talk to me, boy. Like I'm some kind of stranger or sickness that gonna rub off on you. Not after all those long hard prayers I sent up asking God to keep you and protect you, and to make sure you got back here safe and sound. And from the looks of things He's heard and answered every one of them too. So even if you don't think your own mama is good enough for one of your hugs, the least you can do is to come over here and love on those prayers I sent up for you.

BONZ

(Rushing to Grandma and tightly embraces her.) MAMA!! (Embraces her grandmother passionately. Begins to cry.)

GRANDMA

(She continues to embrace her son as she speaks to him.) Aw-w-w-w! Go ahead. It's alright. Sure it is. You're home now. And as long as you're at home among family, you ain't got to pretend to be nothing that you're not. See . . . when you're home . . . and you're hurting . . . you cry . . . and it's alright. 'Cause you're with family, son. And tears shed among family are some of the most precious tears ever. You don't have to be a superman or a super woman. You don't have to be a thug or a preacher. All you ever have to be at home is just *you*. That's the beauty of home, baby, it's the one place in the whole wide world where you can just be *you*.

BONZ

(Finally breaks the embrace. Dabs tears from his eyes, then acknowledges and speaks.) Zeeke . . . Bipsey.

ZEEKE

(Half mesmerized by what he's seeing.) Albert, it's good to see you, brother. Even though I still can't believe it's you I'm seeing. How did this miracle happen?

GANG MEMBER

Albert? All this time I thought his name was Bonz, dog. What's up with that?

TERROR

Hey, you heard the man, dog. Albert, alright? Bonz is the brother's streetname, man.

BIPSEY

Bonz, you have no idea (begins to cry) just how much me and Zeeke and Mama have cried and worried and prayed since you've been gone. It seems . . . (buries her head in her husband's chest, sobbing)

ZEEKE

It seems like our prayers have all just been answered . . . somewhat.

GRANDMA

We just got the news (glancing at the cop) about J.T. God knows what happened to him sure wasn't in any of our prayers. But you know, you have to be careful what you ask God for because even though you can pray for results, you can't tell him how to bring the results into being. (Pauses. Tearful.) We prayed for you to come home, but we didn't know your coming was gonna come at the expense of JT's life though. Good child J.T. was. Lord knows that boy was one *good* child.

MOTHER

Now, Mama, don't go get all worked up and excited and send your blood pressure through the roof now.

GRANDMA

Ain't many more J.T.'s in this world. I can promise you that. (Wipes her eyes. Door bell rings a second time.) Well don't everybody just stand around here crying your eyes out. Somebody go see who that is at the door.

(Enter other gang members. Family sees them and reacts to their presence.)

ZEEKE

What the heck's going on here? Who the . . . (Notices one of the gang members) Helen . . . Is that you? (To one of the female gang members.)

HELEN

(Shyly) Yes sir, Mr. Johnson, it's me alright. Shame to ask, but how you doing? I can imagine not too good right now.

BIPSEY

Girl . . . where have you been so long? Why . . . It's been a minute since we last seen hide or hair of you. Where have you been hiding? I haven't seen you in a month of Sundays. Every time I see your mama I ask about you . . . but she just drops her head and says you're just around the neighborhood doing what children do.

HELEN

Yes ma'm. I guess she's kindda right about that. But you're right too. I mean it's been a minute, huh? I guess I shouldn't have stayed gone so long.

BIPSEY

At least a year and two or three months if not a year and a half since I last saw you or even spoke to you. You mean to tell me that your old god mama and god daddy ain't even worth a phone call and quick "hello how y'all doing" no more? Guess now that she's too old for us to take out to the park or to the amusement center or even to church or the movies on Sundays, she just doesn't need us anymore, baby.

HELEN

Naw. It ain't even like that, Auntie.

GRANDMA

Say it ain't, huh? Then what's the real reason we ain't been seeing you around here then? Go ahead. I'm listening. Gone listen real good too, and see if you gone be honest with us or if you're gonna try to pull a fast one over on this old biddy.

HELEN

We talking the truth, right?

GRANDMA

Nothing but.

HELEN

Man, been a little while since anybody, outside the law that is, cared whether I told the truth or not. OK. Alright. The truth. Well, I kindda went out there (gesturing to the street) . . . and got myself caught up in a little some some.

COP

Something like a gang, you mean?

HELEN

We've all made mistakes before, officer. But today we're all here to heal mistakes and not to condemn folks just for making them.

GRANDMA

Helen, I know nearly all of your people. Your grandparents. Your aunts and uncles. Your cousins. And Rossie, your big mama, was my best friend in school. Your mama stayed right here in this house many a nights while she was carrying you in her belly. She ate at (pointing) that dining room table and laughed until she out right cried watching some of them dumb video tapes on that television. (Reassuringly) You come from a really good family, Helen. Strong and respectful people. God fearing. And full of honesty, integrity and family pride.

HELEN

You're so right. You're totally right, and I know all of this.

GRANDMA

(The doctor re-enters carrying his bag. He looks somewhat surprised at the number of visitors at the Johnson's house. He goes over to the couch where Grandma is sitting and begins to perform routine checks on her. She is cooperative, but continues to talk.) So what happened? Who . . . er . . . what did this to you? How did it come to the point of you leaving your good family and going out and joining up with some gang?

BLADE

She don't know. And neither do the rest of us. I mean . . . I don't want to sound disrespectful or anything, but it's the simple truth . . . None of us don't really know. So how can any of us truthfully answer that question? I mean was it too much discipline or not enough discipline? Was it too much criticism and too little praise or none of either one of them? Was it love or was it tolerance? What happened? (Pause) I guess if I had to narrow it down to just one thing, I would say it all started with either broken dreams or maybe abandoned hope. Then, too, it could have been because of lost faith or maybe even no love being shown at home. Shoot, I don't know, it's hard to say.

CATHY

We didn't mean to. None of us set out to become a member of a gang.

GRANDMA

Catherine?

ZEEKE

Catherine? You mean (holding his hand about waist high) Little Cathy? Maryland's and Ray-Ray's baby girl?

CATHY

Yes ma'am.

GRANDMA

Girl-l-l, if you don't bring your little hips over here and give me a hug I'll be forced to get up out of this chair and whip you clean 'round this whole room with my cane.

DOCTOR

And even though she's a little bit weak right now, don't put it past her to try it.

GRANDMA

Oh, there you go again! You just do the doctoring 'round here and let me head up the loving department. (Hugs the child.) Girl, you look and feel like a brand new gift at Christmas time. It's so good to see you and just to have the peace of knowing that ain't nothing bad done happened to you out there on them streets.

CATHY

It's good—really good—to see you too—Auntie.

GRANDMA

Baby . . . what is it?

CATHY

What is what, Auntie?

BIPSIE

The cause behind all y'all young people today running away from ya' homes . . . and families . . . and ya' whole life . . . just to join one of those street gangs. What is it?

CATHY

Mainly, Auntie, it's all about love. Love. Most of the time we are just looking for someone to really and truly love us . . . with our faults, immaturity, bullheadedness, and even our stupidity. We just want somebody to love us through all of that.

GRANDMA

Well who done went and told you that don't nobody love you and won't nobody love you through all of that? Who told you that?

BIPSEY

Alright, Mama. Remember your blood pressure now. You know it doesn't take a lot to get your steam kettle to whistling.

GRANDMA

Don't you worry 'bout me none. I got my blood pressure right where I want it. It's these here children I ain't quite got where I want 'em to be yet. And that's what you ought to be worrying about if you 'gone worry 'bout anything at all, Missy. (To the child) Now go on and tell me that answer to my question. Who in the dickens went and told you that don't nobody love ya'? Who?

HELEN

In words, no body actually told us that. But in action—everybody tells us that all the time and in a number of ways.

GRANDMA

Hmm-m-m. And that hurts, don't it?

FREEZE

You better know it. You know what's it like to be a boy and not to have a daddy to come home to or to take you out to the park or to throw balls with you or watch a good boxing match with on T.V? You know what it's like to have your grandma and mama constantly yelling and screaming at you because the truth is they're mad with your whore mongering, dope slinging, womanizing, jailbird daddy? And just because you look like him, they treat you as if you are him. Oh yeah, they ain't never had to say it in words—at least not to me anyway—I could feel it. Everytime I looked at them, I could feel it in the hate I saw in their eyes. I could taste it in the burnt up meals I had to eat every evening. I could feel it, every time I tried to hug my mom, but she was too preoccupied or tired—or concerned—to even hug me back. Naw. They never did say it, but then too, in a way they constantly screamed it out at me and the rest of us, every day.

BONZ

Mama, it ain't easy being a young person in this day and time. It's hard. I'm talking seriously hard. A lot of stress and responsibilities.

GRANDMA

So what you think being a parent must be like then? After all we ain't only stressed and responsible for our own lives, but now we are stressed by whatever is stressing you and responsible for however you react to whatever it is you think you're responsible for?

BONZ

But that's different. Y'all are adults. Y'all suppose to know how to handle the pressures of life.

ZEEKE

Right. And we suppose to know how to teach and prepare y'all to be able to do the same thing . . . if you would just give us a chance.

TERROR

I gave my old man a chance, and what did he do? He beat my face bloody. And she gave her moms a chance too, but all she did was to neglect her for some old drunkard of a husband. Two of the girls joined this gang because they gave their step-dads chances, and ended up molested. So how many chances are we suppose to give people?

GRANDMA

That depends, baby, on how badly you want to find love.

POLICEMAN

Listen. I really hate to break up this touching family session, but duty calls.

GRANDMA

You go on, son. We can handle anything that needs handling in here.

POLICEMAN

Thanks, but I did have a few questions concerning your grandson's . . . er . . . death.

GRANDMA

No. Not now. No questions. Today we want to heal wounds, not inflict more hurt. What's done is done. And we'll deal with that when we have to. But right now, I just want to love these children. All of 'em. At least when I'm gone, I'll know one thing for sure, and that is that everyone of y'all would have had at least one person in your life to truly love you—regardless of anything you're ever done.

HELEN

What you mean by when you're gone? You planning on cutting out us and heading some where?

GRANDMA

Nope and yep. Nope it ain't my plan, and yep I still gotta go anyhow.

DOCTOR

Hey, hey now. Enough of that already. What did I tell you earlier?

GRANDMA

And what did I tell you earlier, Mr. Smarty Pants? Doctors! They think they know everything!

BIPSEY

Mama! Now there you go again!

GRANDMA

Well, they do—sometimes anyhow. But y'all children. Don't y'all be so bullheaded. Listen and learn. Talk a little bit . . . but listen a whole lot. If you 'round some people who know something, you can learn a whole lot just by listening—ain't got to say a word. Just listen. 'Cause when you talk, you can't hear what nobody else is saying 'cept yourself. And if you already knew the answer to what you were talking about chances are good you probably wouldn't even bring up the subject anyway. So just listen. Kindda like y'all doing right now. And another thing. Don't just expect to receive love. You have to learn to give love out too. Stop judging and learn to love people unconditionally. Too many young people today got that "if you" kind of love.

HELEN

If you?

GRANDMA

Yeah. Y'all know what I mean. I'll love you "if you." I'll be your man or woman "if you." I'll do such and such for you "if you . . . ." That ain't love. That's just making a deal. And deals and love ain't the same. That's why you young folks keep looking for love in all the wrong places. 'Cause where y'all look for love, there ain't no love there at at all. Ain't a thing in the world there except a whole lot of "if you's" and a bunch of deals to be made.

HELEN

I know that's right.

GRANDMA

Sure I am. You don't think I live to be this age being no fool now do you?

HELEN

Oh, no ma'am. I didn't mean to sound like I was calling you a fool.

GRANDMA

Oh, I know you didn't, Baby. And ain't no harm taken either. I just want to pass on a little bit on the insight I managed to store up over the years; that's all. 'Cause I sure won't need none of this earthly knowledge where I'm headed. Now one more thing then I'm going to leave y'all to have a conversation with that policeman over there. He got a list of questions he gone need some answers to, and I believe y'all just the ones to help him too.

BIPSEY

Mama, you look like you're getting a little tired and winded. Why don't you rest a spell now?

GRANDMA

I'm about to, Honeybunch. I am. But I got one last thing to say to these children, and that is y'all got to learn how to love people for real. Y'all got to learn to love through the good times and through the bad ones. Through your tears as well as your smiles. Through your nights just like you do during your days. When people treat you right and when they treat you wrong—sometimes for no reason except your day was just going too good for them to just leave you alone. Yeah, love and forgiveness are two of the most powerful things you got, children. And if you don't learn how to share them with others, you're die without ever experiencing them in your life from the rest of the world. I'm through now, and I'm tired too. Guess I done talked y'all enough for one day. Policeman got some more talk for y'all and I got a bed in that back room just hollering out my name. Think it's time to rest now.

BONZ

That's all you gone say to us?

GRANDMA

Sure it is, child. If y'all were listening to everything that I just told you, and you do it, you'll see a big change in your lives for the rest of your lives. Then other people's lives will take on more value to you, and you'll protect it and not take it. Especially for no good reason at all. Just think about it. It'll make sense to you later on. (Nodding her head as if to say good night.) Ladies. Gentlemen. So glad I got a chance to see each one of y'all again. (Grandma and Bipsey exit together.)

POLICEMAN

It's a bit crowded in here. Why don't everybody step out on the front porch. (Policeman and kids exit. Zeeke busies himself with domestic tidying chores. Suddenly a sobbing Bipsey rushes onto the stage and collapses into her husband's arms. The doctor walks slowly behind her.)

ZEEKE

Baby, what is it? What's the matter?

BIPSEY

It's Mama. It's Mama. She just died.

ZEEKE

(Shocked) What?

BIPSEY

She sat on the side of the bed, took in a deep breath, smiled, and said "Yeah, here they come for me again. My angels. And this time they show do aim to take me back with them." Then she smiled and she looked at me and she grinned, and she said softly, "I sure do pray them children were all paying some close attention to what I just told them. It was too important for them to miss." Then she said, "Just love'em, baby. No matter how much it hurts you or what they did; they did it because they didn't know love." Then she smiled and said, "OK now. I'm ready. Let's go home." And just like that, Mama was gone.

DOCTOR

Zeke . . . Bipsey . . . I'm so sorry. She was the best friend I ever had and the best person I've ever known.

BIPSEY

We know. Thank you for trying. I know this is as tough for you as it is for us.

DOCTOR

What do you mean by you and us? When it comes to your mother, it will always be "us."

BIPSEY

Sorry. I didn't mean it that way. Just a little bit mixed up right now is all.

ZEEKE

It's okay, baby. It's okay.

POLICEMAN

I'm sorry for another loss of a family member, Ma'am, Sir. I really am. And I hate to talk police business at a time like this, but I have a confession here in reference to your son's murder. I'll need one of you to come down to the station with me to fill out the necessary paperwork to press charges.

ZEEKE

(Staring off into space. Speaking reflectively into the air.) Just love 'em. No matter how much it hurts you or what they've done. Just . . . love them.

POLICEMAN

Say what, Ma'am?

ZEEKE

She was saying we won't be pressing any charges or going down to the station with you officer.

POLICEMAN

But I've got . . .

BIPSEY

We know. But let's just say you've got what you've got and we've got what we've got.

POLICEMAN

And what is it that you have, ma'am?

BIPSEY

It's a long story officer, but it's perfectly alright with us if you would let them all go now.

POLICEMAN

Are you listening to yourself, Ma'am? Are you? I'm talking about a confession to your own son's murder. A confession. I've got . . .

ZEEKE

And like we said, we know what you've got. And we've got something we've got to hold on to as well, officer.

POLICEMAN

I don't get it. I don't understand that. How could you just . . . .

ZEEKE

We have to. It was the last thing she said. She knew you would find out who did. She knew everything—that she would die; that our child was dead, and that they were associated with his death. Yet she never told us to seek revenge or to rely on the justice system or to take the law into our own hand. Instead she told us to love them . . . and as hurtful as it is, and it is hurtful you know, (looks over at his wife, then at the front porch where most of the children are standing) we're going to do just that. Call an ambulance, baby, will you? And wait here for attendants.

BIPSEY

You going somewhere, honey?

ZEEKE

Yeah. To tell some kids, we know what they did, but we've decided to love them instead of pressing charging against them. Is that alright with you? I mean, you okay here alone until the ambulance comes?

BIPSEY

Sure. I'm fine, but somehow I just know I'm not alone. I love you.

DAD

I love you too, Babe. Be back soon. (Points to a some of the kids) You, you and you, come ride with me. You and you, my wife's gonna need some help while I'm gone. Go inside and help her tidy things up before the ambulance gets here. Let's go guys. We'll going to make a stop at the morgue to identify and claim

J.T.'s body. But the most important thing for all of us to remember is that this is the day we all get a second chance at a new life. So let's go get started right now. (exit)

CURTAINS

MAMA . . . CAN WE TALK?

(A CHRISTMAS TALE)

CAST OF CHARACTERS

Alexis—The mother
Frank—The father
Will—The son
Miffy—The daughter
Peco, Hayes and PJ—Teenage runaways
Officer Grant—Police Officer
Angel/Homeless person

(Street extras as needed)

ACT I

SCENE I

The action begins in the kitchen/dining room of the family's home. The setting is somewhat opulent in appearance, and clearly announces the middle to upper class status of this family. It is obvious that the mother and father are "busy bodies" as they constantly glance at their watches throughout the dinner meal as if preoccupied with meeting a demanding schedule. There is no discussion by family members during the meal.

The family is seated at the table. Will's countenance is depressed as he looks back and forth from one parent to the other during the silent "family" meal. He is sullen and appears detached from his surroundings. His voice (recorded) or a (live) voice can be heard reading the poem "My Hurt."

MY HURT

I'm hurting, but nobody seems to care
It seems so—unfair—that my family would let me bear
All this pain I feel alone, and without coming to my aid
What kinds of folks must they be—stupid or afraid?

They never ask about my grades or why I refuse to eat
They never ask why I'm always quiet nor notice that I never sleep.
They never see the signs of depression written all over my face
They never notice the tears in my eyes after something as simple as the
    family's grace.

They never notice how irritable and detached my mannerisms always are,
They never notice how much weight I've lost or that I'm always staring afar.
They never notice how I nearly never ever smile.
They never consider last year I ran cross country; this year I can barely run a
    mile.

They never notice that my piggy band no longer stays filled with change
They never notice how illogical I am at times, almost as if I'm deranged.
They never notice the excuses I come up with for all my failures and misdeeds,
But let me leave a single vegetable on my plate and a bushel of admonishment
    they would heave.

You see, it's not important to me that they notice all of these things I said,
But to notice none of them makes my baffled mind beg
To know how can my family not look at me and see
The hurt, the pain, and the poorly disguised agony
That walks side by side each day with me,
And should be as visible as the branches of a an oak tree.
How can they not see the pain etched upon this face
Just imploring their help to please make this place
Home . . . again . . . home sweet home
And let the practices of neglect and drug abuse lone be gone.

For the hope and will are sincere and are here
But what I need most is the strength I receive from my family so dear,
That it waters my faith seed with each dripping tear . . .
Which gives me the courage to go on and to face the fear
Of any obstacle, trial, and even tough tribulations
I have no doubt because my family is my confidence and jubilation.

Can't you hear me? Can't you hear the pleas of my heart?
Begging for you to help me to start
Anew, refreshed, refocused and revived
Loved by you, revered, and once again alive.

All these thing and more we can do
If only I can make this point to you
I have succumbed to drugs and am strung out strong
I'm sorry I did and I know it was wrong
But now more than ever I need a miraculous rescue
You gotta forget what I did and think about what we've now got to do
I need y'all . . . FAMILY . . . I need y'all to stand by me
But for starters tonight I just need y'all to look at me . . . and see

Someone who gave you all the clearest signs
Of a loved one desperately seeking help for a long time
An innocent child cleverly seduced by a wicked deception
Now permanently entangled in a weave of needed corrections

I need you to see what my world has become
I need you to feel the pulse of my heart as it drums
I need you to hear the words of this mole
I need you to resurrect the life in my soul

I'm hurt, but no one seems to care
Please don't talk to me about right or wrong, just or fair
Don't let me bear all this pain alone
I need you to guide my soul back to a happy home.

After the reading of the poem, Mother checks her watch and rushes out of the door. The phone rings. Sister answers and gives it to Dad. He checks his watch, gets his brief case and leaves. Sister goes over picks up the phone, dials, and exits as she talks with a friend. Son remains seated for a few seconds then exits. Stage remains bear and quiet for several seconds.

Son re-enters the stage carrying a tote bag which he places behind a chair (in the living room). He is prancing back and forth and displaying very nervous and anxious behavior. He mimics rehearsing for a very difficult speech. He is constantly observing his watch as if waiting for something or someone. Finally mother enters. She appears obviously tired and does not care to be bothered. She grabs a magazine and reclines in her seat. Meanwhile, the child continues to pace and pace pausing occasionally to give action to the poem as it is being read aloud. No words are spoken on stage. His voice (recorded) or a (live) voice can be heard reading the poem "Mama Can We Talk?"

MAMA, CAN WE TALK?

Mama, can we talk?

We don't have to just sit here.
We can listen to music, turn on the tube, or even go for a walk.
We can even play a game . . . rummy, scrabble or even pitty pat
You know, maybe we could do a little something while we talk
Something really simple like that
Most of all, Mama, I just need to talk . . . whether we watch the tube, walk,
    or play pitty pat.

It ain't got to be no long talk, no lecture or no fussin'
And Lord knows, Mama, I don't need no yelling or no cussin'
All I want to do is just here and now sit and talk
'Cause there are so many things that need to be brought
Up between us so we can say what we see and what we feel
And finally learn how to talk with each other and how to be real
About all this stuff life's just throwing in my face
Lord, I need to talk to you, Mama, before I let go and disgrace
Your perfect name and impeccable church and community reputation
And I'm trying hard not to, Mama, but I need your concern and cooperation

Every day the world seems to just keep closing in on me
Showing me all the ugly things I just don't need to see
Sex and rape and prostitution and crime

Whore mongering and killing and young folks happy to be serving jail time
A national budget that's completely out of control
Preachers ministering to congregations themselves with wickedly corrupt souls
An educational system that's fallen from the world's grace
People so full of hate that they forgot we all belong to the same human race
Children defying all authority while parents are fighting with their own kids
Women sleeping with women while men are wearing high heels, breast
    implants, and wigs.

Now I know this is boring and you sort of don't want to listen
But I wish you would because it feels so much like I'm fixin'
To explode and just blow up and do all kinds of stupid acts
Some of them I understand and the rest makes it looks like I'm smoking weed
    crack!

But if you give me five minutes just to share with you what's on my mind,
Then maybe me and you can put our heads together and combined
We can lick this thing that's bothering me so and eating away at my last gut,
Come on, Mama, talk to me! Give me some help! I don't want to fight this
    thing on luck.

What is there to talk about you look like you want to ask
Well, let's see now, Mama. Let's see if we can un-sort this mass.

Well . . . there's drugs and pregnancies and aids and gangs
And violence and incest and abuse and world leaders who are insane
There are fears, and thoughts and prejudices and world strife
There are cults and easy money and subliminal messages saying "Go ahead,
    do it, take your own life."
There's t.v. and guns and politics and the ongoing war

And even the U.S.-based hate groups that have taken the 5th Amendment way
  too far.
There's religion and science and aliens from out of space
And Lord knows there's still a lot to be said about the deteriorating human
  race.

I truly don't care where your interest lies
I just want to talk so that we can take the time to get inside
Of one another's mind and one another's soul
And find out what it takes for us to help make and keep one another whole.

I need to talk, Mama. I need to talk to—no—WITH YOU.
It's such a terrible thing, Mama, you don't seem to need to talk with me too.

*Mama dozes off during the poem, nearly drops the magazine, wakes up, glances at
her watch, gets her coat and notes and rushes out again. Son follows mom to the door
and watches her leave. Goes over and places a note near the telephone then returns
to his seat just as the final line of the poem is being read, retrieves the bag, pulls out
a hypodermic and administers drugs to himself. He is dazed, but manages to grab
his bag and stagger to the door. There he stops, turns and glances around the LR
then staggers out of the door. Door closes softly behind him.*

ACT I

SCENE II

(Action takes place in the family's living room. It is obvious that the family now knows Will has run away. Alexis (the mother) appears very distraught over this discovery. A uniformed policeman is present collecting information from the parents. Frank (the husband) is providing the officer with the information. Alexis, the very temperamental and image—consciously wife and mother, is visibly upset and paces back and forth. She is a very dramatic and attention seeking individual who works hard at protecting her image and reputation in the community and among her socialite acquaintances. Suddenly . . .)

ALEXIS

But how could he? How could he? How could that boy just run away like that? Haven't we always been there for him? Haven't we always shown him love, understanding, devotion, commitment and all the other things it takes to make us good parents? (Becoming angry again) How on earth could Will have ever hurt us this way? How?

FRANK

It's okay, Sweetheart. It's okay. I'll never understand it either. How could a child who has everything (gesturing) just get up and run away from it all without a reason? Why it's the absolute dumbest thing I've ever heard of in my life!

ALEXIS

I can't believe we've given this child the best years of our lives and *for what*? To have him runaway and humiliate us in front our friend and family and only God knows who else? To have him leave this beautiful home to run out (pointing outside) and sleep on the streets? To have him defy our reputation and image in the community and church? I ask you, for what have we given so many good years of our lives for, Frank?

FRANK

Now, now, Dear. Please don't' go and get yourself all worked up and upset over this. Surely this is nothing big. I'm sure the boy's just out having fun . . . you know playing a practical joke or something.

ALEXIS

(Furious) Practical joke! Practical joke! What do you mean practical joke?! Do you call packing up your clothes and leaving during the middle of the night a practical joke? Do you call leaving a run-a-way note a practical joke? Do you call staying out on the streets on a night like *this* a PRACTICAL JOKE? (Intended to insult her husband) Wise up, *Dad!* It's no wonder the boy isn't here right now. With that kind of masculine wisdom what boy in his right mind would want to stay here?

OFFICER

Ms. Johnson, why don't you have a seat over here before you become any more upset . . . (Tries to take her by the arm)

ALEXIS

I am NOT (snatching away) upset, Officer! Now please do your job and get out of here!

FRANK

Officer, I think you already have as much information as we can possibly give at this time. (Takes the officer by the arm and leads him in the direction of the door) Please keep us updated on anything and everything, won't you?

OFFICER

Certainly I will, Sir.

FRANK

And, Oh, Officer Grant . . .

OFFICER

Yes sir?

FRANK

Please forgive my wife. She's . . . well just a little upset about all of this.

OFFICER

Perfectly understandable, Sir. Maybe you'd better get back over there with her. I can see my way out from here.

FRANK

Thank you, Officer Grant.

OFFICER

My pleasure, Sir. Good night.

FRANK

Good night. (Turns and notices Alexis who is primping in a handheld mirror. Removes his glasses and ponders deeply for a few seconds. Starts to exit but stops and places his hand on Miffy's shoulder who is now entering the room. She looks at her father as if to ask if there is any news. He sadly shakes his head no. Suddenly and without warning . . .)

ALEXIS

Aa-a-e-e-e-e!! (Alexis leaps to her feet and rushes across the stage and begins barking at her husband.) JUST . . . YOU . . . WAIT!! JUST . . . YOU . . . WAIT! Why I'm going to break that boy in half with my bear hands just as soon as I lay my little beady on his body! No. No. I know what I'll do to him. I know exactly what I'll do to him. Why, I'll hang that boy upside down by his big toes.

FRANK

Now honey . . .

ALEXIS

O-o-oh no! Don't you now honey me. How could this child possibly do this to me? How could he?

MIFFY

So . . . Is that what this is all about, Mother? Is it? Is that all that matters? (coming more c and d stage) How could he dare do what he has done . . . to you? To you, Mother? What about him? Why did he do this to himself, Mother? Why did he decide to live on dirty, violent, smelly streets with pimps, drug users, prostitutes and other so called terrible people instead of living here at home with me . . . you . . . Dad. Why? You want to know why? (Becoming emphatic and emotional) Because the streets and the hoodlums are more of a real home and a true family to him than we've ever been! Don't you see, Will didn't just RUN out there! We PUSHED him out there!!

FRANK AND ALEXIS

PUSHED HIM??

MIFFY

Yes Mom. (To Dad) Yes Dad. Pushed. We pushed him out of our lives and into the lives of others. Can't you see that? Can't you see that every time you remembered to condemn him but forgot to praise him you were pushing him away? And can't you see every time you were too busy or too tired to listen to him or spend time with him that you were pushing him away. And can't you see that every time a ballgame, sale at the mall, social event or television show was given more attention than he was he felt PUSHED away. For goodness sakes folks . . . what on earth does it take to make you see this?

ALEXIS

(Arrogantly and defiantly walks over to her daughter and stands nose to nose) And just how do you know so much about how *he* felt, Missy.

MIFFY

(Stares boldly into her mother's eyes) Because he's not the only child in this house who's felt "PUSHED AWAY" before. (Music begins softly. Exits)

FRANK

I never knew my children were feeling that way.

ALEXIS

I guess I didn't either.

FRANK

I thought all they wanted or needed were pretty clothes, X-Box videos games, and an allowance every week so they could go straight to the mall and spend every penny of it right up then ask for more.

ALEXIS

Yeah, I never knew we were pushing our kids out of our lives . . . and onto the streets.

FRANK

Neither did I Alexis. But now that I do . . . (Goes over, gets his hat, coat, and scare. Puts them on as he is heading for the door.)

ALEXIS

What are you doing? Where are you going?

FRANK

To get my son.

ALEXIS

Your son? But how can you do that, Frank? You don't even have the slightest idea where he is.

FRANK

I'll find him, Alexis. I have to. It's either find my son or lose him forever to the monster call the streets. And I refuse to do that. (Exits. Music. Alexis sits slumped in her chair with her face in her hands.)

ACT II

SCENE I

(Setting: The street. Will enters onto the street carrying his bag with him. There's another kid sitting nearly in his path.)

PECO

Hey!! YO!! Where do you think you're going? Get out of here! You're on my turf . . . and I didn't give you permission to be here.

WILL

Your turf? I don't see your name on it nowhere. So where I come from that makes it nobody's turf.

PECO

Oh yeah? (Gets up, goes over and writes his name on the ground with his finger. Spells out his name aloud as he writes it.) P-E-C-O. Peco. Now there's a name on it . . . and it's mine. So I guess that means you're standing on my turf, just like I said earlier.

WILL

(Goes over and erases writing with his foot. Writes his own name with his finger. Two more youths have entered onto the stage while he is writing his name on the ground. Stands up and announces defiantly . . .) And like I said earlier, dude, I don't see your name on no turf 'round here. Only name I see is Will. And that's me. So the way I see it, Slim, it looks to me like you're walking right on top of my turf. So why don't *you* get off *my* turf?

PECO

OK. OK. I can already see what the deal gonna have to be with you. (Pushing up his shirt sleeves as if preparing to fight.) I can tell you're one of those smart mouth ones, huh? You know the kind. Don't believe sugar sweet 'till you've tasted it. Or fire is hot 'till you get burned, huh, Mr. Smart mouth?

WILL

Ain't looking for no trouble and I wasn't trying to be smart either. Just want you to see this ain't really nobody's turf, man. That's all.

PECO

Okay, Mr. Smart mouth. I just want you to see this!! (Boys begin to tussle. The other two youths run over and break them up immediately.)

PJ

Yo! Chill! Chill! Chill out, man! Y'all chill with all that, man? What's up with that, brothers. I mean what's going on? What gives, man?

WILL

(Struggling to free himself from the grasp of the other youth who has separated him from Peco) What's up? And what gives? I'll tell you what gives AND what gives. (Closing his fist and shaking it in Peco's direction) I was just about to give him one of my world famous knuckle sandwiches right up side his big Donald Duck looking head.

PECO

(Also struggling lightly) Oh yeah? (Dismissing Will's threat likely.) Please. One of y'all remind me later on to be scared of this little wimp's threats . . . that is if I don't have anything else to do later on. But now if you really think you're all that, you can just go ahead and try your luck out right now, tough guy. (Shoves Will in his chest. The two begin wrestling again. The others quickly separate them.)

HAYES

Hey, man, like I told y'all a minute ago. Y'all gone have to chill out with the wild west cowboy act, man, before y'all two bring the heat down on all of us run-a-ways. Know what I mean? (Suddenly notices a policeman slowly heading their way.) Oh no! Speaking of the heat here comes one now. See I told y'all to chill with all the fighting and stuff.

PECO

(Remembers he has a ball in his pocket. Pull it out and nervously whispers to the others . . .) Quick! Sit down. Here catch. (The boys begin tossing the ball as if engaged in an innocent game of catch.)

WILL

Why are we doing this?

ALL THE BOYS

(To Will) Sh-h-h-h.

HAYES

Just toss the ball and go with the flow, man (police enters). No time to explain.

OFFICER GRANT

(Officer Grant walks about the stage generally inspecting everything within his immediate view. Finally to the boys . . .) Everything alright boys?

BOYS

Oh yeah. Sure thing, Officer. Never better.

HAYES

We just thought since it was Christmas and all that maybe we should take time out of our busy, busy schedules just to do a little bit of Yuletide male bonding, Mr. Officer.

PJ

Come on now, Mr. Officer. Even you can't say that ain't a real good idea now. I mean we're just bonding, right? We ain't robbing nobody or stealing or doing nothing wrong. Right?

HAYES

(Before the officer can reply) That's right, Sir. All we're doing is just a little male bonding at Christmas time out here, Mr. Officer. You know how that goes, Sir. We males just gotta continue to bond. Feel me?

ALL THE BOYS

(Chiming in with support for Hayes' comment. They are still tossing the ball and trying desperately to conceal their faces from the policeman's glance.) Right on, my dog! That's what I'm talking about. Real male bonding.

OFFICER

(Looking at the boys very skeptically) Sure thing, son, but right now I want all of you to listen up carefully. You listening?

PJ

Oh yeah.

HAYES

Full attention.

PECO

We straight.

WILL

Yes sir.

OFFICER

Listen, you boys better be extra careful out here. The streets are always dangerous, but for some strange reason it seems like they get even more dangerous—especially for women and kids—during this time of the year. So don't overstay your welcome out here tonight because these streets ain't nobody's friends . . . And especially after dark.

PJ

You don't got to worry about us, Mr. Officer. We all got the same family rule. Gotta be inside by the time the street light comes on.

HAYES

But we're be careful anyway.

PECO

Yeah. As a matter of fact I'm on my way home right after we finish this last game of catch anyway.

PJ

(With his hand to his ear) A-a-ah!! Speaking of home I do believe I hear my dear sweet little old mommie calling me for dinner right now. What about your mom, Hayes, can you hear her calling you too? (Winking to indicate he's playing a joke on the cop)

HAYES

Oh yeah! I believe I do! Coming Mom! Coming! (To Will) Are you still coming to dinner with us today, Christopher? (Winking to indicate to Will that a trick is being played on the cop; however, he is obviously lost.)

WILL

(Confused) Christopher? Who's . . .

HAYES

(Interrupting quickly) Don't you remember yesterday your mom said it would be okay for you to eat at our house tonight?

WILL

Yesterday? Man I don't even know . . .

HAYES

(Quickly placing his hand over Will's mouth and pulling him off stage.) . . . know what we're having for dinner tonight. I know. And neither do I but don't worry it's all good brother. You know my mama always knows exactly what to do in the kitchen. Now you just wave good night to the policeman. Good night Mr. Policeman and thank you so much for making our neighborhood so safe. (All the kids exit. Officer Grant thinks hard for a moment.)

OFFICER

Something strange is going on here . . . and I'm going to get to the bottom of it too. (Pauses and thinks) Come to think of it, I've seen that one kid's face some place before. I better go run a quick check. (Exits briskly. Stage is quiet. Peco sticks his head out, examines the stage, determines it's safe and waves the others back onto the street.)

WILL

So what all of that about just now?

HAYES

Better yet, brother, why don't you tell us what you're all about?

WILL

Whadda'ya talking about what I'm all about? Whadda'ya mean by that?

PJ

Listen, buddy. We're all street kids. You understand? We didn't just come out here today either. We know the streets, the cops, the system and everybody that's somebody on these streets or in the system. Now we don't know you . . .

PECO

YET!!!

PJ

But we will . . . and in just a few minutes . . . (pounding his fist into the palm of his hand) . . . Or else.

WILL

Alright! Alright! But don't think you scared me into telling you anything though. (Obviously somewhat intimidated) It's just that I'm a talkative kind of guy. That's all. Well my name is Marcus William Johnson but everybody calls me Will for short. (Enters an old man in the background. He says nothing but takes a seat on the ground nearby and observes for a few seconds. Old man pulls a sketching pad and pencil from his sack and begins doodling. He remains quiet.)

PECO

Okay Marcus William Johnson, let's get back to some real business, brother. I want to know why you come here busting up on my turf.

WILL

I already told you it's not your turf . . . (looks away and speaks more softly) and because I'm . . . running away from home.

HAYES

You're what? Are you crazy? Why on earth would you want to do something like that?

WILL

What do you mean am I crazy? You're out here aren't you?

HAYES

Sure am and regretting it every day. Hey, man, this is no way for a kid to have to spend his childhood.

PECO

So talk to us Marcus William Johnson. What's the real deal? I mean what's the real reason you decided to pack that pretty little bag of yours and run away from your family? Your old man booted you out or something?

WILL

'Booted me? Shoot! I wish. (Music begins very softly in the background)

PJ

You wish?

WILL

Yeah! That's what I said, alright? I WISH!! At least if he had booted me out I would know that he at least paid me enough attention TO boot me.

PECO

(More sympathetic) Hey, man. Been there, done that, felt those same pains before. Dude, where's your home.

WILL

Ellis Estates. But that's just it, man. Yeah it's a big beautiful house, but I wouldn't call it a home. But to answer your question my house is over on Hampton Pond Road. Over on the north side of town.

HAYES

We know that area. Kindda ritzy ain't it?

PECO

Word dog. Y'all got some REAL cribs out that way. Ellis Estate ain't no joke. Yo' old man must be really hustling up the Benjamins to be able to camp y'all out in that area.

WILL

(Ignoring Hayes' remark and continuing to voice his feelings.) I guess you could say he's doing alright, but like I said before, personally I wouldn't call anything about where I live a home though. OK, look at this thing like this. I wouldn't call neglect and self centeredness and arrogance the qualities that make up a home? Would you? (They mumble among one another.) I mean shouldn't a home have just a little bit of love? Shouldn't there be just a little bit of concern? Shouldn't there be communications? Shouldn't there be some genuine caring and not just the image of someone who cares because it's the politically correct way to appear to all the people in the church, social clubs and neighborhood? Hey, but what do I know? I'm only a child, right? So maybe what I think or how I feel really doesn't matter anyway. But what does matter to me is that I hate having a big, beautiful, expensive house to run into a sit in my huge bedroom and cry all by myself because my parents are too busy being professionals and looking good for everybody else except my sister and me. I may be a kid, and I may not know very much but trust me guys, I know when I'm lonely and I know when I'm hurting. And I also know when people don't seem to care about my loneliness or my pain. So now, you tell me. Does that sound like much of a home to you? I don't know. I'm not even sure I even know what a home is anymore.

PJ

Hey, man, check this out. It's kind'a easy to tell you're a newbie out here.

WILL

Newbit?

PJ

Check this out, brother. Newbie! (accenting the bie) Meaning somebody new to the streets. With me now? (Will nods yes) That's why we pulled you away from that cop because you wouldda said the wrong thang and got us all turned in.

WILL

Turned in? Turned in to who?

HAYES

In our case to the State Department. You see, Marcus William Johnson, unlike you, we don't have a home in the estates. There are no moms and dads out looking for us. Only the cops and social workers. To you these are the streets until you decide you want to go back home. To us this IS our home.

WILL

(To Peco) Oh, so that's why you call this your turf?

PECO

(Sad looking) Yeah. That's why.

WILL

Sorry, man. I didn't know. (extends his hand) Friends?

PECO

Under one condition, brother?

WILL

And what condition is that?

PECO

That is you go back home . . . and right now.

WILL

What?

PECO

Will, this is no place for you to be if you don't HAVE to be, brother. Listen to me, Will. Right now there are approximately 15-20 million teenagers. They're . . . no WE'RE eating anywhere we can find food. We're sleeping anywhere we can bed down for a night. Our hope is dim and our futures fade a little more every morning the sun comes up. I know you may be saying that all's not perfect at home . . . but there's far less perfection out here than in your home.

PJ

Yeah, Will, just go home and give yourself a little time to think about what you're doing. This could be crucial brother. Trust me. I know. I made that same mistake three and a half years ago.

HAYES

Will where are you going when you leave here?

WILL

I don't know.

HAYES

You've got to eat. How are you going to eat?

WILL

I don't know.

PECO

It's suppose to rain and get cold tonight, Will. Where are you going to sleep?

WILL

I don't know. I don't know. I don't know. I don't know anything anymore! So please just leave me alone. Please!

(Old man is putting away his sketching materials and lying down for the night. Other bag people wander into the area and bags down as well.

PECO

(Very calm) Let's go guys. I know a place we can sleep tonight and not get wet. As for you, Mr. Tough guy, (walks over to where Will had written his name on the ground, erases it with his foot and re-writes his own name) ain't nothing changed. These are still the streets and this is still my turf. So don't let me and my boys catch you here when we come back come sunrise. (The trio heads for the exit. Once nearly off Hayes turns and reminds Will . . .)

HAYES

Oh yeah, remember what the po'lice man said . . . streets ain't nobody's friend . . . especially after dark. (Winks. Exits. Music is playing softly as Will kneels down and prepares to bed down for the night. He looks homeward. Stuffs items back into the bag. Takes a few brisk steps then stops. Returns to his original location. Slowly unpacks the necessary gear for the night, kneels and prays, Finally he beds down and immediately dozes off. Evening persons can be seen conducting business about him.)

ACT II

SCENE II

(Act II Scene II takes place in the family's LR. Alexis is still seated with her face in her hands. She begins to speak to God.)

ALEXIS

Dear God . . . if you're there then please hear me tonight. I know—and you do too—that I've never been one who has relied on prayer or miracles in my life. But now . . . I guess . . . I need both, huh? Well . . . you've always said you were a forgiving God. I guess now I'll really get a chance to see. God I don't mean to sound as if I'm bargaining with you or anything like that . . . I just want to ask you to please look after my baby out there on those dark and lonely streets. God, it's so dangerous out there! He needs you. (Begins to cry harder.) He's my baby, God. My own flesh and blood baby! Mine! I desired him. I conceived him. I carried him. I birthed him. I raised him. And now I'm praying for him. Lord, you know there is no love like that of a mother for her own child. Don't take my baby away like this God. (Miffy has quietly entered the room and stands staring at her pleading mother. Her mother is yet to notice her there.) Please don't do this to me. God, I don't know why you would let my child just get up and walk away from this beautiful home and his family. And I don't know why you would . . . (Startled when interrupted)

MIFFY

HE WOULD?! HE WOULD? You mean you are really trying to blame this on God? No mother! Not HE . . . YOU . . . YOU . . . and DAD . . . and ME . . . WE . . . WE let him walk away from us and this home. Can't you see that? Can't you understand that when a child leaves a home it's not because God let's him, but because the child chooses to because he's simply unhappy about something that's going on there!

ALEXIS

(Enraged with anger, Alexis crosses swiftly to her daughter) Young Lady! Why you have no idea . . .

MIFFY

(Miffy cuts her off by promptly raising an envelope eye level) Mother I have more than an idea . . . I HAVE PROOF!!!

ALEXIS

(Emotions visibly diminishing) Proof? What are you talking about?

MIFFY

(Remains frozen in her position but very solemn in speech) Proof, Mother.

ALEXIS

(Nervously snatches a wrinkled, folded sheet of paper from her daughter's hand, hesitates, then begin reading it silently, and, eventually, aloud. Alexis begins reading from the final stanzas of the poem "Mama Can We Talk." Her voice fades into that of son's. She concludes her reading. Silence. Eyes darting about room. Finally . . . sorrowfully . . .) I never knew. (Stands up collects herself and wipes her tears.) I just . . . never knew. I mean . . . I never figured it out. How could he not be happy. I mean . . . look at all of this. What child wouldn't be happy with this . . . and proud too. I just never knew. (Starts across stage to where her coat and hat are hanging on a rack.) But now that I do . . .

MIFFY

What are you doing Mother?

ALEXIS

I'm going to find your brother . . . er . . . my son.

MIFFY

But, Mom, you can't. I mean you don't even know where he is.

ALEXIS

It doesn't matter. I know he's out there and now I have a choice. I can either go get him or leave him to a vicious monster known as the streets. Tell me, Miffy, if you had a child out there, which would you do?

MIFFY

You're right. (Starts over to the coat rack to get her coat and hat.) I'm getting my coat and purse. I'm coming with you. I'm sure I can help find him.

ALEXIS

You are not! Those streets out there are dangerous and they're no place for any child to be.

MIFFY

It doesn't matter . . . I'll be safe . . . protected . . . I'll be with my mother.

ALEXIS

Oh, no, Miffy. I need you here. After all, what if the policeman should call and we're not here?

MIFFY

(Getting her purse) The answering machine will pick up, Mother.

ALEXIS

What if your father comes back and doesn't find us here this time of night?

MIFFY

I'll leave him a note.

ALEXIS

What if . . .

MIFFY

(Interrupting her mother firmly) I'm going with you mother . . . and that's all there is to it. Don't forget he's my brother too. (Scribbles a note and goes over and double checks the answering machine) There! There's the note and the answering machine is set to pick up on the third ring. I'll be waiting in the car, Mother. (Soft music. Starts out then stops and glances over at Mom. Goes over and gives her a big hug. Miffy exits.)

ALEXIS

(Looks up and resumes her talk with God) I guess it's true . . . You do work in mysterious ways. One of my children just walked out of my life and the other one just hugged me for the first time in . . . only you know how long. God had this much really gone wrong with my family and I hadn't even taken the time to notice it? Lord, send a protector to Will and a teacher to me so that I can learn what I must do in order to re-establish a true spiritual and family relationship with you and within this home. And Lord, I promise You, the first chance I get I will have a family prayer and tell all of my family that I love them. And, God, thank You and I love You too.

(EXIT. LIGHTS)

ACT III

SCENE I

(The action opens on the streets with the father showing a photo of his son to street patrons and inquiring if they have seen him. None has. He continues to inquire vigorously. Visibly disappointed and disgusted, he gives up for the night and dejectedly returns home. Upon entering the house he goes to the phone and notices the note left by Miffy and Alexis. He reads it then tosses it away. Dad then turns on the answering machine. There are no messages. Exhausted and perplexed, he flops down into a chair and eventually dozes off to sleep. Meanwhile, mother and daughter are now canvassing the street for assistance. Like Dad, they find none and, also like Dad, return home tired and disappointed. Immediately upon entering the house, Miffy hurriedly tosses her coat and hat aside and rushes over to retrieve the messages from the answering machine. She has barely noticed her father at all.)

MIFFY

I'll see if anyone has called from the police department.

FRANK

No message, Pumpkin. I checked it half an hour ago and I've been sitting right here every since waiting for it to ring. (Dad is very drowsy and lethargic in his speech.)

120

ALEXIS

You mean nothing?

FRANK

Nothing.

ALEXIS

No word?

FRANK

No word.

ALEXIS

Not even a clue?

FRANK

Not even a clue.

ALEXIS

(Sounding more and more worried) Not even an idea where he might be?

FRANK

No idea.

ALEXIS

Well for goodness sakes, Frank! Please don't let me keep you awake with all of these unimportant and aggravating questions! After all DAD, (becoming agitated again) we're only talking about our son living out there on the filthy and dangerous streets of this city!! And during Christmas no less, Frank!! In case you'd forgotten what time of year this is.

FRANK

Alexis, please! Not now! Can't you understand that? (Getting up quickly) NOT NOW!!

MIFFY

Mother (trying to calm the situation) I think you're just a little bit tired, perhaps it would be (going over to her) better if you . . .

ALEXIS

(Cutting her off abruptly) Perhaps it would be MUCH better if you just stayed out of this young lady!

FRANK

(Sounding very tired) Alexis it's not the child's fault . . . don't yell at her that way!

ALEXIS

(Very angrily) I will yell at her anyway I please! And as for as *you* are concerned . . .

MIFFY

Mother, please!

ALEXIS

If you were any kind of a father at all you would never had allowed any of this to happen in the first place!!

FRANK

(Jumping up) *ME!! ME!! WHAT ABOUT YOU, ALEXIS? WHAT . . . ABOUT . . . YOU!!??!!*

MIFFY

Daddy!

ALEXIS

ME?!! So now it's my fault is it? (Face to face with Dad) Well, I should have known you'd say that.

FRANK

(Pointing to the sky and very emotionally) ONLY . . . BECAUSE . . . IT'S . . . TRUE!!!

MIFFY

(Aside as if to the audience.) I can't believe it! It's happening all over again and with a son out on the streets at Christmas no less.

ALEXIS

(Continuing to argue with her husband and ignore the daughter's plea.) YOU'RE A FINE ONE TO TALK! An anorexic daughter! A run-a-way son! A depressed wife!

FRANK

AA-h-h-ha!! (Turning and pointing) But NEVER too depressed to go shopping!

ALEXIS

Shopping?! Shopping?! Is that what we're talking about now? Shopping?

MIFFY

(Facing the audience) Please stop. (Mom and Dad are yelling at one another.)

FRANK

Yes we are since YOU brought up the subject!!

ALEXIS

I brought up the subject? I brought up the subject?

FRANK

Yes you did!!

ALEXIS

You have lost your mind, man.

FRANK

No! No, Miss Perfect. It's not ME who's crazy! It's YOU!

ALEXIS

Oh, so now I've got to be all perfect, huh? It's like that, huh Just because you couldn't do your job as the father of this family and keep us all together. Now you want to shift the blame to me!

FRANK

I DID my job, Alexis. It's you who didn't do your job—MOTHER. And you know why you didn't have the time to do your job in the house, in the family, with your children? Because you were too busy with your image and reputation and your dinners and ladies' tea parties. That's why you didn't have time to do your job as a mother and a wife!

MIFFY

Oh . . . my . . . God! I really don't believe this is happening! I don't!

ALEXIS

My job? For your information, Mr. Man-of-the-house, my job is to support you in doing your job as the head of the family and house.

FRANK

Then why won't you support me, Alexis and stop trying to *be* me!

ALEXIS

Be you? Frank, are you crazier than usual? Did you fall and bump your ego-swollen head on a stupid rock or something?

FRANK

Aw-w-w, so we got jokes now, huh, Alexis? At a time like this my *brilliant* wife come up with *jokes*! Well, I've got an idea for you, Alexis.

ALEXIS

You? An idea? Get real, Frank! You wouldn't know an idea if one sat down and at the dinner table with you.

FRANK

Well, I'll share it with you anyway! Why don't you just save your poor attempts at jokes for your next uppity and boring ladies' tea party? Alright?

ALEXIS

Uppity . . . and boring? MY tea parties?

MIFFY

Oh, my Lord, not the tea party thing again please!

FRANK

You heard me! Uppity *and* boring!

ALEXIS

That's why I can never support you, Frank.

FRANK

Why? Because I'm not uppity and boring like you?

ALEXIS

Oh-h-h-h, trust me, Frank. Uppity? No. Boring? You bet'cha!

MIFFY

(Looking to the sky) All I want is my brother. That's all.

ALEXIS

You listen to me, Frank Johnson. You want to be the man of this house? You want me to support you? You want to be something more in this house than a live in business partner? THEN GET OUT THERE AND GO FIND OUR BOY—DAD!!! Isn't that what daddies do when their kids run away, Frank? Isn't it?

FRANK

I wouldn't know, Alexis. My kids have never run away before. But since you're son knowledgeable about the subject why don't you tell me what mothers do when their kids runaways.

ALEXIS

I swear it, Frank Johnson. I swear there are times when I could just . . .

FRANK

What? Just what?

ALEXIS

When I could just . . .

MIFFY

STOP THIS MADNESS NOW!!! STOP IT!! STOP IT!! STOP IT!!!

(Both parents are now quiet and look at their daughter quizzically. Father goes over to her and leans over her shoulder very tenderly)

FRANK

Pumpkin, why are you yelling so loud? (She looks shocked he would ask that.)

ALEXIS

Is something wrong, Honey? Is it something your daddy said?

MIFFY

(Totally disgusted) Why am I yelling? Is it something daddy said? Don't you guys see? This is it. *This* is why Will isn't here. Because the two of you are so full of yourselves that there isn't any room or time for anyone else . . . to include your own children—*AT CHRISTMAS TIME.* This isn't about a sale or shopping or how good a mother or father either of you are. This is about us bonding together as a family unit . . . during a period of crisis . . . in order to save our family. It's Christmas Eve, Mom, Dad, and my brother's not here. I don't want to know who's anorexic or who goes shopping or who's the best parent, or uppity or boring . . . all I want is my brother! My brother, people! WILL!! WILL!! My God, folks, must we BOTH run away before you two learn *anything*? Forget it!! It doesn't matter. I'll do this myself! (Turns and heads for the door briskly) You two can just sit around here and argue over who's the best parent! (Runs off stage.)

ALEXIS

Miffy! Miffy! (Running to the door) Miffy where are you? Miffy come back here! Miffy! Miffy! Oh no not my daughter too! Quick, Frank! Grab your hat! We've got to catch her. We can't lose both of them in the same day. Hurry, Frank! Hurry! (They both run out behind Miffy.)

LIGHTS

ACT III

SCENE II

(Miffy is on the street showing the photo of her brother. She finally hears the desperate voices of her parents calling her name. She does not answer. Finally they catch up to her.)

ALEXIS

Miffy!! (She's out of breath) Didn't you hear your father and me calling you for the last quarter of a mile?

MIFFY

What are you two doing here? Shouldn't y'all be at home clawing away at each other's throats trying to figure out who's the better parent?

ALEXIS

Miffy . . . (pause) I'm sorry.

MIFFY

No luck, Mom. No one has seen him.

ALEXIS

Miffy, did you hear me? I said I was sorry.

MIFFY

Funny isn't it, Mom? There was a time when you wouldn't even let Will and me come over here in the south central part of the city and tonight here you are looking for one of us over here.

FRANK

Pumpkin, your mother and I realize how wrong we were and how . . .

MIFFY

It doesn't matter now, Daddy. You know, Dad—I wonder if I followed a star in the east . . . like the three wise men did . . . I wonder if I will find Will just like they did the Baby Jesus. You think so? You Mom? You think so?

ALEXIS

Miffy . . . (places hand on Miffy's shoulder who quickly brushes it away.)

MIFFY

Oh well here goes! I think I'll just follow *that* one! (Pointing skyward)

FRANK

Miffy I have had enough of this foolishness. I want you to cut this childishness out right now!

MIFFY

Here goes! (Looking skyward and pointing to her chosen star. She does not look down to see where she is walking. She is only observing the star.)

FRANK

Miffy, I said stop it right this moment! (Miffy trips over a bag person. He is totally wrapped up in his bed gear. She does not know this is Will.)

WILL

(Uncovering his head as he is speaking) Hey!! Yo!! What'cha doing on my turf? I didn't . . . (Sees it is his sister)

MIFFY

Oh my God! WILL!! WILL! Mom! Dad! I found him!! I found him!! It's Will!!

FRANK AND ALEXIS

WILL???

FRANK

Why, son, you scared us all nearly half to death!! We've been searching all over the city for you. But as long as you're okay that's all that matters. Come on. Get you bags and let's go home. It's damp and cold out here and we can all sit down and talk about this tomorrow night after I get home from my meeting.

WILL

No, Dad. (Gets up and starts down stage)

FRANK

No? What do you mean no?

WILL

I mean I'm not going home with you. Not tonight, not tomorrow, not ever.

ALEXIS

Will, what on earth are you saying?

WILL

(Soft music begins) I'm saying as far as I'm concerned, I AM home, Mom. And this (pointing to his sleeping bag and the street) is it. I know it's not what you want for me. And I know this isn't your choice of neighborhoods either. But right now it's the only place in the world where people listen to me. It's the only place in the world where people care about me. It's the only place in the world where I don't come second to everything else. I'm happy here. Here on my own little piece of the turf. All I want is for you all to know that I am fine and for you to please go home and leave me alone.

MIFFY

(very sympathetically) Will let's go home. I'll listen to you. I promise. We'll sit and we'll talk. And we'll have fun and share secrets. And open presents tomorrow too.

WILL

Thanks, Miffy. But I can't.

MIFFY

What do you mean you can't, Will? I just promised you I would listen and talk and be there for you.

WILL

(Exploding) But it isn't YOU that I need that from, Miffy!! IT'S THEM!! (pointing to his parents) Can't any of you see that? Can't you? (To his Sister) Miffy, you're not the person I bonded with before I was even born. My mother is. And you're not the person I dream of throwing footballs or riding motorcycles with. My father is. You're not the mother who makes me cry because she's too tired or too busy to listen to my feelings or even pretend she's listening to them. (To his parents) Mom, dad, I don't have microwaves and snacks and color tv's . . . and I don't have a beautiful home out in the estates with a picture perfect picket fence, but here on the hard, dirty dangerous city streets, I do have someone who thinks my feelings are worth hearing. Just look (pointing to other bag people sleeping on the street) these folks are my new family now . . . and anytime I feel I have the need to talk I have someone to talk to. And even if I didn't . . . it wouldn't matter anyway. You know why? Because they're only the substitutes. You see you're the ones I've always wanted to talk to but never got the chance till tonight. Sad isn't it? I've lived with you all my life and I never got the chance to really talk with you until I ran away to live on the streets.

ALEXIS

Marcus William Johnson, you just stop this nonsense right here and right now. Now you grab that bag this very moment and let's go home NOW!! Is that clear young man?

WILL

(Highly agitated) For goodness sakes, Mom!! Didn't you hear anything at all that I just said? Or do you think this is all just some kind of act?

BAGPERSON

Sh-h-h!! Have a little respect will you? Can't you see people are trying to get some sleep around here!

ALEXIS

Oh sh-h-h yourself you filthy street bum!! How dare you even speak to me.

MIFFY

Leave him alone, Mom. You don't even know who he is.

ALEXIS

And what's more is that I don't care, young lady. What I do care is that he goes and finds himself a job, and not lie out here on these streets and waste my hard earned taxed dollars. Bum!

MIFFY

Mom!!

ALEXIS

Quiet, Miffy. You just stay out of this! I don't have the energy to deal with your brother and homeless, jobless, rude people too!

BAG PERSON

Sorry, ma'am.

ALEXIS

Yes, and you should be too! Now, Will, as I was saying . . .

WILL

Mom don't you understand? I don't want to come back home. Not tonight. Not tomorrow. Not ever again. EVER Mom. That's the whole reason I left home was because I didn't want to be there anymore. (Moving about the stage) Mom, I'm just tired of you and dad fighting. You and Miffy fighting. You and me fighting. I'm tired of the screaming and yelling. I'm tired of eating at a table with people I feel like I don't even know. Mom I'm tired of sharing a home with strangers and I'm tired of having to call our house . . . a home. I'm tired of Oprah Winfrey getting more of your time each day than I do. And I'm tired of you, dad, calling me only when you want me to bring you another beer or a dark suit out of your closet because you're packing to leave on another business trip. And I'm tired of Miffy having to try to make up for both of you in my life. I'm tired folks. I'm tired to the bone. And so I chose to leave your house and come . . . (pointing to his sleeping bag) home.

ALEXIS

Will surely you're not serious about this little charade.

WILL

This is not a charade and I am very serious, Mom. It's just something I've got to do.

FRANK

But son (starts for Will but Will immediately puts his arm out and halts his progress)

WILL

No dad! It's no use. My mind is made up. Even if you took me back tonight . . . I'd only run away again and again and again. Please just go now and leave me alone. It's been a long day and I'm very tired.

MIFFY

Will . . .

WILL

I love you, Sis. (She runs over and gives him a hug and kisses him on the cheek) Please take them now. This is hard enough without having them here. Please . . . for me . . . please.

MIFFY

I love you Will. (Nod nods his head yes. Miffy goes over and extends her hand to Mother and Dad. They take one each and start off. Stop. Turn and look back. Mother snatches away and goes back! She is highly emotional.)

ALEXIS

Will, son, I'll change. I will. I won't yell anymore. I won't fight I'll listen. I swear I will. A-a-and we'll talk . . . and go for walks . . . and pitty pat . . . you know and stuff like that. (Will does not acknowledge her at all. He remains with his back to her and seemingly oblivious to his mother's comments. She becomes more emotional . . .) My God Will!! Why are you doing this to me?? Why? Don't you see I'm trying? Won't you even let me try?? Won't you? Come home, son! Please don't do the, Will! (FRANK approaches from behind and takes her by the shoulders. She maneuvers free.) Will . . . Will . . . (softly and crying) Guess what? I'd said all of these things I was going to do when I saw you again . . . I was going to pounce on your chest with two feet (trying to laugh jokingly through her tears) . . . a-a-and string you up by your big toes (still trying to laugh). Funny isn't it? Isn't it? Well it was until I say you and then all of a sudden I realized that all I wanted was . . . my son back. That's all I want for Christmas Will is you back home with us happy and safe. I prayed tonight Will that God would send you back to home safely. Will, please (extending her hand) let's go home.

WILL

(Coldly and without visually acknowledging his mother) Go home, Mama.

ALEXIS

But son . . .

WILL

Please! Just go home.

(Father turns mother away successfully this time. Family leaves stage slowly and dejectedly. Heads are hung. Affects are sad. Will goes back to bed. As Will sleeps the three runaway teenagers return to rob him. However, as they approach him, the old street bum quickly stands up and [with hand gestures only] abruptly stops them and sends them on their way. A second person of the evening contemplates robbing Will as well; however, the same thing happens again. Will tosses and turns then finally sits up on his pallet. He is visibly frustrated. He glances toward home. It's obvious he is wrestling with returning there. He is now standing and pacing. His confusion is mounting. Will quickly snatches up his belongings, stuffs them into his backpack, and starts home. He stops. Despondently he returns to his spot on the street. Will sits and ponders for a minute, then begins rummaging through his bag. He pulls out a hypodermic needle and begins to prepare his arm for an injection. The street bum (who has been watching him all along) rushes over to him and places his hand between the needle and Will's arm. Then he sits and talks (mouths) with Will. He extends his open hand to Will, and Will slowly places the needle in the man's hand. The street bum then rubs his heart then rubs Will's arm with his hand. He repeats this 2 or 3 times. After the third time, he gives Will's arm a stinging smack with his open palm. Will jumps then inspects his arm as if something strange has happened. The street bum throws the needle to the ground and stomps on it. He invites Will to join him. Will jumps up immediately and does so. The duos pounce on the hypodermic until it is thoroughly crushed, then laugh until they literally fall down. The old man stops laughing first, returns to Will's area, and beckons Will to sit down again next to him. Will obliges. He commences talking to Will, and when he is done, he returns to his accommodations, and returns to sleep. Will does likewise, but rises shortly thereafter and packs his belongings. He glances at the old man, the streets, and his arm and exit in the direction of home. (Song/Music) Family enters the house and all sit around in LR. Dad's examines his watch and gestures that he is going to bed. Miffy does the same shortly thereafter. She gives Mom a hug then exits. Mom begins pacing the floor. She goes over and picks up a copy of the poem "Mama Can We Talk". Mom is dabs away tears as the poem is read. She places the poem down on the table and grabs her purse. She heads off to the door then stops just as she is about to open it. She comes back. Ponders a moment. Then heads back to the door. She snatches the door open preparing to go back on the streets to her son, but standing in the door holding his bag is Will.)

ALEXIS

Oh . . . my . . . God!! Will! Will! Oh my God! Will, it's you. (Alexis is pulling Will on stage from "outside" as she speaks. My son! You've come home! Oh, God! Thank you, Lord. My baby is home. Will, you're home!

WILL

Yeah. I am, Mama. The old man who bedded down next to me on the street had a long talk with me right after you guys left. He made me see and understand a lot of stuff I guess I hadn't even thought about before. He even took away another problem I had too. I know he did because I could feel it when it left me. I know you don't have any idea what I'm talking about, but . . . well . . . well, let's just say miracles at Christmas still happen. He also made me understand that the making of a happy home isn't 100% the parents' doings either. We—the kids—have a lot to do with it too. How well we obey. Our decisions. Our behavior . . . discipline . . . friends . . . habits. He told me that we play a big role in the quality of our family lives and our homes just like our parents do. And you know what else he said? He said to tell you that if you lend me your ear, you will probably earn my heart. But he also told me to be sure not to forget to tell you that unless you are patient enough to truly listen to another person's side of a story and to try to understand their frustration, confusion and feelings—not agree with them—just understand them—you'll never truly understand that person—even if that person is your very own child. And finally he told me to tell you *and* Dad to always remember love is not in your possessions or your reputation. Love, he said, is ONLY in what you do for people. And then he said I was suppose to just say END OF MESSAGE and you'd know what I meant. Mom, you do remember who I'm talking about don't you, Mom? He was that little homeless man that you spoke so rudely to on the street. The one you called a street bum. Anyway it seems like he already knew a lot about you. But you know what was even more strange about him? He wasn't from this city, but no one asked him why was he treading on their turf like they did me. Wonder why?

ALEXIS

I don't know, Will. I don't. Maybe because he's been there so long everybody just knows him and doesn't say anything to him. Anyway, you're home! And we certainly can't spend this valuable time talking or thinking about some homeless street bum . . . er, person . . . now can we?

MIFFY

(Enters from her bedroom with robe and slippers on. It's obvious she was asleep. Rubbing her eyes until she sees her brother.) Mom, I just wanted to ask you . . . Will!! Will!! (Runs to the door) Dad Will's here!! (Enters Dad with robe on)

FRANK

What? Will? (Notices Will) Will!! Son, you're home! Man! My son is home! And just in time for Christmas. I'm so glad you decided to come home! Now there can be a real Christmas in this house. I'll tell you, son, Christmas without you here is like Easter without the bunny. It just wouldn't be right. You know what I mean. Oh, thank God you're home, Will. I'm just so glad you're here! (Big hug)

WILL

So am I, Dad.

FRANK

You know something, Will? I guess I should be ashamed to say it, but I'm not. You really made me think tonight. You said a lot of things I think I needed to hear. Son, I'm glad you were man enough to stand up to the challenge and to educated me—and your mother—tonight. I'm sorry, Son. I'm truly sorry for all the times I've hurt you and I promise I'll try my best to never let that happen again.

WILL

That's all I ask, Dad is that you—well—all of us—try our best. After all, we're a family, right? So what's wrong with families trying to make each happy? Oh, and

Mom, that guy said something about don't forget to have that family prayer that you promised this family would have if we all got back together for the holidays.

ALEXIS

Did he really? That's creepy. How did he ever know . . . Oh well. It doesn't matter now. He's 100% correct. I promised it and there's no way I'm going to fall short on this promise either. Family let us pray. Father we are glad you sent your guardian angel our way to guide, protect and reunite this family in greater love than it has ever had before. Now more than ever before we all now know the real meaning of Christmas as well as what it means to be loved, listened to, and understood. Thank you for teaching us this very valuable lesson this Christmas day. Amen. (The family says amen too. Alexis begins going to each member of her family individually and saying to them . . .) Frank, I love you.

FRANK

I love you, Alexis.

ALEXIS

Will, I love you.

WILL

I love you too, Mom. But today I have much love for EVERYBODY!!

ALEXIS

You're right about that, Will. I'm so happy right now I feel like getting dressed and going caroling right now.

MIFFY

I love you too, Mom, Dad, Will. But I am not about to go caroling at this un-Godly hour of the night! I've spent enough time out walking the streets tonight anyway!

FRANK

I love you guys too and I'm happy to see that we are all finally happy together. But I'm with you, Miffy. I'm not about to go caroling at this hour of the night or morning.

ALEXIS

Well, Will. Should you ever see that old gentleman again, you can be sure to let him know that I absolutely did not forget to do that prayer I promised to do. Alright family! That's enough sharing love for one night. Will's tired. Mom and sister are sleepy and Dad has a business meeting early tomorrow morning. He should be done before noon and once he gets back here we'll begin opening our gifts and officially celebrating Christmas in our home.

FRANK

No meeting, Alexis!! I just thought about it and made a command decision. Tomorrow's Christmas for crying out loud! Christmas Day. No meeting. Not for me. I'm cancelling first thing in the morning. Tomorrow's Christmas AND father and son day ALL day long in this house. All day long—and nothing's going to get in the way of me spending it with the whole day with the most important people in my life. Especially with you, Son.

WILL

ALRIGHT!! What are we going to do, Dad?

FRANK

I don't know. I haven't exactly thought it far enough through to have planned it all out. But who cares? It's Christmas! Christmas! We'll just wing it.

WILL

Wing it?

FRANK

Yeah. That's right. You know, do whatever we feel like. We're entitled to do that every once in awhile—right? Once a year. Like on Christmas Day. Right? Tomorrow is OUR day, Son, and nothing or nobody is ever going to come between that again. (Arms around each other's shoulders, they head off stage. Miffy trails them.)

MIFFY

Hey what about me, guys? I mean aren't I included in this too? (following them off stage) I mean I can fish, water ski, skeet shoot, catch the football, skate, hand glide . . . . hey guys what about me?

ALEXIS

(Alexis remains on stage alone.) Well, I guess if I ever had a single doubt in my mind about what Christmas is all about, you just straightened it right out for me, didn't you? You sent an angel to watch over him and to tell me that which I needed to know in order to keep my family in-tact. I don't know how you run the department called blessings, but YOU do. And I just want you to know that this was truly a Christmas blessing for this family. Thank you for putting my family back together again . . . and God . . . thank you so much for letting all of us know what the real meaning of a family and Christmas are all about. (Starts to exit) Oh yeah, listen. Next year could you make my Christmas gift a little less stressful? See you in church Sunday, alright? (Gives a thumbs up and exits. The old man sits up on the street removes his oversized street clothes and reveals his white angelic attire and angel wings. He flaps his wings and flies away. MUSIC UP. LIGHTS.)

CURTAINS

NOW THAT I KNOW

SETTING

The action is set in or around a police holding cell at the town's local precinct. Much of the action, however, is presented by way of period flashbacks.

CAST OF CHARACTERS

POLICEMAN

HORFECT

(Horfect's) MOTHER

MIME

ANGEL

VOICE OF GOD

MOSES

CHARACTER #1

CHARACTER #2

CHARACTER #3

W.E.B. DUBOIS

BOOKER T. WASHINGTON

MALCOLM X

MARTIN L. KING, JR

DANCERS

POETIC PERFORMERS

SLAVE #1

SLAVE #2

SLAVE #3

HARRIET TUBMAN

(The stage is black and silent. A spotlight shines into the jail cell which is situated upstage. Inside the cell is a mime dressed in black with his back to the audience. He is not discernable until he slowly and carefully raises his head and turns his face to the audience. He suddenly leaps up and snatches on the bars, attempting to gain his freedom. The attempt continues for several, but to no avail. He sinks back down onto the bunk and rests his head in his hands. Suddenly, music can be heard. Dancers enter and perform. The mime watches with intense interest as the dancers perform. The dancers exit and the mime re-assumes his previous posture. The lights fade (mime exits) as a husky voice can be heard entering from off stage L.)

POLICEMAN

This way, kid. Straight back. All the way. (Policeman is leading a young man in handcuffs to his cell. The youth is clad in typical street clothes. Though he is handcuffed, he offers no resistance.) Alright. Stand fast! (Opens the cell) Get in there and back up to the door so I can remove those bracelets off your arms. (The sound of the clanking steel as the door slams shut is very distinct. The youth follows his instructions, and the officer leaves after retrieving his cuffs. The youth is obviously and visually distraught. He stands and sits. Fidgets and bangs. Stands and sits. Then starts over again. Finally he takes a seat and rests his head in his hands just as did the mime.

HORFECT

Officer! Officer! I need to write some notes. How 'bout some pencil and paper? (Pauses. Officer enters and hands Horfect pencil and paper through the bars. No words are exchanged. He sits and begins writing. The officer leaves.)

OFFICER

The husky voice can be heard entering again from off stage.) He's this way, ma'ma. Just follow me. (Approaches the cell) Visitor for you, Murphy. Your mom's here. (The child shows no interest in visiting with his mother. He does not move from his seated position.) Darn children today! Excuse me, ma'am. But

153

sometimes you just have to wonder, what's going on with them. You know what I'm saying? What's in their minds? What will they ever turn out to be if they keep up the non-sense ways they're following these days? Know what I mean, ma'am?

MOTHER

(A nervous smile) Yes, officer, I do. Trust me. Sometimes I just say . . . well, to tell you the God heaven truth, officer, sometimes I just don't know *what* to say. I just don't know. Er, officer, do you mind if he and I . . .

POLICEMAN

Oh, excuse me! Of course not, ma'am. After all that *is* why you're here. I'll just get on back to tidying up some paper work I've got to get done, and I'll come back her to escort you back up front in about ten minutes. (Looks at his watch) To tell you the truth, Ma'am, there's not a whole lot of traffic in and out of here today. You can just take your time and visit with your boy, and when you're ready to leave, just give me a loud holler. I'll be up front at the desk. It's the least I could do for you, Ma'am. Kind lady like yourself and all. Enjoy your visit, ma'am—as best you can that is. I'll keep an ear out for ya' call. (Exits)

MOTHER

(Mother goes over and tries to give her son a big hug. He resists her.) So this the way my own shoplifting child greets his own mama, who done caught three buses and made two transfers just to get downtown to see his crummy little butt sitting up in a jail cell for stealing some stupid shoes and CD's. You ungrateful little bastard! I ought to call that cop and tell him to come open up this cell and walk out of here and never lay foot in this or any other jail cell to visit you ever again! Think you'd like that, tough guy? Think you'd like calling this place home for a little while? Do you? Just how would you feel then? (Youth drops his head) Yeah. That's exactly what I thought too. Now get over here and give your mother a hug. (He does so) And a kiss. (He reluctantly pecks her on the cheek.) Bigger. (He does not move.) If you want Mama to help get you out of this cinderblock castle, you'd better start listening to her a lot closer, son. Now let's try that one . . . more . . . time. I *said* bigger. (He obeys) And now even bigger. (Pause. He obeys.) Good Horfect. Now sit down. (He goes to sit on the bunk) Not there! I'll sit there. It looks like it's probably the most comfortable place in this hell hole to sit. Listen. There's no sense in making this long or difficult. Truth is I don't have any money. And if I have no money, you, my dear son, as a natural consequence, have no lawyer. And it's probably just as well anyhow since from the looks of things right now we've got less of a chance of winning a court case than some who's walking through hell with gasoline drawers on stands of getting burned. I know it ain't exactly great news for somebody locked up in this sardine can, but at least you know your chances. Winning just doesn't look good for the home team in this game. (Notices her son is writing and paying her no attention at all.) Hey! Hey! Ain't you even listening to nothing I'm saying to you, boy? That's exactly how you landed in this . . . this . . . 21st century Alcatraz in the first place.

HORFECT

(Never looking up at his mother.) No need for you to be overly concerned about me *or* Alcatraz, Mama. From the looks of it, both of us are doing just fine for ourselves. Ain't no need for you to sweat it. I'll be alright. I can feel it in my bones.

MOTHER

You look a'here, boy. Your bones ain't what determines whether or not you get off when you go to court . . . a good lawyer is, and I just told you that neither one of us or both of us together don't have enough money to get you a good enough lawyer to get you off this time.

HORFECT

(Very unconcerned with the conversation.) Yeah, I heard you when you said it the first time, Ma. Loud and clear. I heard you when you said it the first time.

MOTHER

(Notices the youth's strict attention to his writing. Goes over and snatches it from him.) You over here writing like you're crazy and I'm up here trying to talk to you about a lawyer. Aren't you at least *concerned* about a lawyer? Say? What's this mess anyway that's got your brain so tied up and involved that you can't even take time out to talk about your own representation in the courtroom room? (Glances down at the pad. Her face shoes subtle surprise. Then enlightenment. Then slight angry. She suddenly throws the tablet back at the youth and yells at him to . . .) Read it! (He stares but says nothing.) I SAID READ THAT *MESS* YOU JUST WROTE ABOUT ME! READ IT OUT LOUD. LOUD! LOUD!!

POLICEMAN

(From off stage) Ma'am, is everything alright?

MOTHER

(Altered demeanor) Why of course, Officer. Everything is just fine. Dandy. Just fine. (Then to the youth beneath her breath.) I want you to read that stinking crap . . . and I want to hear every blasphemous and unappreciative word on that paper come off the very end of your tongue and through your lips. Now you read that crappy poem to me right now. 'Cause I know it's talking about me. Now read it! READ I said!

HORFECT

(Begins to read the poem in a lifeless nearly inaudibly.) Yo! Yo! What up dog? How the sister be? Sho 'nuff . . .

MOTHER

(Places her fingers beneath his chin and lifts his face bringing them eye to eye.) Don't make me leave you in here 'till the day you *rot,* boy! Now I said twice already, and for my blood . . . three times is just TOO many for me to have to ask you. (Stares him in his eyes. He lifts his chin from her fingers, and begins to read more forcefully.)

HORFECT

YO! YO! What up dawg?
How the sister be?
Sho' nuff can't believe you done come way down here just to yell at some old jailbird like me!

How come, Mama, how come?
What brings you this way NOW?
Sho-o-ot! Don't go worry yo' pretty little self bout it. Ain't nothing but a thang. I mean you being here to see me anyhow!

So what's up, Mama? How come you look at me like that?
And don't go fronting on me either;

You ain't got to worry 'bout nothing. I ain't gonna cheese on you like some big fat rat.

Cell . . . Toilet . . . (patting his bunk) Bunk . . . Bars
This is where you landed me . . . when you shot for the stars.
Long days . . . longer nights . . .
Broken dreams . . . blinded sights . . .
Smiles of lies . . . Hopes of sighs . . .
Dreams of defeat . . . and a future in which I cannot compete.
Cell . . . Toilet . . . Bunk . . . . Bars
This is where you landed me . . . when you shot for the stars.

You winked at men, flirted with boys, and disregarded my feelings and soul
You shaped my thoughts and corrupted my character and for a simple favor from any man, your very dignity and self worth you sold.

You taught me to lie, to cheat, to connive, and to deceive
And every time the game worked you never corrected me—you cheered!
And because my deception earned your approving cheers and smiles
I grew up believing "out the door with honest"
I'm street smart enough to make it on guile.

And so I left your nest and ventured out—and set out to become another you;
But in order to do that, I had to emulate everything I'd seen you do.
And so I grew up lying, and cheating, and beating my way through,
But ironically, I got caught while you managed to slip through "just doing the do."

And so now here I sit . . . in a cell . . . with my bunk . . . . and my toilet . . . and these jailhouse bars;
Here I am, Mama . . . and all because I was you paycheck to the stars.

MOTHER

I see. There's no need for you to explain. Your "poem"—if that's what you call that—that—that thing. Well whatever you call it, IT has said more than enough for me. I'm sorry I landed you here in your cell . . . with your bunk . . . and your toilet . . . and these jailhouse bars. I'm sorry, Horfect, that you were my sorry paycheck to the stars. (Turns and summons) OFFICER! OFFICER!

OFFICER

Yes, ma'am?

MOTHER

(To the officer.) I'm ready now. (To Horfect)
Twinkle twinkle little star, you want me to feel guilty about where you are.
OH! But I can't. Not this week.
You see, my (turns and glares at the youth) worthless paycheck is in jail, with his bunk bars and toilet seat.
Which makes it necessary for me to hit the streets
In order that I might keep food in our house to eat.

(Starts singing "Twinkle Twinkle Little Star." Officer enters and opens the cell door. She stops singing long enough to place her face near her son's face. He hesitates then kisses her lightly on the cheek. She resumes her singing and continues to sing "Twinkle Twinkle Little Star" until she has exited the scene.)

HORFECT

(Begins reading the poem aloud, then in his mind. Stops half way through and throws the paper to the floor. Bangs on the bunk. Kicks the toilet. Jerks on the bars. Then sinks to the floor in tears.) Why, Lord, why? Why me? Why not all the other children out there who do every day what I was caught doing. Why me? Are you trying to tell me something, Lord? That's what I always hear old people say. You know, "Well maybe the good master is just trying to tell you something, boy." They always saythings like that. But is that the truth? Is that the real reason I'm here and they're not. Shoot, this crap sure ain't no fun though . . . whatever the reason is I'm here. Show ain't no fun. (Goes over and sits on the stool. Stands and walks anxiously back and forth. Sits again. Looks skyward. Lights go black then come back up immediately. When they do, the youth has been replaced in the cell with a mime. The mime performs to music then the scene returns to normal with the youth now being back in the cell and the mime off stage.) If I ask (speaking skyward) will you answer me? All I want to know is why me? Why me? Why not somebody else? Why me? (Begins pacing back and forth. Sits. Stands. Sits. Then kneels to pray. Lights dim. "Our Father Prayer" music is praying. An angel enters and dances about the stage. The angel begins his/her dance outside the cell, however during the process the angel touches the lock and opens the door. He/Her dances into the cell, offers his/her hand to the youth and "dances" the youth out of the cell to center stage where he leaves him before the music's conclusion. The youth is mystified and unsure what to do, say, or think as he stands glazing in the direction of the exited angel.)

OFFICER

(Approaching carefully with his hand on his gun as he attempts to persuade the youth to return to the cell.) What the . . . ? Hold it right there now, son. Don't you move one twitch or you're be sorry you did. What the John Brown are you doing outta that cell anyhow? You trying to plan an escape out of here? Huh?

HORFECT

No, sir, Mr. Officer. Please don't shoot. Don't shoot me. I didn't do nothing, Sir. I swear I didn't.

OFFICER

Now boy that's a good one. I'm standing 10 feet away from a jail break and you trying to convince me you ain't done nothing.

HORFECT

But I didn't, officer. You gotta believe me. I didn't do . . .

OFFICER

Boy if I had a judge and jury in here right now, you'd be found guilty on the spot and sentence to at least 25 years for a felony jail break charge.

HORFECT

Officer, you gotta believe me. I didn't do a thing. Really. I didn't do this. Honest.

OFFICER

Yeah. Right. And I didn't just put you in that cells just minutes ago and locked it securely behind me either! You didn't do nothing. HUH!!! That's what every guilty as sin criminal I've ever known before always said. I see you figured out pretty quickly how to pick that lock and make your way outta that cell, huh? Maybe handcuff or maximum security is better suited for you than just a regular cell, huh, boy?

HORFECT

No, sir. No need for that sir. I'm innocent, officer. I-I-I don't even know how I got out here.

OFFICER

It's a bad thing to want to be good at something you so bad at kid.

HORFECT

Like what, officer? Whadda mean by that?

OFFICER

I mean like your lies, boy! That's what I mean. Why you want to try to fool people with such bad lies? I sure hope those hoodlum you hand out with are better at lying than you are. Now shut up and get back in there! Move it!! Move it!! (Horfect complies.) Now turn around and put your hands behind you and back up to the bars. (Horfect does and the officer handcuffs him.) Now sit down and see if that can't hold you in here for a while. I'll be back to check on you in a little while.

HORFECT

But, officer, I swear to you, I really didn't do anything wrong.

OFFICER

Well, if you didn't the first time, then I know you won't the second time since you'll have these bracelets on for a while. Sit down and stay out of trouble, ya hear? And by the way kid, you should be grateful to your mother for being such a wonderful and caring mother. That's the only reason I'm giving you another chance and not throwing you in solitary right now. (officer exits)

HORFECT

(To himself) Yes, sir, officer. I'm sure before the night's over a lot of other gentlemen will think she's wonderful too. They always do. Just wonderful. (Horfect sits with his head in his hands. When he raises his head, he has been transformed into a mime. The mime performs to music then returns to his seat. He lowers his head then looks up again and has been transformed back into Horfect.)

VOICE

Horfect! Horfect!

HORFECT

(Looking around in astonishment) What the . . . ? Hey! Who is that calling me? Who's there? (No answer) Who's there I said? Who are you?

VOICE

Horfect! I am here to answer your questions. All of them.

HORFECT

Oh, man. If this is some kind of joke I wish y'all would play t somewhere else and with somebody else too. I ain't in no mood for no games right now, dog, so why don't y'all lighten up with all the jokes! Alright. This the way y'all treat everybody in here?

VOICE

Horfect, who are you?

HORFECT

What? And why are you asking me questions anyway? I thought you said you were here to *answer* all of my questions.

VOICE

In my questions *are* your answers, Horfect. If you are able to answer my questions, Horfect, then you can teach youself the answers to your own questions. Now, to begin, and most importantly, Horfect, do you *know* who you are?

HORFECT

Of course I know who I am. I'm Horfect. But who the heck are you?

VOICE

I am *you*, Horfect. And *you* are *me*. You and I are all one and the same.

HORFECT

I ain't digging this game you running on me right now dude—whoever you are! Why don't y'all stop clowning up in here man and just tell me what it is y'all want from me. You don't need to go all Hollywood-like just for that man.

164

VOICE

There is no clowning, Horfect. And certainly there is no Hollywood to be found in a your jail cell. Yet you are here, so then, so am I. Because, as I said earlier, we are all one and the same. From the start to the finish. We are not separate. Neither are you and Malcolm X or you and Harriet Tubman or you and Maya Angelou or Mahalia Jackson, Thurgood Marshall or Martin Luther King or even you and Moses or Abraham or anyone else as far as that goes who has given their lives and limbs to make your life and limbs possible. We're all one.

HORFECT

(Highly confused) Aww man! I'm tripping big time up in this steel cage dog and I ain't even been in her one hour good yet! Come on, man! I'm sitting up in the jail yacking like I'm talking to somebody for real. I'm losing it already, dog. Gotta get a tighter grip on my mind—my sanity. At this rate I'll be stone loco by sunrise tomorrow! What's up with me? I'm stronger than this!

VOICE

There is nothing wrong with you, Horfect. Nothing at all except you simply don't understand . . . and I knew you wouldn't. After all, I know all things.

HORFECT

All things? Get real dude. The only person in the whole universe who knows all thing is . . . (pauses and looks around nervously) Oh my . . .

VOICE

Yes! You finally got it! It's me, Horfect, and I've allowed what appears to be a setback to happen in your life at this time so that I might get you alone and teach you more about who you *really* are.

HORFECT

Alone? To teach me who I am? Man please. Chill out with all the nonsense bro—whoever and where ever you are— 'cause if there one thing I know that I know for sure it's who I am. Ain't no doubt about that. I know me—*real* good.

VOICE

Really Horfect?

HORFECT

Really.

VOICE

Then why are you in jail? Why are you failing in school? Why do you steal? Why do you sell drugs? Why don't you pray? It's because you don't know who you are. You only know who people say you are. But today you will be guided through the years, times, and events that I allowed to precede your birth so that at your birth all of the great things, people and events of your past would become an intricate part of who you are as well as who you will mature into the future. Obey and learn, Horfect. Obey and learn.

(Music comes up. An angel enters and dances about the stage. The angel begins its dance outside of the cell, however, during the dance the angel touches the lock and magically the cell door opens. The angel dances into the cell where it touches the handcuff that are binding Horfect's hands and holding his captive. Magically, they fall to the floor. The angel offers his hand to Horfect who calmly accepts it and is danced out of the cell and left standing center stage. He is in the same place as he was the first time the sheriff redirected him back into the cell.)

HORFECT

Why am I here again? Why?

VOICE

So that you will learn, Horfect.

HORFECT

Learn what? What am I to learn here?

VOICE

Horfect, first you must learn that *my* people are lost for a lack of knowledge but . . . if my people, which are called by my name, would humble themselves, and pray and seek my face, and turn from their wicked ways, I will hear their prayers and I will answer them and will heal their land, their hurt, their will, their children, and their futures. and I will make their way prosperous in every way.

HORFECT

But what will happen to a race of people whose members do not humble themselves or pray or seek your face or turn from their wicked ways? What will happen to such a race of people, Lord?

VOICE

Then I will curse them . . . . and their efforts . . . . as well as their present and future generations. And they nor their children shall prosper until they have done as i have commanded.

HORFECT

You will *curse* them?

VOICE

I will allow the curses of the land to come upon them and their children until they learn of and believed in me and are willing to do as I have commanded.

HORFECT

But, Lord, I am ignorant. I am only a child and do not know how to avoid your curse. I have never been taught this.

VOICE

My child . . . many tests and trials will come your way. you cannot avoid them. Some of them will be in the form of drugs. Some in the form of stealing, sex, lying, cheating and other temptations. Some will be in the forms of pain and even hatred. But many will come by way of and because of slothfulness . . .

HORFECT

Slothfulness, Lord?

VOICE

Slothfulness. which means to be lazy.

HORFECT

You curse laziness, Lord?

VOICE

Laziness is a sin. It is the sin which stops you from achieving, succeeding, growing, learning, becoming and changing what is not right. Laziness is a sin which I curse daily.

HORFECT

I see, Lord.

VOICE

There will be other curses to avoid as well. But drugs, alcohol, teen pregnancies, disobedience and rebelliousness are some of the ones you must be extremely mindful to avoid and never to fall victim to. For should you fall victim to them, surely you will bring much shame upon yourself, your family, your race, and your future. My child, do not bring this shame upon your life simply for the love of material things or fleshly pleasures. To do so would not be wise, and in the end, the cost will be much greater than the perceived profit. (Music and dance.

VOICE

Do not be afraid, child. Lo, I am with you always. And this day, I will walk you through the history which has by My design and plan preceded you in order to make you. For you, my child, are not what you think you are. You are not just what you gaze upon when you behold your reflection in the mirror. You are not just what you see on the evening news or on the cover of magazines or on the bulletin boards of post office buildings. You—my child—are of me—from me—for me—but most of all because of me. Follow me through the course of time and see all that I have placed inside of you. You, my little black child, are not to be looked upon with contempt, but to be praised as Ii have created you for my divine purpose and for greatness among men. Lift up your head. Open your eyes. Incline your ears and learn this day that you are my creation. You are in My image. You are after My own heart. (Words from the poem "The Creation" by James Weldon Johnson are read off stage. Horfect is able to stare into the distant past and observe "The Creation" of mankind. [music])

. . . And God stepped out on space, And He looked around and said, *"I'm lonely, I'll make me a world."* . . .
Then God sat down On the side of a hill where He could think; By a deep, wide river He sat down;
This Great God, Like a mammy bending over her baby, Kneeled down in the dust Toiling over a lump of clay
Till He shaped it in His own image;Then into it He blew the breath of life, And man became a living soul.
Amen. Amen.

HORFECT

And that's how I came to be? You mean I started out as nothing more than a lump of dirt scooped up in your hands, and shaped by the precision of your fingers?

VOICE

Correct, my child.

HORFECT

And then you blew life into me?

VOICE

And then I blew me—that is my spirit—into you. And my spirit is what gave you life. But more than a spirit, I blew greatness into you child. I blew victory into you. I blew success into your very lungs. I caused you to inhale challenges and to exhale victories. I caused you to see obstacles yet to walk in confidence. I blew some of all great people into you. I blew the faith of Moses into your spirit. I blew the understanding of Solomon into your mind. I blew the courage of David into your loins. I blew the strength of Samson into your body and the patience of job in you character. You are not just who you see in the mirror my child. You are not just who you read about in the papers. You are not just who the news media says you are, not just who you read about in the papers. But you are many, many, many great and wondrous things . . . magnificently made and fearfully created in my own image. My child, behold who you really are!!

(A short tribal dance is performed around the clay figure which now remains on stage. The dancers are extremely cautious with the figure and it is obvious that they regard it a a treasure. As they conclude their dance exiting stage L, Moses enters leading his followers on from the opposite side of the stage. Much moaning and groaning can be heard before Moses and his followers are seen on stage.)

CHARACTER #1

Moses!! (Moses is emerging from the rear carrying the Ten Commandments on tablets.) Moses!! What will we do, Moses?

CHARACTER #2

Pharaoh's army is quickly approaching from the south and the Red Sea has blocked our path from the north.

CHARACTER #3

Moses, what are we to do? Surely we will die.

CHARACTER #4

Why the death of all shall be on your hands, Moses. It was you who lead us to this place of damnation! How can this be Moses you say you have heard your instructions from God himself?

MOSES

Oh you of a little faith. Stop your wailing woman. And you man, stop your doubting for we are creatures in the image of God himself and never shall he leave us along. Where is your faith oh weak man? Rise. Be strong. And know that you are the child of a mighty king.

CHARACTER #3

That is so easily said, Moses. But how does one show faith in at tie like this?

MOSES

It is called faith woman, and no one shall ever succeed without it.

CHARACTER #1

And how do we get this measure of faith which you speak of Moses.

MOSES

To each man is dealt a measure of faith. It is up to him to develop his faith to the exact level that he wishes to succeed, for God has reminded each of us "Be it unto you by your faith."

CHARACTER #3

And that means?

CHARACTER # 1

Moses!! (Moses is emerging from the rear carrying the Ten Commandments written on tablets of stone.) Moses!! What will we do, Moses!!

CHARACTER #2

Pharoah's army is quickly approaching from the south and the Red Sea has blocked out path from the north.

CHARACTER #3

Moses, what are we to do? Surely we will die.

CHARACTER #4

Why the death of us all shall be on your hands, Moses. It was you who lead us to this place of damnation! How can this be, Moses when you say you have heard you instructions from God himself?

CHARACTER #2

We will die if you do not help us, Moses. Moses, please help us. Don't let us die out here in the wilderness.

MOSES

Oh you of a little faith. Stop your wailing woman. And you man, stop your doubting for we are creatures in the image of God himself and never shall he leave us alone. Where is your faith oh weak man? Rise. Be strong. And know that you are the child of mighty king.

CHARACTER #3

That is so easily said, Moses. But how does one show faith in a time like this?

MOSES

To each man is dealt the measure of faith. It is up to him to develop his faith to the exact level that he wishes to succeed, for God has reminded each of us that "be it unto you according to your faith."

CHARACTER #3

And that means?

MOSES

It means that you cannot achieve beyond your level of faith or belief. Behold you of little faith. "Waters of the Red Sea, in the name of Jehovah the creator, I command you to part and stand fast until these children of the most high have walked across on dry land and are no longer slaves of pharaoh.

CHARACTER #1

WHOAAAA!

ALL

AWWWWE!!

CHARACTER #3

Moses how is it that you have parted the waters? How is this? How could you, a mere man, have done such a thing?

MOSES

This same power is within you my sisters and brothers. Be it unto each of you according to your own faith. Come now. Let us cross over into the promised land. We will talk more once we have safely arrived on the other side. (Exit)

HORFECT

But, Lord, how am I a part of all that was . . . and is . . . and will be . . . all at the same time?

VOICE

It is because of your spirit, Horfect.

HORFECT

Spirit . . . ?

VOICE

Yes, Horfect, your spirit. Your body is a time capsule of sort. And it can only pass through one time period at a time. It cannot be in the past because it has already gone past the past and can never return to it again. It cannot be in the future because it has yet to reach the future and therefore according to the laws which govern it, it cannot operate in a time space that it has not yet reached. Therefore, it can only be in the present. However, my spirit is timeless and ageless. Through my spirit you have lived, you are living, and you will continue to live forever. Therefore, you have lived longer than you know, and I have been with you every step of the way. There was never a time when I was not there with you at every turn along the way. Never!! (Horfect seems to ponder these words then . . .) It is a revelation you should celebrate!

(VICTORY DANCE)

HORFECT

So, Lord, are you telling me that I am a part of the old history that Moses made? That I am not just a part of the history made by Martin Luther King, Jr., Malcolm X, Thurgood Marshal, General Colin Powell, and All the modern day famous people?

VOICE

That, my child, is exactly what I am telling you. You are what you may call a composite.

HORFECT

A what, Lord?

VOICE

You are a composite. You are made up of more than just what happened during the sixties and the seventies and the eighties and nineties . . . and even since the turn of the century. I began making you as soon as I began making the earth and man. With each generation that came about before you, I placed a little bit more and a little bit more of everything that I wanted to be deposited in you by the time you were actually born. You are much like a living, breathing, walking, talking, human puzzle whose pieces are the experiences of everyone who has come before you and whose total picture can only be put together by the very precious and perfect hands of time.

(Dance)

HORFECT

God!! This is awesome! It's finally beginning to make sense now!

VOICE

Behold your past.

(Harriet Tubman advances to the lookout point and intensely surveys the scene. She sees no signs of danger and beckons for the others to join her.)

HARRIET

Sh-h-h-h!! Can't make no noise a'tall out heah now. 'Dem bounty hunters dey be having mo' ears den a field full of corn stalks. And I declare dey dogs could plum sniff darkness right off midnight dey could. (Still carefully surveying the area. Pauses.) We rest for now though. Den we gets up and us be heading north some mo'.

SLAVE #1

How long we rest heah fo', Harriet?

HARRIET

Right hard to say for sho', but jest long'a 'nuff for us to breath a few well rested breaths, den we's gonna move on toward the norff some mo like I done said a while ago.

SLAVE #2

How much further is we got to go, Harriet?

HARRIET

Norff ain't too long a ways off. Jest ahead of us is a bend in da' rivah. 'Bout eight to 10 maybe 12 mo' hours beyond dat bend, ought to put us within another's half day's travel of da norff, I reckon. But oOnce we gits to dat bend in da rivah, I speck we kin easily make the next station on the Underground Railroad by noon t'morrow.

SLAVE #3

Noon t'morrow!! (Grabbing Harriet and speaking to her intensely.) Harriet!!! I . . . I . . . I can't do dis for the rest of t'day and 'till noon t'morow too!! Ain't no way I kin do it. No way.

HARRIET

You's got to, Clarence. You know good and well how this Underground

Railroad werk. I puts my life on the line every time I comes back to get y'all . . . and y'all comes wid me—by yo' own choosings—if you decide you wanna be free that is. But ain't nobody done made you come out heah. But jest like it's always been now, that'the way it still is.

SLAVE #3

What is trying to say, Harriet?

HARRIET

You knows the rules Clarence. I done been over'em wid you mo'n one time now. And you knows'em good too. (Pause) Rule is once you starts on the Underground Railroad to freedom, there ain't no turning back. 'Cause if you do, dem white folks gone beat every word you got in you 'bout this Underground Railroad slap out of ya'. Then me and all of dem (pointing to the others) and every good white person 'long dis heah passageway gon' be strung up and beat like we's all animals 'till we either bleed to death or die from pain. Norff is where this trains be headed, Clarence. And you's goona be on it when it pull in at the freedom station too. Is you heah me?

SLAVE #3

Harriet, jest look at my foots! Go head! Look at'em. Why dey ain't seen hide or hair of a shoe in mo'n two solid weeks now. Dey's all cut up and bruised up. Why both my foots done swoll up more'n twice they regular size. Harriet, I can't go no further. Y'all go on. And I'll jest turn 'round and go back and face the master and the whup by m'self. But I won't tell him nothing 'bout dis hear Underground Railroad or nobody that be on it.

HARRIET

Now you listen to me, Clarence Lee Smith. I done been a slave once in my life. But I done been a free woman many times ovah. Every time I leads a different group of slaves to freedom, I feels like I be set free all ovah again. And if I had to choose one or da' other to be, um telling you, I would choose to be free. And you is gonna choose freedom too, Clarence, just as soon as this hear Underground Railroad gits you to the north and you gits yo'self a taste of it too.

SLAVE #3

I ain't gonna taste no freedom, Harriet. I's turning back rat heah like I done said I wuz.

HARRIET

(With gun in hand) Walking on swoll up foots—that's a choice you got Clarence. Heading north with us in just a few minutes—that's a choice you got too. Giving everything you got so that you and somebody else can be free some day—dat's another one of yo' choices, Clarence. But turning back and staying a slave ain't one of your choices, Clarence. (Puts the gun to his head. Clarence starts to mumble in verbal retaliation then tries to stagger to his feet. He falls back down and wave his hand as if to signal for the rest of the group to go on and leave him. Harriet presses the barrel of the gun firmly against his skull.) I done told you Clarence and I swear it befo' my Almighty God, befo' I let you turn around now and stay a slave I'll shoot you where you sits. Now that's another one of yo choices too.

SLAVE #1

Harriet, no. (Much mumbling can be heard.)

HARRIET

I's done spoke on dis heah topic, and I ain't changed my mind none neither. Either Clarence gits his tied old body up and come go with us now—(deep breath), or I's gonna leave his soul right heah where he sits for the angels to come and tote away to heaven. But I ain't gonna leave not one person that the good Lawd done put in my care to the mercy of no slave master and his ruthless blood thirsty whup. Now y'all gitty up on y'all tide and swoll up feets and let's be on our way to the north where we' be free. (Goes over to Clarence. Looks in his eyes and says to him . . .) Befo' I be a slave . . . I'll be buried in my grave . . . and go home to my Lawd . . . and be free. You ain't gonna never understand how I say that, Clarence, 'till you done been set free yo own self. (He starts staggering to his feet. Others help him. Harriet calls to her followers . . .) Let's go. I kin hear freedom a'callin' all y'all name. (Negro spiritual)

HORFECT

Oh, God! You mean I am greater than what I see when I look in the mirror each day?

VOICE

I do mean that child.

HORFECT

You mean I'm actually greater than my color, my past mistakes, my image, and all these other things?

VOICE

You are.

HORFECT

But, why didn't anyone ever tell me this? Why didn't someone try to let me know all of this before now? Why did everybody just let me go right on thinking and believing what was never true about me?

VOICE

Because they cannot teach what they do not know. If they do not know this about themselves, how could they ever know this about you? They only know you by way of human and scientific theory. I on the other hand know you and have always known you from your inception. That is because I designed you, planned you, and created you. It is my purpose that is within you and my ability which enables you.

HORFECT

Well then why didn't you tell me this about myself . . . before now, I mean.

VOICE

I did, but you did not listen to me as I tried to teach you.

HORFECT

Teach me?

VOICE

Teach you. Who do you think it was that picked you up after each one of your falls? And who do you think protected you as you walked along the dangerous streets? And who do you think it was it that healed you sick body? Time and time again, I raised you up when you could have been destroyed. It was always me, and I was always trying to teach you just who you were.

HORFECT

You mean, I'm really just a human composite of all of the great events that ever happened before I was born. Everything that my people went through before I was born is a part of who I am now.

VOICE

Remember my instructions to you child: Lift up your head; open your eyes; incline your ear; and learn as I show you who you really are.

HORFECT

I will.

(Two gentlemen sit across from one another around a candle-lit table. They are well dressed, and body language suggests intensity in their dialogue. [Poem: "W.E.B. and Booker T."]

"It seems to me," said Booker T.,
"It shows a mighty lot of cheek
To study chemistry and Greek
When Mister Charlie needs a hand
To hoe the cotton on his land . . .

(Authorization not granted to re-print the entire poem in this book.)

(Lights down. Lights up on the opposite side of the stage. A mother is busying herself with unimportant domestic tasks. Her young daughter enters gleefully and hopefully, then presents her request to her mother.)

"Mother, dear, may I go downtown instead of out to play,
And march the streets of Birmingham in a Freedom March today?"

"No, baby, no, you may not go, for the dogs are fierce and wild,
And clubs and hoses, guns and jails aren't good for a little child."

(Authorization not granted to re-print the entire poem in this book.)

(Spotlight dims and comes up on a single female on the opposite side of the stage. She is attired in African garb. She begins to speak as the light comes up on her. She passionately recites a black feminist poem. Before she finishes, another lady has joined her on stage and recites the next poem . . .)

I am an ebony queen
I am beautiful, firm, smooth and black
I give meaning to the mystery of the sunrise
I adorn the firmaments by night.

I am history's guide through many treacherous ordeals.
I am the wings of angels and the harvest of the dream fields.
I ferry your prayers to a divine ear light years beyond the sky.
I am the answer to your enigmas and the riddle which ask why?

I paraded through time before records were ever kept.
I was at the creation and the big band and was with Aristotle and Socrates
And even Jesus when he wept.

I have seen all the beauty eternity has spread before my eyes.
I have observed both, joyful reunions and tearful goodbyes.

Yet I am strong and wise and will never yield my faith,

For in the back of this African queen lies the strength of her race.

I am the mother of life as predestined by the divine
I am the keeper of knowledge and the sentry of time.

I was created your helper and alongside you took my place.
I have honored your authority and have birth the human race.

I am an ebony queen
Beautiful, strong and black in hue.
I am God's gift to all wondrous things.
I am God's gift to you.

HORFECT

All of this, Lord? You mean I—little old me—I am a composite of all of these people and their experiences.

VOICE

Yes, my child. They are like the sugar and salt—the flour and eggs—the butter and grease that all go into the pan in order to get one cake. Time is the oven that bakes these ingredients together. And you are the finished product that time removes from the oven of life in order that you may serve and contribute to the next generation.

HORFECT

Oh-h-h. Now I see why I am the composite of so much and so many. But I never knew this before. Oh my God!! Look!! (Lights are coming up on a hotel room where Dr. King and Malcolm X are seated and in dialogue.) You mean, I'm even a composite of them?

(Dr. King stands and goes over to the hotel window to observe the mob below. There is a faint chant of "freedom" in the background which gradually fades into the Negro spiritual "We Shall Overcome.")

MARTIN

Brother Malcolm, you have posed many great points here today. And I know you are only speaking what lies deep in the recesses of your heart. But we are a poor people who cannot afford the loss of lives to flesh eating dogs, power-hungry bullets and uncaring hearts of our adversaries. And I am sure this will be the result of our attempt to fight violence with violence and blows with blows. I am afraid I cannot agree with your ideology of on how to most prosperously attack the problem of racism in this country. To fight violence with violence will only promote violence. To kill and murder those who would do the same to our people makes us in principal no different than they. To seek supremacy is to take on and pursue their goal and objective. To emulate the adversary is to become a vital part of that which we say we seek to destroy. Injustice is injustice and cannot be justified on the basis of race, my Brother Malcolm.

MALCOLM

And so, Brother King, it would seem to me that you have chosen and justified every possible reason known to you why we should not fight the battle of racism on the exact playing field and moral terms as our adversary. You seem to be of the opinion that it is alright if a man's head is beaten, battered, and bludgeoned as long as it is the black man's head that being done that way—and then by his white counterpart.

MARTIN

Brother Malcolm I assure you that that is not what I am saying.

MALCOLM

But if the black man decides to as you put it, "straighten his back up" (mockingly) because a white man can't ride his black back unless it is bent over, you make sound as if it is the black man who has committed the crime in this instance. You make it sound as if fighting back is a crime within itself. (Becoming angry) Why is it that it is alright for them to bomb our churches but not alright for us to bomb theirs. Why is it alright for them to open up the heads of our young people with their billy clubs but not alright for us to share a common pool of blood? Why is it alright for them to beat the unborn babies out of the stomachs our pregnant young sisters, but they want to lynch every young brother who gives a courteous glance at even that which they themselves call white trash? Our old people are being killed; our young men and women are being lynched, beaten, discriminated against, slapped, kicked, spat upon and shot down on the streets in broad open day light. Why, then, my brother, would you expect us not to fight back against those who would perpetrate such dastardly acts against us? How can you think peace when we are on the verge of being destroyed by violence. Brother King, if we don't rise up and fight this violence with an organized, structured, well informed, and purpose driven violence of our own, unquestionably the black race will be exterminated—totally. Brother—we can't sit here and just let that happen. Force must meet force.

MARTIN

I'm sorry, Brother, but I cannot endanger the innocent lives of so many loyal and faithful supporters of this Civil Right Movement, just to appease an emotional and logical dilemma within my own mind. That would be pretentious, murderous, and indefensibly wrong.

MALCOLM

Brother King, how then? How, my brother, do you think the problem of racism in America can and should be most effectively attacked—and destroyed.

MARTIN

Brother Malcolm, I prefer not to adopt the method that you have expressed here as the most effective way to confront and destroy racism in this country. However, I myself have chosen to employ—in order to gain equality and human dignity for all people in this country—a vastly different approach to this problem.

MALCOLM

Talk brother. And tell me about how you want blacks to stand still and be quiet while vicious dogs are being released on them for committing o crimes at all. Talk about how you want black men and women to turn the other cheek while white men drunk with ignorance and hatred spit in their faces, burn down their homes, rape their wives, and bludgeon their innocent heads with steel-hard billy clubs. Then when we have taken all of the brutality and punishment, all of this pain and frustration, all of this dehumanization and mistreatment, you want us to sit around, hold hand, chant freedom and sing about overcoming. Yes, Brother Martin, you talk—because I'm very interested in hearing exactly what you have to say. Talk, brother.

MARTIN

Brother Malcolm, freedom—and acquiring it—is a (searching for the appropriate word.)

MALCOLM

Fight? A battle? A confrontation? Is that it, Martin. But you, my brother, being non-violent, don't want to call it what it is.

MARTIN

The maintaining of freedom is indeed a fight, Malcolm, but the securing of it is a meticulous process. It is a process that we must die to protect and promise never to abandon. You see, Brother Malcolm. You see, Brother Malcolm, freedom and equality are a dream that I have for all the people of this country. It is too deeply rooted in my conscious and too much a part of my spirit for me to every abandon it. It's my dream, Brother Malcolm, and I will never be talked out of believing in it.

MALCOLM

Dream?

MARTIN

Yes, Brother Malcolm. Yes. A Dream. (To the audience.)

Five score years ago, a great American, in whose symbolic shadow we stand signed the Emancipation Proclamation. This momentous decree came as a great beacon light of hope to millions of Negro slaves who had been seared in the flames of withering injustice. It came as a joyous daybreak to end the long night of captivity. But one hundred years later, we must face the tragic fact that the Negro is still not free.

One hundred years later, the life of the Negro is still sadly crippled by the manacles of segregation and the chains of discrimination. One hundred years later, the Negro lives on a lonely island of poverty in the midst of a vast ocean of material prosperity. One hundred years later, the Negro is still languishing in the corners of American society and finds himself an exile in his own land.

So we have come here today to dramatize an appalling condition. In a sense we have come to our nation's capital to cash a check. When the architects of our republic wrote the magnificent words of the Constitution and the Declaration of Independence, they were signing a promissory note to which every American was to fall heir.

This note was a promise that all men would be guaranteed the inalienable right of life, liberty, and the pursuit of happiness. It is obvious today that America has defaulted on this promissory note insofar as her citizens of color are concerned. Instead of honoring this sacred obligation, America has given the Negro people a bad check which has come back marked "insufficient funds." But we refuse to believe that the bank of justice is bankrupt. We refuse to believe that there are insufficient funds in the great vaults of opportunity of this great nation.

So we have come to cash this check—a check that will give us upon demand the riches of freedom and the security of justice. We have also come to this hallowed spot to remind America of the fierce urgency of now. This is no time to engage in the luxury of cooling off or to take the tranquilizing drug of gradualism. Now is the time to rise from the dark and desolate valley of segregation to the sunlit path of racial justice. Now is the time to open the doors of opportunity to all of

God's children. Now is the time to lift our nation from the quick sands of racial injustice to the solid rock of brotherhood.

It would be fatal for the nation to overlook the urgency of the moment and to under estimate the determination of the Negro. This sweltering summer of the Negro's legitimate discontent will not pass until there is an invigorating autumn of freedom and equality. Nineteen sixty-three is not an end, but a beginning. Those who hope that the Negro needed to blow off steam and will now be content will have a rude awakening if the nation returns to business as usual. There will be neither rest nor tranquility in America until the Negro is granted his citizenship rights.

The whirlwinds of revolt will continue to shake the foundations of our nation until the bright day of justice emerges. But there is something that I must say to my people who stand on the warm threshold which leads into the palace of justice. In the process of gaining our rightful place we must not be guilty of wrongful deeds. Let us not seek to satisfy our thirst for freedom by drinking from the cup of bitterness and hatred.

We must forever conduct our struggle on the high plane of dignity and discipline. We must not allow our creative protest to degenerate into physical violence. Again and again we must rise to the majestic heights of meeting physical force with soul force.

The marvelous new militancy which has engulfed the Negro community must not lead us to distrust of all white people, for many of our white brothers, as evidenced by their presence here today, have come to realize that their destiny is tied up with our destiny and their freedom is inextricably bound to our freedom.

We cannot walk alone. And as we walk, we must make the pledge that we shall march ahead. We cannot turn back. There are those who are asking the devotees of civil rights, "When will you be satisfied?" We can never be satisfied as long as our bodies, heavy with the fatigue of gravel, cannot gain lodging in the motels of the highways and the hotels of the cities. We cannot be satisfied as long as the Negro's basic mobility is from a smaller ghetto to a larger one. We can never be satisfied as long as a Negro in Mississippi cannot vote and a Negro in New York believes he has nothing for which to vote. No, no, we are not satisfied, and we will not be satisfied until justice rolls down like waters and righteousness like a mighty stream.

I am not unmindful that some of you have come here out of great trials and tribulations. Some of you have come fresh from Georgia hills. Some of you have come from areas where you quest for freedom left you battered by the storms of persecution and staggered by the winds of police brutality. You have been the veterans of creative suffering. Continue to work with the faith that unearned suffering is redemptive.

Go back to Mississippi, go back to Alabama, go back to Georgia, go back to Louisiana, go back to the slums and ghettos of our northern cities, knowing that somehow this situation can and will be changed. Let us not wallow in the valley of despair. I say to you today, my friends, that in spite of the difficulties and frustrations of the moment, I still have a dream. It is a dream deeply rooted in the American dream.

I have a dream that one day this nation will rise up and live out the true meaning of its creed: "We hold these truths to be self-evident: that all men are created equal." I have a dream that one day on the red hills of Georgia the sons of former slaves and the sons of former slave owners will be able to sit down together at a table of brotherhood. I have a dream that one day even the state of Mississippi, a desert state, sweltering with the heat of injustice and oppression, will be transformed into an oasis of freedom and justice. I have a dream that my four children will one day live in a nation where they will not be judged by the color of their skin but by the content of their character. I have a dream today.

I have a dream that one day the state of Alabama, whose governor's lips are presently dripping with the words of interposition and nullification, will be transformed into a situation where little black boys and black girls will be able to join hands with little white boys and white girls and walk together as sisters and brothers. I have a dream today. I have a dream that one day every valley shall be exalted, every hill and mountain shall be made low, the rough places will be made plain, and the crooked places will be made straight, and the glory of the Lord shall be revealed, and all flesh shall see it together. This is our hope. This is the faith with which I return to the South. With this faith we will be able to hew out of the mountain of despair a stone of hope. With this faith we will be able to transform the jangling discords of our nation into a beautiful symphony of brotherhood. With this faith we will be able to work together, to pray together, to struggle together, to go to jail together, to standup for freedom together, knowing that we will be free one day.

This will be the day when all of God's children will be able to sing with a new meaning, "My country 'tis of thee, sweet land of liberty, of thee I sing. Land where my fathers died, land of the pilgrims' pride, from every mountainside, let freedom ring." And if America is to be a great nation, this must become true. So let freedom ring from the prodigious hilltops of New Hampshire. Let freedom ring from the mighty mountains of New York. Let freedom ring from the heightening Alleghenies of Pennsylvania! Let freedom ring from the snowcapped Rockies of Colorado! Let freedom ring from the curvaceous peaks of California! But not only that; let freedom ring from Stone Mountain of Georgia! Let freedom ring from Lookout Mountain of Tennessee! Let freedom ring from every hill and every molehill of Mississippi. From every mountainside, let freedom ring.

When we let freedom ring, when we let it ring from every village and every hamlet, from every state and every city, we will be able to speed up that day when all of God's children, black men and whit men, Jews and Gentiles, Protestants and Catholics, will be able to join hands and sing in the words of the old Negro spiritual, "Free at last! Free at last! Thank God almighty I'm free at last!"

MALCOLM

Brother Martin, I do believe in the purity of your dream. This I do. But I do not believe that any man can afford to stand back patiently and non-violently while his wife and children are being slaughtered in the streets of the world's most powerful nation. While your dream is a beautiful one, I for one do not believe that any sane and rational man can truly expect to simply dream his way to freedom. If freedom is a goal—and a goal is a destination—then the right to travel the road to my destination is as much mine as it is anyone else's. And I will walk this road, Brother King. And I will secure the blessings of liberty granted to me by the Constitution of the United States of America. And I will not be denied my right, my privileges or my life's goals no matter what the battle may cost me. I will be free, Martin, and I will help to secure the liberties that my people are entitled to.

MARTIN

How, Malcolm? How will you do this?

MALCOLM

I don't know what techniques we will use to gain these freedoms, Brother Martin. But I do know that we will gain them—by any means necessary.

(Lights)

(The young man is visually taken by all that has been revealed to him. He is virtually speechless.)

HORFECT

This is awesome! Adam and Eve. Moses. The Children of Israel. Harriet Tubman. Booker T. Washington. W.E.B. Dubois. Malcolm X. Dr. King. They are all a part of me, and I'm a part of them. We're all one. (As if he is finally figuring thing out.) They were . . . so that I could be. They did . . . so that I could do. They died . . . so that I could live. (Obvious revelation) I am not their extension. I am our continuation. Each of us has a time, a purpose, and a destiny. And our time, purpose and destiny only lead on to the time, purpose and destiny of others who will come after us. And what they will have and do will depend on what we do with the time, purpose, and destiny assigned to each one of us. Awesome! Now I see how this thing works. It's really quite simple. (The officer comes up and snatches the kid by the arm.)

OFFICER

Hey you! What do you think you're doing? And how did you get out of your cell?

HORFECT

Stop it! Hold it, Mr. Officer! Don't do this. I have something to tell you. (He's struggling to make the officer listen to him.) You've got to listen to me. They showed me who I really am. I know who I am now. Will you please listen to me? Please.

OFFICER

You get back in there (opening the cell door and forcing the child in.) And if I come back here again and find that you're out of this cell again, I'll have your hands and feet chained. The only reason I'm not doing that right now is because you keep getting out, but for some strange reason you don't seem to be trying to escape. But if I catch you out of that cell one more time, I'll have you cuffed hands and feet to the wall and you won't get out for as long as I'm sheriff here. You understand me boy?

HORFECT

But it doesn't matter anymore.

OFFICER

What?

HORFECT

It doesn't matter. Not anymore. You see, I know who I am now. I'm a composite. And as long as I know that, you can cuff my hands, wrists, ankles. It don't matter, sheriff, 'cause you can't cuff my mind and you can't cuff my spirit. And since you can't, I'll always be free.

OFFICER

(Perplexed. Then . . .) Yeah right. Well you listen to me, Humpty Dumpty. If you fall off my wall just one more time, you'll be broken into so many pieces that no even super glue will work on you. So just don't put me to the test on this one. Now stay put I said! (Checks the cell door for security then leaves.)

HORFECT

(To the voice) I don't understand. This is confusing. If I am a composite of all these good things and good people, how did I end up in here again?

VOICE

You have not ended up any place child. You have simply passed through many places on your way to your destination of greatness. After all, did I not say to you that I created you out of and for greatness?

HORFECT

But, I don't understand. If I'm created for greatness, how do I get from here to there?

VOICE

There is only one way to reach the greatness I have created just for you.

HORFECT

And what way is that?

VOICE

If my people, who are called by my name would humble themselves, seek my face, pray, and turn from their wicked ways, then I will hear their prayers and will answer them from heaven and will make them and their children great and prosperous. Man can only lock up your body . . . but I can free your soul and your spirit. No one can take your soul or your spirit except you give it to them.

Stay close to me and I will guide your steps in my way and secure your future this day. (The child sits in the cells. A mime, representative of his spirit, can be seen in the cell with him. Music. MIME. As the mime performs the angel returns and unlocks the cell door. The mime beckons for the child, but the child is afraid to exit. The mime continues to dance and beckon unto the child. The angel finally extends its hand to the child. The child slowly places his hand in the hand of the angel. The angel escorts the child non-stop through the events of history he just visited. When he returns to center stage his cell has fallen apart and now reveals a beautiful kingly throne. (Music) The angel ushers him to his throne. After he reaches the pinnacle, characters from various periods in the past approach his throne and place a "deposit" at his feet. The first deposit is a long flowing king's robe. The second is a crown. The third is a man fashioned of clay. The fourth is the staff of Moses. The fifth is the musket of Harriet Tubman. This continues until everyone has presented him with a "deposit." The sheriff enters escorting the mother. They see the "young king" and bow down to honor him.

VOICE #1

Now he has come to know who he really is.

VOICE #2

Greatness is imminent in his life!

VOICE #3

And so shall he be great in the lives on many others!

VOICE #4

Greatness is his destiny!

VOICE #5

Because he knows who he is!

MOTHER

He shall be wise!

VOICE #5

Because he knows who he is!

SHERIFF

He shall be a man of character and morals and leadership and integrity!

VOICE #6

Because he knows who he is!

VOICE #7

And no one will be able to take away what he knows or stop him from imparting it into others!

VOICE #8

Today he has become a TRUE man!

VOICE #9

Forever he will be a king! For this is what happens when they know who they are!

VOICE #10

Now that he knows who he is and his greatness no one can imprison him!

VOICE #11

No one can deny him!

VOICE #12

No one can frighten him!

VOICE #13

Greatness has come upon his people through him today!

VOICE #14

Let us celebrate our young king and hail him as one who now knows who is truly is!

VOICE #15

The wisdom of the ages has come upon him. This king is due honor!

VOICE #16

Then let us all honor him!

ALL

LET US DANCE FOR OUR KING!!!!! DANCE FOR HIS VICTORY!!!! DANCE TO HIS WISDOM. LET US CELEBRATE OUR KING AND DANCE, DANCE DANCE!!!!

(FESTIVE MUSIC IS UP. ALL ARE DANCING AND HONORING THE YOUNG KING. EVEN THE OFFICER AND MOTHER ARE DANCING AND HONORING HIM. HE IS WAVING AND SMILING. LIGHTS.)

CURTAINS

THE POWER OF "NO!"

(Scene opens with Tangela and Vance on stage. They are channel surfing and not really watching any show in particular. Tangela is a 16 year old female. She is fairly attractive with an average build. Seventeen year old Vance is a cool acting, slick talking guy who is convinced his masterful conversation will win over the favors of his childhood sweetheart, Tangela. Tangela is relaxing on the couch next to Vance. His arm is around her shoulder and his fingers slowly and suggestively snake a path through her hair. Suddenly their favorite song can be heard playing on the radio which is also on in the background. They both jump up and begin to dance and sing along with the music. They are both ecstatic and obvious taken by the music. The music finishes and they return to the couch laughing and joking. Vance slides over closer to Tangela and returns to running his fingers through her hair.)

VANCE

Yo, like Tang, baby . . . so . . . you know . . .

TANGELA

Know what, Vance?

VANCE

You know. (A bit more suggestively) You know.

TANGELA

Oh, Vance. I *don't* know and I wish you would stop trying to tell me I do because I really have no idea what you're talking about. So, now what is it that you obviously *want* me to know that I *don't* already, but you already seem to *think* I do? What's up, Vance?

VANCE

I'm just trying to say, Tang. You know. We've been at this thing for a minute now, you and me. You know . . . what I'm saying. And I was just starting to wonder . . .

TANGELA

We've been at what *thing* for a minute now, Vance? What thing you talking about and where are you going with all this?

VANCE

I'm just saying, Tang . . .

TANGELA

Yeah?

VANCE

Alright, Tang. Here it is. Straight talk. No sugar coating or beating around the bush. Here's the deal. We've been at this relationship thing for a minute now and it just seems to me like we don't (Tang looks at Vance inquisitively) . . . it just doesn't look like we're ever going beyond where we are. Know what I mean? So I was just wondering . . . thinking . . . no, wondering—like when are you *ever* gonna let loose and come on over to the players' side, Tang? And that's on the real!! Alright now I've said it.

TANGELA

Players' side? Players' side? Vance, I don't *even* know what you're talking 'bout. Talking like you all that or something. Talking 'bout some players side. Come on, Vance! Are you crazy? You really do think you're all that and a bag of chips, don't you?

VANCE

Check it out, baby. Look at it like this. I mean . . . I *MIGHT* just be all of that; but you ain't gonna ever know unless you finally get the nerves to (tapping on her chest) answer that sweet little knock at your heart's door that you get trying so hard to ignore. See what I'm saying? I mean . . . you're my girl and I'm your guy, right? So I should be all that . . . and if I'm not then whatever I'm not . . . then it's your job to make me into that. Follow me? Know where I'm going with this? I mean if you gonna be my girl, then you ought to be my girl all the way and in every way. See what I'm saying, Tangela? I've got to be your oasis out here in this love-dog—eat—dog desert of mistrust, lies, deceit and selfishness. That's me, Tang. Your Oasis, baby—out here in this brutal desert of love.

TANGELA

My oasis, huh? Out here in this sprawling, mean, cruel, brutal desert of . . . how did you describe it now . . . . uh, mistrust, lies, deceit and

VANCE

Selfishness.

TANGELA

Oh yeah. Sure. Don't want to leave out the big S do we? Selfishness. Vance! You *are* crazy! Anyway . . . for the one millionth time, listen to me PLEASE!! I'm not ready and I'm not going to have sex right now at this point in my life—not with you or nobody else . . . OK? Alright? (Shyly) Because I don't even know if you or anybody else is the right one for me yet.

VANCE

Whoa! Whoa! Whoa! Put that in the big R (pretending to be driving in reverse) and let's back that thing up girl? What you mean you don't know if I'm the right one, Tangela? What kind of foolishness is that girl? (Becoming more and more angry as he speaks.) Hey listen, baby! If I say I'm the right one for you then I'm the right one! And that's all there is to it. Now I don't know where you get off fronting on me like that. And check this out. What you mean if I "or anybody else" is right for you? What you mean by that? Hey, hear this baby. Alright? I don't need this, Tang! And I don't *need* you. Understand? See old Vance ain't gotta sit around here and just keep holdinghis britches waiting for Ms. Goodie Two Shoe to come around to seeing things his way. You feel me? And I sure as heck don't have a good enough reason to just sit back and watch all my young life go drifting by while you play the role of the good little girl. No sweat off my back, baby. You can just chill here, Ms. Goody. Old Vance'll just go out there (pointing) and fine a woman who knows a good thing when she's got it. (Primping) Maybe she won't be scared to walk those burning sands with the brother. Does that make the picture a little clearer for you now, Miss Perfect?

TANGELA

Vance, please, don't you think you're taking all of this just a little too far and much too fast. I mean I'm sorry, Vance, but I just don't understand . . .

VANCE

Understand? What is there to understand girl?

TANGELA

Not *what,* Vance, but *who*! Who! And the who is *you*. I don't understand *you* anymore, Vance!! I don't understand *you*!!

VANCE

So now it's me, huh? How about that? Little Miss Sweet Thing says she doesn't understand plain and simple old Vance. Alright, my little angel, help me understand what it is about bad old Vance that your pure and perfect little moralistic mind can't seem to figure. (Pauses) OK. Go ahead. Talk to me. What about me don't you understand?

TANGELA

Vance, listen. Why it's always got to be like this? Why can't I just "stay on my side of the sands and you stay on yours" just a little while longer?

VANCE

Oh. So that's what you don't understand. Why we just can't stay on opposite sides of the sands . . . and just be—well you know—friends—so to speak. You know—one of those long distance reach out and touch someone kind of relationships. OK. I get it. Old Vance understands now. (Turns to her suddenly pointing) And you're absolutely sure this is the way you want it? Me on my side and you on yours? And every once in a while we'll just reach (reaching his arm out as if trying to touch someone) out and touch someone . . . ooops . . . I mean each other. If that's alright with you, that is.

TANGELA

(Pleading) Vance.

VANCE

NO! Just *tell* me! Is that what you *want*? Is that *exactly . . . what . . . you . . . want*?

TANGELA

Vance, listen to me! Why the big rush all of a sudden? For the last two weeks all you've talked about is sex, sex, sex. You don't seem to care anything at all about *me* anymore. Seems like all you're interested in is sex. Listen, baby, (goes over and takes his hand) can't this sex thing just wait a little while longer?

VANCE

(Snatching away) No!! No!! No!! No we can't wait! No *it* can't wait!! No I can't wait!! And no, Little Miss Perfect and Pure, YOU CAN'T WAIT EITHER!!!

TANGELA

(Calmly and reassuringly) But, Vance, I *can* wait. It's *you* who says *you* can't wait.

VANCE

I'm sorry, Tangela, but this waiting thing can't happen anymore. (Pause) Sorry but that just ain't what I'm all about no more. I'm outta here. Chill.

TANGELA

VANCE . . .

VANCE

Gotta go. I'm out. Later

TANGELA

Vance . . .

VANCE

I'm outta here, Tangela. Peace out, baby. (Exits. Tangela goes over and puts on music then flops down and continues channel surfing. Relaxes. Falls asleep. Entes Mother, Grandmother and younger sibling. They are carrying bags. Sibbie goes over and plays with his sister's hair while she is asleep. He is an obvious prankster. He carefully removes the remote from her hand, changes channel and then . . .)

SIBBIE

B00-0-0-0-0-0-0-0-0!! (Tangela jumps. Obviously frightened.) A-ha-ha-ha-ha!! Girl if you wasn't so black you'd be white as a ghost! A-ha-ha-ha-ha!!

TANGELA

Grandma did you see that? You saw that! Why did y'all let him do that? Why I bet I'll beat your little butt!

MOTHER

Alright you two cut it out I say. And Tangela, you watch your mouth before I wash it out with warm water and soap.

TANGELA

All I said was I'll beat his little butt, Mama.

MOTHER

Say it again and you'll be blowing bubbles.

GRANDMA

You get your room tidied up, baby girl?

TANGELA

Sure did, Grandma.

SIBBIE

NOT!! (Licks his tongue and makes a face at his sister.)

TANGELA

See there he goes again messing with me.

MOTHER

Leave your sister alone, Sibbie.

SIBBIE

Good grief. All I said was "not".

MOTHER

And if you keep on saying it I'm gonna knock a knot right on your big noggin.

SIBBIE

I don't know why she always got to be the one right and I'm always wrong. (Tangela changes TV channels. Sibbie runs over to her and snatches the remote.) Hey don't change that!! I was watching (singing) Power Rangers.

TANGELA

You were not.

SIBBIE

Was so!!

TANGELA

Was not!

SIBBIE

Was so!

MOTHER

He-e-ey! Quit it. Cut it out already. Didn't I just say that a minute ago? For goodness sakes. You'd think three families lived in this one house sometimes!

SIBBIE

But I always watch (singing) Power Rangers.

TANGELA

Well guess what? You're not watching any (singing) Power Rangers today buddy!! (They begin fight over the control again.)

SIBBIE

Am too!!

TANGELA

No you're not bubby!

SIBBIE

You wanna bet?

GRANDMA

(Slams a book to the table and stands pointing from one to the other.) Didn't your mama just tell both of you to cut that nonsense out! Now if I have to tell either one of you about it again I bet I'll come over there and knock pure fire out of both of you! Now quit it! And I don't aim to say it again! (Turns and winks at her daughter who smiles approvingly in return.)

MOTHER

Baby girl, give that controller to your brother and come on over here and talk to me. Go ahead. Give it to him now. You know he watches (singing) Power Rangers every single day.

TANGELA

But, Mama, Sibbie's too old for Power Rangers. He's already big enough to be in college!!

GRANDMA

Don't argue with your Mama baby. Just do what she says. (Sibbie holds his hand out for the remote. Tangela throws the remote on the couch and crosses to Mother.)

MOTHER

Now talk to me. You're not your old self. What's the matter. (Pause) And, Sweetie Pie, I mean what's really the matter.

TANGELA

(Pauses, looks down and begins talking) Ma . . . it's Vance.

MOTHER

Vance?

TANGELA

Vance, Ma. Vance. He came over while y'all were gone.

GRANDMA

Come over here? While we were gone? Now look a here, girl, ain't no hanky panky been going on in this house while we were at the Piggly Wiggly I know!

TANGELA

Of course not, Grandma. But hanky panky is exactly what *Vance* wants to go on between us. It's all he ever talks about anymore. No matter how often I say no he always comes (drawing a circle with her finger in the air) back full circle to the topic again.

GRANDMA

Then just get rid of the no-account rascal. Quit him and go find yourself a good respectful church going boy. Now there's the kind that can appreciate a nice girl like yourself.

SIBBIE

I been told her to drop that no count bum like a hot potato! But does she listen to me? No-o-o. She thinks all I know about is (singing) Power Ranger.

TANGELA

(Dismisses her brother with a wave of her hand.) Oh, Grandma! I just can't do that.

GRANDMA

And just why can't you?

TANGELA

Because I love him. And he loves me. But I don't understand why he's in this great big rush to have sex all of a sudden though. I mean I know he has my best interest in mind. And all he wants is to express his feelings for me in the most intimate way, and . . .

MOTHER

(Goes over and starts to lightly slap TANGELA . . .) Snap out of it child. What in the world are you saying? Do you hear yourself? Get real here girl!

GRANDMA

Yeah! You better *snap* her out of it 'cause if I come over there I'm gonna *slap* her out of it. Girl you know what you're saying? You ain't got no time for all these cool boys' stories. They don't want but one thing from you. And you don't want but one thing out of life . . . and that's a chance to become *anything* you want to be in life. And you ain't about to throw that chance away falling for no fancy sounding sweet-to-the-ear-home-made-lie. Anybody who don't understand that it's alright for a sweet young thing like you to stay that way and to save herself for someone real special in her life—like her husband—is a plum fool and ain't worth the ground you spit on. Now you know the future is gonna be tough enough without you having to worry yourself with a baby and no child support check. So don't you be no fool and think that just 'cause some boy tells ya'that he *loves* you that he's got your best interest in mind . . . 'cause his real interest just might be what you got in your britches.

TANGELA

But grandma! It's not that easy. And besides, I think you're being much too hard on Vance.

SIBBIE

(Yelling from the couch) Right on, Grandma. I think you're right on time!

TANGELA

SHUT UP, SIBBIE!! I wish everybody would just leave me alone for awhile. Nobody understands me or what I'm saying or what I want or . . . (she is interrupted by the sound of the telephone ringing. She and Sibble race for it. Sibbie wins.)

SIBBIE

Hello. Sure. Just a minute. (Offers the phone to Tangela. She takes it then he says . . .) Mom telephone. Tangela's holding it for you. (Returns to couch. Sister passes and hits him on the head. They begin passing licks. Action stops when grandma clears her throat very harshly.)

MOTHER

Ms. Jackson. How nice to hear from you again. We were just talking about Vance a few minutes ago. He just left from over here seeing Tangela. (Her voice and expression change noticeably.) Oh no. (Tang notices the change in her mother's appearance and voice and is trying desperately to hear the entire conversation. Mother constantly turns and pivots away to avoid allow Tang to hear what is being said.) Oh my God!! No-o-o! Ms. Jackson, I'm so sorry. How? When? Where? But . . . but . . . but . . . aww-w-w!! Oh my heavens no. Yes. Yes. I see. Oh, poor child. I feel absolutely awful, Ms. Jackson. Sure. Sure I will. Sure I will. I will, Ms Jackson. Thank you so much for filling me in. Ms. Jackson . . . I'm sorry. God bless you and if there's anything we can do please don't hesitate to call. Thanks for calling. Good bye.

TANGELA

Something's wrong, Mother. What is it? Is it Vance? What is it, Mother?

MOTHER

(Goes over and touches Tangela's face softly.) Yes, baby, it's Vance. (Tang slowly seats herself on the couch as her mother begins talking.) Honey, would you like some soda or cake or something? Ice cream?

TANGELA

(Firmly) No. What is it, Mom? (Long pause. Then emphatically) WHAT . . . IS . . . IT?

MOTHER

(Retorting quickly. Nearly interrupting Tangela) Tangela! It seems Vance was unable to get rid of a nagging cough he'd had for a couple of months so he went to the doctor's for a routine check up and hopefully some over the counter medication to help him get rid of the cough. The doctors were a little concerned . . . so they ordered some extra tests be run on Vance . . . and three of four tests came back positive for AIDS.

TANGELA

AIDS?!! Oh . . . my . . . oh my. AIDS. Mom . . . AIDS? How could he? I mean . . . Oh Gosh . . . I'm confused. I'm confused. (Grabbing her cap and preparing to exit) I've got to find Vance, Mom!! I've got to help him. Where is he? I have to go to him.

MOTHER

You can't!

TANGELA

No, Mother. I have to go where he is. I have to help him. I've got to go.

MOTHER

(Moving quickly between Tang and the door) Tang, you can't. You can't help him.

TANGELA

Mother I have to and I'm going now!! I'm sorry you don't understand. (Trying hard to get past her mother.)

MOTHER

I *DO* understand, Tang!!! I *DO*!! I *DO!!* VANCE IS DEAD!!! DEAD!! Dead!! He's dead, Tang. (Tang falls in her mother's arms and weeps.)

TANGELA

(Starts to laughs hysterically.) This is all a dream. This isn't real. (More laughter) This can't be. (Laughter) Ok alarm clock. You can go off now and wake me up from this nightmare. (Laughter)

MOTHER

There is no alarm clock, Tangela. This is no nightmare. And it *is* real.

TANGELA

But, Mom, how can Vance have AIDS when he's still a virgin? And if he has AIDS why would he be asking me to have sex with him? And how can Vance be dead when he was just here an hour ago? How Mom? How?

MOTHER

Single gun shot wound to the head. Self inflicted. In his suicide note he said he didn't want to fight the long, never ending painful battle of AIDS—alone. So he tried to "share it" with the one person he loved most. (Takes her hand

and forces Tangela to look at her.) So I guess the reason Vance felt as if the two of you couldn't wait (gesturing with fingers as if to make quotation marks) for this sex thing to happen between the two of you was simply because he knew he really couldn't wait much longer—before the truth came out about him, I mean. Anyway he said tell you he loved you in his own special and unique way. And even though he has to cross over to the other side of life alone—in his heart and spirit, he's glad you said no. He was really a nice kid, you know.

TANGELA

Mama?

MOTHER

Yeah, Tangela, baby?

TANGELA

Mama . . . can I please have just a few minutes alone here in the living room?

MOTHER

Are you sure you don't want to go to your room and lie down, Baby?

TANGELA

No. I prefer the living room . . . since that's the last place I spent time with Vance. May I please?

GRANDMOTHER

(Interrupting.) Aw-w-w absolutely you can, *Baby*. We'll just give you as much time as you need. Me and your mama got a little talking to do between ourselves anyway, (winking at mother) don't we girl?

MOTHER

Oh yeah. Sure do. Just take your time and relax baby and if you need us just call. We'll just be in the next room. Okay?

TANGELA

Sure, Mama. Sure I will. (Family exits. Tangela sits and drops her head in her hand. She bursts into tears. Her mother rushes back on stage but is quickly stopped by her mother after entering the stage approximately two to three steps. She silently coaxes her offstage. Tangela rises and crosses upstage. Suddenly she blurts out . . .) HOW COULD YOU DO THIS TO ME, VANCE? HOW COULD YOU? HOW . . . HOW . . . HOW??? (Mother enters on the edge of the stage. She wants to rescue Tang, but Grandma quickly emerges behind her and silently guides her back off stage.) YOU TOLD ME YOU LOVED ME. YOU TOLD ME YOU WANTED TO MAKE LOVE TO ME . . . NOT KILL ME?!? I TRUSTED YOU!! I BELIEVED IN YOU!! I *LOVE* YOU!!! (Looking skyward) DID YOU HEAR THAT? DID YOU? WELL LISTEN VERY CLOSELY THIS TIME BECAUSE YOU'LL NEVER HEAR IT AGAIN IN YOUR LIFE . . . thoughtfully) . . . or death. (Calmly) I said I loved you, Vance. Don't you understand that? (Vance has entered wearing all white. He is very pale and has obviously returned from the dead. Tangela is very shocked to hear him speak and twice as shocked to see his spirit.) Don't you understand what it's like to not only love someone but to be betrayed by them as well? Don't you?

VANCE

(Very compassionately) I do. And I'm very sorry. I was wrong.

TANGELA

VANCE!!! (Recalling he is dead) V-V-Vance??

VANCE

Yes, Tangela . . . but don't be afraid. Everything's okay. You might say I have permission to be here.

TANGELA

You might have permission to be back on earth, buddy boy, but you sure as heck don't have permission to be back here in my living room or to (turning and crossing to get away from him) ever speak to me again . . . YOU TRAITOR!!

VANCE

It wasn't that way, Tangela.

TANGELA

Oh no? Then why don't you just explain to me the way it really was . . . or is . . . or was suppose to be . . . . or will be one day . . . or whatever!!

VANCE

Tangela, you must listen to me. My time with you is very short. But there is something very important you should know.

TANGELA

And that is?

VANCE

I never meant to hurt you. I just loved you so much and was so sure that AIDS was going to take me away from you that I couldn't bear to let that happen. So I . . . selfishly . . .

TANGELA

Selfish? Selfish? Did I actually just hear you use the Big S in reference to yourself, Vance?

VANCE

Yes, Tang, you did. I selfishly and stupidly . . . thought that since I loved you and you loved me . . . and if I had to go . . . . then . . . maybe . . . we could just go together. I mean I know it sounds stupid to you and all but it's the truth. Look, Tang, why should I lie to you now? I'm already dead, right?

TANGELA

Hold on just a minute there *ghostbuster*. Are you telling me that you were going to kill me just because you were sick and were going to die? Vance, I didn't do this to you. I didn't give you AIDS. I *loved* you for goodness sakes. Can't you get that through your thick . . . thin . . . ghostly . . . whatever . . . head? (Tenderly) I *loved you*.

VANCE

I know, Tangela. And I'm sorry . . .

TANGELA

(INTERRUPTING) SORRY?!? YOU TRIED TO KILL ME AND ALL YOU CAN SAY IS I'M SORRY?!? No Vance!! That's what you say when you bump into a little old lady with bags in both arms! That's what you say when you step on somebody's new Air Jordans! That's what you say when you talk too loudly in theater and disturbs the person sitting next to you!! (Yelling) BUT YOU DON'T SAY I'M SORRY AFTER YOU'VE *TRIED* TO KILL A PERSON!!

VANCE

(Calmly and thoughtfully) Tangela, you have it all wrong.

TANGELA

Do I? Do I really Casper the Friendly Ghost? Well let's just put that no-life theory to the test, shall we? Did you not know you had a deadly virus.

VANCE

Yes.

TANGELA

Did you not try to talk me into having sex with you inspite of knowing this?

VANCE

(Deep breath) Yes.

TANGELA

Did you not know that I could have contracted the virus which you were carrying and were aware that you were carrying through sexual intercourse?

VANCE

Yes.

TANGELA

Would you not have had sex with me had I said yes instead of no?

VANCE

Yes.

TANGELA

Then you tried to kill me, Vance. And, truth be known, I'm sorry too. (Their eyes meet.) Sorry I trusted you; sorry I loved you; sorry I ever met you. (Moving across stage) Yeah, Vance, like you, I'm sorry too.

VANCE

Tangela . . .

TANGELA

See, Vance, this is bigger than me and you. Listen. If we had "done it" and let's just say I would have become pregnant and given birth before I died don't you see that even our baby could have been left here to pass on this deadly virus; then end his life just like his daddy did because he didn't want to suffer either. And on and on it could have gone, Vance, from one generation to the next. Just like a curse flowing through the veins of our family and our race.

VANCE

And *that's* why I was allowed to come back to your world . . . to speak to you about that very thing.

TANGELA

What thing? What are you talking about, Vance?

VANCE

To show you the power of your no. Your no couldn't stop *me* from having AIDS, but look at the people it *did* save . . . to include *yourself. Can't you see that?* Because one young lady had the will . . . the courage . . . the determination . . . . the strength to say "no" just one crucial time look at number of people whose lives she saved and made happier.

TANGELA

Vance, what are you talking about?

VANCE

When you said no, you were just talking to me you were talking directly to the AIDS virus. You were saying no to passing it on to another generation. You were saying no to having it passed on to you. You were saying no to making doctors and nurses and dentists having to work on dangerously infested patients. You were saying no to having another human being eaten to the bone to the point that they *look* like walking death and do little more than sit and wait for death to come and relieve them on their frustrations and pains.

TANGELA

(Shocked but enlightened) Oh boy! I said no to all of that? I had no idea.

VANCE

Not just that, Tangela, but you were saying no to adding another victim to the rapidly growing list of AIDS sufferers and death count. You did a great thing, Tangela! GREAT!! You have no idea just how great the power of your no was. I didn't know either until I died and was able to rise above then look back down on the whole picture. That's something you can't see while you're here . . . er there . . . er . . . alive. But someday you will. I'm glad you said no, Tang. I really am. Now . . . someday . . . your little kids will be able to play in the park without other parents keeping their children from around him as if he's a disease himself. And when he goes to the pool, all of the other kids won't have to get out because they're all afraid to swim in the same water as "the little boy with AIDS". And his dentists and doctors won't be afraid to do doctor things on him for fear of being infected by "the disease" from him. And his friends won't be afraid to hug him when he does something good. Speaking of good. You did REAL GOOD today, Tangela. REAL GOOD. I'm proud of you. I'm sorry. And I love you. Just as in life, I was given only a certain amount of time to be here with you. My time is up now and so I must go now. I will always remember you, Tangela. Always. And you should always remember the power of no. (Exits. Stops and blows her a kiss before leaving the stage.)

TANGELA

Vance!! Wait! Wait!! Please wait I have something to tell you!! Vance!! Vance!! (Starts off stage after him. Family enters quickly. They hear her calling his name and are able to catch her before she can exit the stage.)

MOTHER

Sweetheart!! Sweetheart!! Please. Let it go. Let it go. It's going to be alright. I promise.

GRANDMOTHER

Awwww. Come here, Baby. (Hugs her) It's okay. It's okay. You're with Grandma now, and everything's okay. It's okay Everything's just fine.

TANGELA

(Sobbing as she speaks) But he was just here, Grandma, and he told me that he still loves me. What kind of love is that? I could have caught AIDS . . . and so could have the baby if I had gotten pregnant? What kind of love IS that, Mama?

GRANDMAMA

(Ignoring the child's questions while posing her own.) Baby Doll, who was just here? And who told you that he still loves you?

TANGELA

Vance was, Grandma. Didn't y'all hear me talking to him just a few minutes ago? He was here explaining to me the power of no.

GRANDMAMA

(Glances at mom . . .) Explaining the what, honey?

TANGELA

He said that if I hadn't said no I could have passed that virus right on down to many many more and to several generations of our family as well. He said he was proud of me for saying no and that it was best decision I could have made.

MOTHER

Sure it was, Tangela, because you're not only deciding for yourself but for the lives of little ones who are not yet born and can't speak or decide for themselves.

GRANDMA

I still think that boy had the kind of love for you that us old folks are always trying to tell y'all young folks to be on the look out for. It's a love of the flesh and not the spirit.

TANGELA

I don't think so, Grandma. Like I said, he said he still loves me . . . even in the spirit world. Now *that's* pure love, wouldn't you say?

GRANDMA

Well, baby, here's what I *would* say. You're still young. You got a lot more growing and learning and saying no to do. This *is not* the end of your world. This is just your first stop on your way to a far, far destination. Be glad you were smart enough and brave enough to say no and not to fall to peer pressure. You see, baby, you don't always know everything about a person . . . you just know what they tell you.

MOTHER

Come on, Tangela, let's just sit down and relax for awhile. I think we all can use just a little bit of rest. Tang, I'm so proud of you for saying no to sex before it was really your time. Because you had the strength to say no, you not only saved yourself from a dreadful disease but many more innocent people as well. The power of your no today saved the lives of many people you'll never know you saved. I'm so proud of you, baby, because anyone could have said yes, but only a real woman could have summoned the strength and courage to say no . . . especially to someone she loves so much. (embraces her tightly) I love you, Tangela.

GRANDMOTHER

So do I, sweethert.

SIBBIE

Hey, Sis. You're cool with me too.

TANGELA

You know. It was a tough decision when I had to do it. But now that I did, I'm proud of myself for doing it. And you know what, now that I've done it, I love me more too. Mom?

MOTHER

Yeah baby.

TANGELA

I feel much better already because I know I did the right thing.

GRANDMA

Sweetheart, doing the right thing seems hard at times, but in the end it's always the best thing you can do in nearly any situation. Hey! What say we celebrate your decision to say no.

TANGELA

How are going to do that?

MOTHER

We have loads of cake and ice cream. I'm just waiting for you to say the word.

SIBBIE

What's the word? Tell me. I'll sure as heck say it!

TANGELA

Oh shut up, Sibbie. Nobody's talking to you. Mom, I'll take a bit of ice cream now . . . if that's okay with you.

GRANDMA

Oh it better be ok with her! Shoot, I was just thinking about some of that orange sherbet for myself. How about you Mr. (singing) Power Ranger?

SIBBIE

I want sherbet *and* cake.

TANGELA

You are such a greedy little pip squeak.

SIBBIE

AM NOT!!

TANGELA

ARE TOO!!

SIBBIE

AM NOT!!

TANGELA

AM TOO!! AND GIVE ME THAT REMOTE NO MORE (SINGING) POWER RANGER FOR YOU TODAY!!! (They begin wrestling over the controller)

MOTHER

Will you two please stop it? (To Grandma) They're started it up all over again!

GRANDMA

AW-W-W-W let'em fight. They ain't gonna hurt each other. Sibbie's just messing with his sister. Kindda like his own pesky way of saying he's glad to have her back to normal.

MOTHER

Normal??? Ma, when they're in normal mode they fight all day.

GRANDMA

Ever known either one of them to hurt the other one?

MOTHER

Of course not!

GRANDMA

(Heads to kitchen table) So what's the worry then? Come on child, let's you and me go over here and fix some bowls of ice cream and slices of cake so there'll be a snack ready for'em when they come up for air. To tell you the truth, I've been waiting for this sherbet so long I can already taste it before I even *get* to the box! (Curtains begin closing slowly.)

SIBBIE

GIVE ME THE REMOTE!

TANGELA

No, Sibbie. *You* let go. No more (singing) *Power Rangers* today, buddy!

SIBBIE

Hey, you know I watch them every day. Mom! Mom! Tell Tangela to let go of the remote! Mom!

TANGELA

No! *You* let go!

SIBBIE

Mom tell her to give me the remote. Mom! Mom-m-m-m!!

CURTAINS

STREET KIDS

CAST OF CHARACTERS

VOONA —A strong willed 17 year old street wise female. Outwardly strong, but compassionate and discerning inwardly. She is an orphans who would like nothing better than to have a family of her own. She is willing to accept replacements as long as they understand and love her for what she is.

NANA—A recovering teen age addict. She is the product of a good upbringing but the results of several bad personal decisions. She is remorseful in nature and very much ashamed of her past choices. She seeks for one good friend and is a good friend to others.

NIKI—The youngest member of the group. Emotional, confused, honest, and pensive about many things that have happened in her life. Growing in experience and knowledge. Innocent but full of pain. A rape victim.

MEKA—A good kid gone bad due to peer pressure. Desires much for herself but unsure of just how to achieve it. Streetwise yet quite benevolent when given the opportunity to show it.

SETTING

An urban city street

(Scene opens with a small group of young black females entering (l) on stage. They appear to range in age from approximately 16 to age 18. They each carry a pouch which secures the total of their personal possessions. There is little dialogue among the girls as they enter onto the stage. The frigid elements appear to be their collective nemesis for the moment. The girls spot a fire burning in a large steel drum (right center) and all make a mad dash toward it. They drop their belongings and began desperately trying to warm themselves. Setting is urban and destitute.)

NANA

Burn, baby, burn!!!

VOONA

I heard that, sister girl! A girl needs all the help she can get out here fightin' this hawk.

KEMA

Hey! I know that's straight! (Becoming dramatic) Roar, oh mighty flames of fire! Roar! Roar to my lonely heart's desire!! (She laughs at her own humor.)

NIKI

That's tight, girl. Check you out and all. I mean like the sister's a poet . . .

NIKI AND KEMA

And don't even know it!! (They laugh and high five one another).

VOONA

Shoot man, this is alright here. Feels good don't it? (She pauses and looks from one girl's face to the next awaiting a response. No response.) Hey! Hey! Said the fire feels better'n this old hawk out here, don't it? Don't it feel good y'all? (Her youth and innocence is obvious.)

NANA

Yeah girl! You bet! Sure would feel even better to have a warm bed, hot meal, and a loving family right about now.

KEMA

(Shouting and pointing) Hey! Hey! Don't you do it, girl! Don't you even do it! Just don't go there on me tonight, alright? Just don't do it, man, 'cause I ain't up for all the sad drama tonight. Alright? I don't care what else you do just don't take that trip on me tonight! It's cold. I'm hungry. I done had a long day, and I just ain't down with it! Straight up real talk, man. (Calming down) So just chill with the wish list, girlfriend. Everythang's straight. All good. It'll be alright for all of us one day. We just got a little some-some we got forge through, but sooner or later we gonna all have the good lifestyle and good stuff again. Huh? Y'all know I'm right. But I just ain't up to the fantasies tonight. I just ain't with all them emotions and memories and stuff right about now. Been a long tough day. (Looks her in the eye and asks) Alright? We straight? (Extends her fist in an offering of "dap." Dap is returned.) Cool! That's what I'm talking about! Now that's my girl! I'm there with you girl. I can feel you, dog. I know where you coming from though. We straight.

NIKI

Hey, check this out man! I don't know why you always gotta go out like that anyway. Know what I mean? Um saying it's always *you* man. YOU. See what I'm saying? Hey, dog, all us out here on these streets. All of us! Hey, it's tough on all of us, not just you. I mean we out here too. You hear me? So we all got to do what we got to do to make it. Hear me, girl? So why don't you just accept that and quit going out like a wimp every time we come up against a little something. Alright?

KEMA

Back off, Niki. Let it go. It ain't worth it. Let it go. She'll be alright. She's cool. It's all good.

NIKI

Yeah, but why she always got to bring up some home . . . and family . . . and house . . . you know . . . and (becoming angry and emotional) stuff like that?!

KEMA

Hey, dog!! Stop perpetrating' man. I told you she's cool and we all know what time it is with the little sister. Ain't no harm done. It's all good. Ain't no thang, my sister. Ain't no thang. Everything's everything, Niki. Don't stress yourself none. Alright? Okay? Now just let it go and chill!!

NIKI

(Visibly upset, storming across stage) Naw, Kema, naw. Shoot! What you mean no harm done and everything's cool? Who said so? You? Everything's everything

242

just because everything's in a chill status with you? Not hardly. I don't think so, sister! Not even.

VOONA

Niki, what you talking 'bout, girl? What's up with all that? Kema and Nana neither one ain't done nothing worth all this. What's up with you? You know Nana is the youngest and newest one of us to hit the streets. You know she's adjusting to being a real street kid. So what's up with you, girl? What's going on in that noggin (point to her head) of yours?

NIKI

It just ain't like that, man. It just ain't.

NANA

Ain't like what, Niki? 'Cause you show 'nough got me all crossed up up in here. I can't follow you with a radar gun right now.

NIKI

It ain't all so much like y'all always play stuff down to be.

VOONA

What?

NIKI

It's not all about just her and her newness to the streets. It's about us too!!

NANA

What the freak are you talking about girl?!?

NIKI

I'm talking about (pointing) HER!! Come on now. Don't y'all go dumb on me right now. And don't EVEN try to pull that innocent "I don't know what you talking about either" on me. Like I'm the only one who noticed how insensitive she really is.

VOONA

What the devil did she just say? Did I just hear you mumble something about insensitive? INSENSITIVE? Niki, what the heck are you talking about insensitive? For goodness sakes, girl. Are you serious? These are the streets and everybody out here is trying desperately to survive. Of course, she's insensitive! But then whose not out here man? These are the street!! Not a finishing school— not a good manners class—not a institution for grace and social skills—BUT THE DIRTY, FILTHY, NASTY, BACKBITING, DANGEROUS STREETS WHERE YOU HAVE TO LEARN TO BECOME INSENSITIVE OR BE TAKEN ADVANTAGE OF AND EATEN ALIVE AND SPIT OUT BY THOSE WHO ALREADY ARE. You know that better than I do. Who out here isn't at least a little bit insensitive from time to time? I know I am sometimes. And so are you . . . (pointing to her peers as she speaks) and you . . . and you and you. And so is everybody else out here who want to survive for just one more day. It's just part of being part of the street.

NANA

Man shoot! Y'all slipped right past me 'cause I'm here still trying to figure out how y'all eased this *insensitive* kick in on me without me ever seeing it coming. Niki, what you really moaning 'bout, girl? I know you better than this. What's up with you? I mean on the real too, sis. What's up with you?

NIKI

(Pointing) Her! That's what's up with me . . . Her. You got it now? Do you?

NANA

Naw, sis, I don't. But I'll listen if you want to talk about it though.

NIKI

Alright. I'll talk. I'll say it. I'll tell you straight up. I got a problem with her.

NANA

I'm still hearing you, girl. Keep talking.

NIKI

The way she always bringing up stuff about home . . . and . . . and . . . family . . . and hot baths and the cold showers. If it ain't that then she's always talking about some warm, clean pajamas, or some soft (kicking the sidewalk) mattresses! Hey man, I mean these streets are it . . . IT . . . IT. Right now these streets are all we've got and she just can't get that little bit of truth in her big thick noggin. Can't you understand, Vana? Can't you? This is it! Get that in that big hard jarhead of yours. This is all the home and family and soft beds and warm pajamas you're going to see or have for a long time, friend. So get off that pity pot and get real for once in your runaway life. All the memories and tears in the world ain't gonna ever put you back where you came from. So just let it go, girl, PLEASE. Give it up. Forget about it. And accept the fact that when you ran away this was what you ran away to. So just forget about all dem daydreams you got wandering 'round up there in your cute little head 'cause ain't none of them gonna ever come true for you again. None of them! Just let'em go and face life out here on these mean, nasty, cold, streets with us like a real woman and not so much like a little sissy wimp! Alright? So just let it go and learn to deal with what we got to deal with every day to survive, alright. I'm tired of the whining and talking about what use to be and what you use to have and how you remember your house and family and friends and all that kind of foolishness? Okay? Now . . . I said it. So now you know.

VOONA

(Goes over and very calmly lays a hand on her shoulder.) Niki . . . what's up with you? Why you tripping like this, girl? This ain't even you, Boo. Insensitive? Niki, what in the world are you talking about? I mean you got us all confused.

NIKI

(Knocking her hand away) The heck you say. Don't you square up on me and then play that innocent role like you don't know what I'm talking about!

VOONA

(Becoming quite stern in her voice.) I don't, Niki. And neither does anyone else here either. So why don't you just tell me, er . . . us what's eating away at you then we'll all know.

NIKI

(Becomes loud and emotional. Shoves Voona away, then yells . . .) Alright sister girl! You want me to tell you? Huh? Is that what you want Voona? (To the other girls collectively) And you too I suppose. You want me to tell you? To tell you all? Huh?

VOONA

(Calmly) Yeah. That's exactly what we want, Niki. We want you to tell us why you're tripping so today. And it looks just like you've got the world by the ear. So go on my sister. Do your thing. (The girls are now nearly nose to nose) Let me hear what it is that's got so far under your skin that you can't even think straight no more. Talk to me!

NIKI

(Nervous. Anxious. Deep breathing) Okay. Okay. (Then crosses to Nana and speaks directly to her.) I'll tell you, little miss innocent. Since this whole thing seems to be between me and you anyway. I'll be more than happy to tell you. (Nana lifts her eyebrows and nods yes but yes nothing.) I'm tired of you whimpering, and moaning, and groaning, and complaining about a soft bed . . . and hot food . . . and bubble baths . . . and clean clothes. I'm tired of that crap! And I don't want to hear you moan, groan, or complain or cry about any of those thing anymore. Ever!! You understand? I don't want to ever hear about any of those things ever again. Case closed, sister!

VOONA

(Very calmly and thoughtful) Case close? H-m—m-m. Not quite, your honor. You see . . . you lied to me.

NIKI

What? I did what to you?

VOONA

Lied. L-I-E-D. You straight out lied to me, Niki.

NANA

She what? Lied? Oh my god! I just don't believe what I'm hearing! You mean to tell me you're actually standing out here on this cold behind street complaining about the fact that somebody LIED to you. Oh my god! Allite. Go ahead. Tell this sister (pointing to herself) what makes you (pointing to Voona) think she (pointing to Niki) LIED to you—princess. What?

VOONA

Don't worry about it. She knows. She knows exactly what I'm talking about. Don't you, Niki?

NIKI

No, I don't know what you're talking about either for one thing, and for another, I don't take too kindly to being called a liar. So maybe you just better take that comment back, my sister.

VOONA

I said it because it's true. And I ain't about to take back one single word of the truth.

NIKI

So it's like that now, huh? You're gonna call me a liar right to my face, huh? (Rising slowly and menacingly starting over to Voona.)

VOONA

Already did.

NIKI

Oh yeah?

VOONA

Yeah. That's right. (Her face is violently turned by the force of a hard slap. The other girls instantly race over to prevent any further confrontation between the two girls.)

NANA

(Totally outdone and in disbelief.) Chill out with them blows, man! What's with all that? What's up? Come on now. We're family. Tight. Niki what's up girl? You tripping some hard tonight dog. What's up? And don't tell me nothing either 'cause I can see better than that. I mean . . . what the . . . ? Lied to you? Insensitive? (Throwing her hand up and walking away.) Aw man!! Y'all show 'nough way out there tonight. Too much for me. I can't see it. I can't see it. (Mumbling) Lied to her?. Insensitive?

VOONA

Why don't you just shut up, NANA!! JUST SHUT UP AND STAY THE HECK OUT OF THIS.

NANA

Oh so that's the way it's gonna be, huh? Big chief here wants me to shut up while little Indian Forked Tongue speaks many more great lies. I get you. I see what's up with you now.

VOONA

No you don't. None of you do. None of you get my drift at all. (Looking inquisitively) None of you understand why I want Niki to tell the truth about what's going on with her tonight . . . right now . . . this very minute. None of you do. Not a single one of you—not even she (pointing to Niki) understands why I want that sister to tell all of us the truth . . . THE WHOLE TRUTH AND NOTHING BUT THE TRUTH SO HELP HER GOD!!! NONE OF YOU UNDERSTANDS WHY. NONE! NOT A SINGLE ONE OF YOU SO CALLED FRIENDS!

NANA

Who-o-oa-a, Voona. We might have our differences but we ain't never measured our loyalty to our friendship on them. That *"so called friend"* thing landed a little south of the belt for me. And I ain't trying to speak for nobody else either. But now I feel like you just moved this conversation to a new level—you know, like this a trial or something and you done made yourself the lawyer, judge and jury. But I'm saying . . . (she is forcefully interrupted)

VOONA

WILL YOU JUST SHUT YOUR BIG MOUTH!! WILL YOU? HUH? (Starts towards Niki but is waved back by Nana and Kema. Stops and goes down to one knee then asks . . .) So, my angry little sister, you decided to talk yet? You decided to tell us the truth? The whole truth? And nothing but the truth so help you God? (Pauses as she drops her head, lifts her eyebrows in a questioning fashion. Only an intense stare is returned as her answer.) Are you ready to really let us know why you get so mad with every mention of home . . . or family . . . or anything other than these nasty, dangerous, stinking streets? Are you ready? (Pause) Can you do it? Can you? Go ahead. Why don't you sound off my sister? Never known you to be without a word to say in any situation. We're all waiting. That's all I want you to do for me right now is to be honest with us about that one simple little thing. Now go ahead. Like Nike says, "Just do it."

KEMA

What's up with you, Voona? You crazy or something? This ain't no psychology office or nothing like that! You spastic or something? These the streets, girl! You see any psychologist's couch out here on the curb anywhere? Check you out. You're going 'round here sounding like a psychiatrist or psychologist— or whichever one of'em it is that suppose to be dealing with your head when you start acting weird —talking 'bout some (mockingly)"Are you ready to really let us know why you get so made every time there's a mention of home or family or anything other than these wretched and pitiful inner city street? Are you ready? (Pause) Can you do it? Go ahead. We're waiting. That's all I want you to do right now is to be honest with us about the at one simple little thing, sweetheart. Now go ahead and just do it for us." (Erupting with madness) What's up with all the psych talk, fool? Ain't nobody out here about all that college talk. Let's be real since that's what you talking about being. Right? Real. Allite. What the heck do YOU think is bothering the girl? Why do you think she hates it when anyone mentions things like home, family, clean clothes, and warm baths? Huh? Why? BECAUSE WE'RE RUNAWAYS, VOONA!! DA-A-A!! RUNAWAYS!! WE DON'T HAVE ANY OF THOSE THINGS! WE DON'T HAVE PARENTS—WE LEFT THEM!! WE DON'T HAVE NICE HOMES WITH HOT RUNNING SHOWERS AND WE DON'T EAT NICE WARM BALANCED MEALS THREE TIMES A DAY EITHER IN CASE YOUR BELLY FORGOT TO TELL THAT TO YOUR OBVIOUSLY NON-FUNCTIONING BRAIN!! WE RAN AWAY FROM ALL OF THOSE NICE, DESIRABLE, BEAUTIFUL THINGS. Don't you remember any of this? Did you think you were out here just because you came over to play with us? Naw, baby. Naw. That ain't how this thang is. Gosh, girl, I don't know how you could even ask her what's the matter with her? You tell me, Voona, what do you think is the matter with her?

VOONA

(Staring at Niki. Very calm and collected. Totally unmoved by anything she has just heard) I don't know. Just like I said before. But she does; and that's exactly what I want her to tell us right now.

KEMA

(Starts right in without being prompted) DON'T KNOW? DON'T KNOW? You don't know—and can't figure out—what's eating away at her like a cancer? You really don't know. For goodness sakes, Voona, I'm only fifteen years old and even I can figure this one out. You silly fool! Here, here (taking her by the shoulders and turning her around) Maybe I should just help you to understand what it is about those words that you keep repeating that get her so upset. Check this out. Hey! Wanna go to the movies tonight? Sure I would. Okay. Go ask your father. Look around now girls. You see dad out here anywhere? I don't. And what little girl—or big one for that matter—doesn't want the security of having daddy in her life? I know. I know. I'll wait until after dinner and see if mom wants to go check out a flick at the movies with me then. (Banging her fists against her head as if she suddenly remembered something very important.) Oh my goodness . . . now where on earth is mom? Mom! Has anybody seen mom? Mom! Mom! (VOONA prepares to speak but is quickly silenced by Kema with a firm and quick raising of her hand.) AA-H-H-H!! No, no, no, no, no!!! You see, I'm not quite done yet sister. (Looking up at the sky) Looks like tonight might be a bit nasty and cold out here on these old nasty and cruddy streets. Think maybe I'll just take a warm shower, put on my clean pajamas and just lay back on my comfortable and relaxing bed and watch a little HBO or Showtime. You think? No-o-o. No. Why? 'Cause we have a slight problem with that picture. And the problem with that picture is there ain't no showers, there ain't no pajamas, there ain't no HBO or Cinemax or Showtime . . . or even showers or hot meals or pajamas out here? Why? 'Cause these are the streets and this is the way we decided to live once we decided to run away from all of those nice things. And at 15 years old she's having a hard time accepting the reality of her decisions and actions. She's split. Torn. Confused. Frustrated. Bewildered. Because she wants all the pleasures of home out here on the streets . . . and the truth is it just don't happen like that. So-o-o, what's she to do, y'all? Jump up and down and turn cartwheels every time one of us mentions anything about a home or a family or any of that other stuff? What? What's the sister to do?

NANA

(Trying to invoke an emotional change in the environment) Hey! Hey! I swear I think all y'all need to just chill out with all of this non-sense about stuff all of us use to have in the past. After all, I mean . . .

VOONA

(Interrupting Nana and remaining emotionally unmoved) Don't matter what you mean, Nana. Not one bit! I know exactly what I'm doing. Exactly!

NANA

Well, shoot then, Voona! Maybe you do know EXACTLY what you're doing; but one thang's for freaking sure, sister girl. We sure ain't got the slight notion on how you operating out here tonight. Not the slightest! (Again trying to interject some humor so as to relieve the emotional tension.) 'Cause as for me, I'm just as lost as a bedbug in a cotton patch. (Forcing herself to laugh an obviously fake and nervous laugher) Y'all get it? Bedbug—cotton patch. (Begins singing, rocking, clapping in old Negro spiritual style) O' Master, he be real good to me. (Mock cotton picking) O' Master he be real good to me . . . why the ol' master he couldda done hung me up by my neck from way up in dat dare tree. Dat's whiles I says O' Master he be real good to me. O' Master . . . .

VOONA

CUT THE CRAP, KEMA!! This ain't no joke. This is for real!! It ain't about pretending no more! It ain't about the old master! It ain't about no old slave! It's a new day, sister! A NEW DAY. Bad thang is we just still living like old time slaves. And we keep losing and killing and hurting ad destroying because we won't talk about what's really making us lose and kill and hurt and destroy. So we just keep going on killing, hurting, and destroying . . . trying to run from what it is that make us that way in the first place. But you can't run away from your past—and you can't run away from the truth. But you can learn how to stand up to both of them and deal with them the right way—before they come together and turn your rage inward on you and cause you to destroy yourself. And that's what sister girl ain't learned how to do yet. She ain't all hyped up and mad because somebody said the words family, home, pajamas, showers. (Moving about as she speaks) Truth is, there ain't a runaway in this country—out here living on the streets and trying her best to make ends meet—who don't want a better situation than he or she is already in. Shoot!! What makes you think she's any different? Ya'll better get real. (Nana goes over and gently places her hand on Niki's shoulder. Niki begins to wipe tears from her eyes, then suddenly bursts into an emotional cry.)

NANA

Aw-w-w-w!!! (Sympathetically) Now just look at what you did to her. (Voona points at herself as if to ask "Me?") Yes you and that big insensitive mouth of yours. Now just look at poor little Niki.

VOONA

What are you talking about? I ain't done nothing to her.

KEMA

You ain't done nothing? You ain't done nothing? Look fool! (Pointing to a crying Niki) Is that what you call nothing? Is it? Niki is one of us and she's crying like a baby because of you and your big SELFISH mouth! And now you got the guts to stand up there and say you ain't done nothing.

VOONA

(Still unmoved) You listen to me . . .

NANA

(Becoming emotional and serious for the first time) Listen to YOU? Listen to YOU? (Pointing to Niki) SHE listened to you and now look at HER! And now you want me to listen to you TOO? I don't hardly think it, baby!

NIKI

(Jumping up and screaming) ALRIGHT!! ALRIGHT!! So you want me to be honest with you? To tell you the truth . . . the whole truth . . . and nothing but the truth so help me God. (She crying and wiping tears as she talks) Okay. Then that's just what I'll do. Here's what y'all been waiting to hear all evening long. So listen up . . . cause I'm only going to tell you this story just one time, then I'm gonna move on with my life.

NANA

Don't pay any attention to any of this foolishness, Nana (tries to put her arm around her in comfort but is shoved away forcefully) you know . . . .

NIKI

NO! NO! Voona's straight. She's right. Besides I think it's time my friends knew some things 'bout me anyhow. (Walks about then begins very emphatically) I hate it when you talk about family, mother, father, showers, pajamas . . . and all that kind of mess!

NANA

Why? 'Cause you have some many memories of all those things with your family?

NIKI

Memories? Shoot. Memories? That's what I hate most. The memories.

VOONA

You've started. Go on and talk about it.

NIKI

It's the memories. The painful, secretive memories. That's really why I'm out here. The memories. Not so much the memories I've had since I've been a street kid, but more so the memories I had before I ever became a street kid. (Turning and facing her peers.) You see, I'm not out here on these streets JUST because I ran away from home. I'm out here on these streets because I ran away from a family that did not believe me when I said my very own stepfather was touching me in a bad way. They never believed me when I said his drunken buddies were always staggering up against me and rubbing on me and saying things to me that they had no right or reason to say to any child. They never believed me when I said it wasn't safe for me to stay at home alone with my stepfather nights while my mother was working. They never believed anything I said. Not even my own mother. The one person I always thought I could turn to . . . trust . . . count on. Even she did not believe me. Truth is, I believe she KNEW what was happening all alone. It's just that she deserted me and supported the very man that raped and molested her own daughter. And you know when he did it? You know? Listen carefully, girls, and this just might tell you a lot. It's my dear, dear pleasure to tell you that it happened one night while my mom was out of the house at work, and it just so happens that when it happened I had just taken a nice long, hot shower . . . put on my comfortable pajamas . . . and laid across my nice soft bed to watch an HBO original movie. He came to my door and said he was just checking to see if I needed anything before he went to sleep. I said no. He said okay. Then suddenly he remembered there was one other thing he needed to tell me before he turned in for the night. Said it was important and that he didn't want to yell it to me through the door, so I told him to come on in. And he did. In more ways than one. That's exactly what he did. He came right on into my bedroom— and raped me. He threatened to hurt me, my mom, the dog, the cat, and anybody or anything else he thought I loved if I told anybody.

VOONA

But you did tell someone, didn't you?

NIKI

Sure I did. But what for? I was thirteen years old and nobody believed me. Nobody. That hurt me more than the rape. And damaged me twice as much. Can you believe it? A thirteen year old girl raped by a 43-year-old man, and her mother having the gall to ask her, "Well what did you do to him while I was gone to make him do this to you?" Tell me, what does ANY 13-year-old do to ANY 43-year-old to MAKE him rape her? Huh? WHAT? WHAT? What? My bed, my pillow, my family, my pajamas—all ruined, defiled, destroyed. And I was asked by my very own mother, what did I do to cause my own rape. So I grew to hate the sound and the memories of the words family, pajamas, bath, bedroom, dad . . . and now . . . even mom. I hate them all. I do. And I always will. (Pause) And now you know why I drift out like a wild child when I hear you guys mention those words.

NANA

It really makes you wonder, doesn't it?

KEMA

'Bout what?

NANA

People.

VOONA

What about them?

NANA

Thirteen. Crying rape. (To Kema) Did your mom take you to the doctor's to have you or your story checked out?

NIKI

(Shakes her head no, then replies softly.) No. I think she was too afraid that I was telling the truth and that she wouldn't be able to live without that molester and rapist in her life—and in her daughter's bed.

VOONA

Never examined. Claim never confirmed or denied. I mean when it comes to things like THAT, why won't people listen to us kids? I mean, like for real, you know? What do they have to lose? Why wouldn't they just listen?

KEMA

That's serious, man. Can you imagine how many lives are destroyed every year behind stuff like that?

NANA

Can you imagine how many serial killers and rapists kill and rape because they were violated as kids and no one took the time to seriously listen to them and get the help they needed at an early age?

VOONA

True. True.

KEMA

So the anger and hurt and frustration and the disappointment and sorrow all just fester and grow and fertilize each other. And each one of these breeds more and more and more of its own kind until ultimately it breeds a copy of the perpetrator.

VOONA

Bingo! Hurt breeds hurt. Pain breeds pain. Destruction breeds destruction. And perpetrators breed victims who themselves will become perpetrators unless they get help.

KEMA

You're one hundred percent right, Voona. You're right. This is a very serious matter. Just think, any child could be going through something like this right now.

NANA

Sure they could. And how would you know? I mean ANY kid. Quiet kids . . . shy kids . . . depressed kids . . . runaway kids (pointing to them).

VOONA

Defiant kids. Rich kids. Black kids. Hispanic kids. Oriental kids. White kids. (Thoughtfully) Oh, man, this is awesome!

NIKI

And check this out. Even though talking about it is hard enough, you should have to live with the memories and pain. Then you'll see just how hard it really is!

KEMA

No, Niki, now that's where you all the way wrong, girl. No child should ever have to live with the pain of being molested, raped or rejected. I'm sorry, but I just don't think that's a necessary part of anybody's childhood.

VOONA

Think you'll ever go back home?

NIKI

Would you? If you were molested, would you? If you were raped, would you? If your mother—the one person you always felt you could count on—had turned her back on you already—in your most desperate moment of need—would you? Would you really go back and risk the same pain and memories happening to you again? I'm a child, Voona, but I'm not a fool.

VOONA

So how you manage to deal with all the pain and agony so good everyday, Niki?

NIKI

I don't. I just try to pretend it's not there and keep going. Just that sometimes I lose it and fall apart, though. Kind of like I did tonight, I guess. Some days are a little harder than others, you know.

NANA

Don't you worry about it, girl. We're still here for you and we still love you too.

NIKI

Yeah! I know. And I love you guys too.

VOONA

(Jokingly and more jovial than her previous speeches.) Well if you love me, how come you slapped me so hard? (Laughter)

NIKI

Oh-h-h, Voona. I'm so sor-r-ry. I really didn't mean to do that. Something just . . . I don't know. It just happened. But I really didn't mean to.

NANA

Didn't mean to? Girl you nearly took her head off with that Mike Tyson like right cross. (Shadow boxing) Shoot! For a minute I thought I was going to have to start calling you MT for short.

NIKI

MT?

NANA

Yeah! Miss Tyson. (Laughter. Still shadow boxing)

VOONA

Well, you can be Miss Tyson if you want to, but if you slap me like that again, I'm going to schedule you a re-match with Evander Holyfield.

NANA

(Instantly stops shadow boxing.) Evander Holyfield?! Child, no. It's time for MT get out the ring now and go look for another line of work (shadow boxing, then mimicking as if biting Holyfield's ear) 'cause my ear biting days are long over now. Girlfriend you know I always say, ain't no sense in getting your head pounded on if you just don't have to do. Sorry, MT, but I do believe this is the end of your very short lived boxing career. But at least you can say you're a legend—in your own mind. (Laughter)

NIKI

Oh, well, easy come easy go.

VOONA

You alright now, Niki?

NIKI

Most of the time, yeah. But like I said, there are times when the pains are more than I know how or what to do with.

VOONA

I'm sure they are, Niki. But then you don't have to handle them all by yourself anyway. That's what we're here for. To help you through those tough times.

NANA

Speaking of being here . . . I mean out here on these (jokingly) nasty, grindy, mean old unforgiving streets . . . why are you here? Why aren't you at home on a cold nasty night like this?

KEMA

Me?

NANA

Yeah. You. I always kindda wanted to know, but all and all at the same time I didn't really want to pry too much. Feeling me?

KEMA

Yeah, I'm feeling you. I know what you mean. You're not prying. And the quick and short answer to your question is Roger. (Quickly) And yes that the truth, the whole truth and nothing but the truth so help me God. (They laugh)

VOONA

Allite. Sounding like the key witness for the defense or something. But you still ain't told you who the devil Roger is.

NIKI

Yeah. Out with the dirt, girl. Come on now. Don't be holding out on us now. We in the confession mode now so just let it all hang out while the hanging is good. Now go on and tickle our ears with something juicy about Roger. First of all who the devil is this roger character anyhow and second of all what does he have to do with you being out here?

KEMA

That's really an understandable question for someone to ask me, but it's still a hard one for me to answer, even though I really don't know why it would be so hard. But anyway, I'll tell you who Roger is. They've always told me that talking about things is sometimes your best form of therapy. (Deep breath) OK. Here goes all or nothing. Roger is the fool who lied to me and convinced me to leave home and my family to be with him . . . as he told me . . . forever and ever.

VOONA

Then where is lover boy now?

NIKI

Yeah, and what happened to forever?

KEMA

Well, let's just say everybody's meaning of forever ain't necessarily the same. For some folks, forever is a long, long, time. Then for others . . . well, let's just say it not as long. As a matter of fact, let's just say it's not long at all. Sometimes it takes longer to make the promise of being with someone forever than the two of you actually stay together as a couple. Anyway, that was Roger's and my case. But I was in love with him and I believed him, so I trusted him and took him at his lying word. (Reflectively) I admit—now—it wasn't a smart thing to do at all—actually, it was a completely dumb thing to do, but you know how it is when the heart tells the head what to do. I believed him. I really did. So I listened to everything Roger told me, and ignored all the advice and lectures my parents kept giving me. Kema don't. Kema do. Kema you ought to. Kema you shouldn't. Kema this. Kema that. Kema. Kema. Kema. They'd spend hours and days talking common sense into me and Roger would call and spend just minutes telling me why my parents were all wrong and why he was all right and why my parents would never be able to understand and relate to us, our generation, our problems, our feelings, and a bunch of other foolishness. But it worked. It worked. And I became a martyr for Roger's cause. I couldn't see anything . . . any truth . . . any love . . . any compassion . . . any concern . . . ANYTHING . . .

for seeing him. He became my demi-god and I literally worshiped the ground he walked on. "Temperance!" My father would always say. "Learn to do all things in moderation—not in excess." Oh but no. Not Roger. Roger was my love toy. He deserved excess. He was too good for mere moderation and temperance. That stuff was for somebody else, but definitely not for Roger. Or so I thought at that time anyway. After all what the heck did my dad know? I mean, sure he's a smart man, but he's a parent. And, tell me, what teenager doesn't know twice as much as their older, wiser, more experienced parents, right?

NIKI

I hear you, girl. Been there done that.

VOONA

Amen! Haven't we all?

KEMA

And so I made Roger the very reason I existed. And I did whatever he asked, whenever he asked, just like he asked. After all, why shouldn't I? Why wouldn't I? Weren't we going to be together—FOREVER anyway?

NANA

Child, I can see this one coming a mile off. But go ahead. Ain't gon' steal yo' thunder. This yo' time to talk. Go ahead.

KEMA

See, that's my point. Everybody else could see the doom coming from a mile away. But me? Hey, man, I just gonna be real and up front with y'all. I couldn't see jack! I couldn't hear jack! I wouldn't believe jack! All I knew was Roger and I loved one another and he promised me we were going to have a couple of kids and be together forever and forever and forever. And I got so caught up in his promises that nothing else anybody told me mattered at all. Nothing. Roger was my whole world, and I was willing to do whatever it took to keep him.

NIKI

So how'd you get here?

KEMA

Roger and I grew desperately in love. So much so that I had started breaking all the rules and telling all kinds of lies to my parents so that I could meet up with him at different places. I'd even taken a big chance on a few occasions and had him in my bedroom after school before my parents got in from work. I mean, I just had no limits with him. I loved him and would do anything in the world he asked me to prove that to him. And finally one day he did. He talked me into stealing the keys to my aunt's brand new Lexus and stealing a charge card and cash money out my mom's purse. Then we took the money, the card, and the car and eloped from Denver here.

VOONA

Well that explains how you got here, but I don't see hide nor hair of "Roger."

KEMA

I know. You know the truth is always so obvious, yet so hard to accept. Deep down inside I knew I had moved too fast with Roger. I knew he wanted something other than just love from me. I mean, he was always full of himself and convenient excuses and other stupid stuff that should have told me that I was being made a fool of. But did I listen to common sense?

VOONA

Well you know what they say about common sense, don't you?

KEMA

No, what?

VOONA

Common sense is sense that is not commonly used

.

KEMA

Well, true in my case anyway. Anyhow, Roger and I arrived here a few days after we left Denver. Couldn't drive straight through because the cops were onto us now. So we drove back roads—mostly at night—until we finally got here. Then while I was in the station paying for the gas and drinks he'd told me to get while I was inside, he drove off and left me. I was so much in love that I couldn't smell, see, taste, or feel his obvious betrayal.

NIKI

Betrayal?

KEMA

Yeah. Little did I know that all Roger really wanted from me was free and easy sex along with some cash and a car to get him across country to his real love.

VOONA

His what?

KEMA

Straight up Jerry Springer action girl. You heard it right. His real love. I found out that Roger had a girl friend named Marshal. Seventeen. Pregnant. Dropout. In love with him too. They'd plan to be together "forever" too. Only thing was he was more determined to be with her forever than with me. So he used me to get him some money and a car so that he could get to where she was.

NIKI

O-o-o-o, sounds to me like somebody deserves a serious beat down.

KEMA

For real. Don't you know? I felt so much like a big dumb fool because I also learned that she helped him to plan it all out. But how could a seventeen year old outsmart me? I mean I thought I always handled my business real tight too. Know what I'm saying? And Roger was my business. My only business to tell you the truth. Anyhow, I guess I should have listened to my parents when they told me I would be much better off to just leave him alone. But I just wouldn't hear it. I just had to see for myself.

NIKI

And now that you have seen?

KEMA

Believe me when I tell you; some pain just ain't worth the experience.

NANA

Why are you still out here? Why don't you just go back home?

KEMA

Can't. Been out here two and a half years now. Mom died and dad's moved and remarried. Both sets of grandparents are dead and my mom and dad were only children; so I have no grandparents, aunts, uncles or cousins. Right now you guys and the streets are the only family I've got. This is my home and you're my family. And that's the way it is—all because I thought Roger loved me.

NANA

I use to have a home and a family . . . and a puppy dog and cute little outfits that I wore to school everyday. (Smiling and recalling) I did. But . . . well . . . drugs took all of that away from me before I ever knew I was really hooked. I mean first it was just marijuana. Then before I knew it, I was drinking, doing crack and LSD, then finally snorting and mainlining. In no time flat I was up to $400 a day.

NIKI

You? Four bills a day? How could you support that?

NANA

How else does a sixteen year old attractive and sexy female support a $400 a day habit? That really don't quality as a brain teaser you know. You know the answer. How else? I hit the streets. And, baby, they hit me right back. HARD too. I was arrested five times and served eight months in a youth center for prostitution, six months in boot camp for truancy, failed two dry out clinics, and stayed on house arrest for over one year. Finally, my parents . . . oh, yes, I had parents. Good parents. Concerned parents. Involved parents. Church going, PTA attending, Saturday morning soccer game van driving socially involved politically correct parents. Yeah. Parents I had. But I just wouldn't listen to anybody. Authority and rules just didn't matter to me as long as I got what I wanted because I thought the whole world was my oyster. I thought everything in the universe was created just for me and nobody else. So why shouldn't I be above the rules? Defiant? Self indulging? Out of control? Well, I was . . . for a long while at that. Then, finally, my parents got to the point where they felt they had taken all they could. They had been pushed to their limit. And rightfully so. And they felt as if there was simply not enough progress being made on my part. So they were getting ready to put me in some hospital for drug abusers.

VOONA

Isn't that exactly what you needed?

NANA

You obviously never been hooked before. And besides that, were you listening to me just now? I was above the rules, not governed by the rules

VOONA

Just answer the question. Isn't that exactly what you needed?

NANA

Now in retrospect. Sure . . . to sober me up and to dry me out . . . you're doggone right that's what I needed. But I was a different me at that time. They weren't talking to a sober dried out me. They were talking to a drug hungry me. They were talking to a totally irrational me. They were talking to strung out me. Drug crazy me. And to an addict, the ONLY thing he or she needs is another high. Anything other than another high, is just a waste of time. And that's where I was when my parents offered me their help.

KEMA

So, now, let me ask you what seems to be the most popular question going today. So how did all of that land you out here on these streets with us?

NANA

I knew it was coming. Alright, now it's my turn to take the witness stand. And yes I do solemnly swear to tell the truth the whole truth and nothing but the truth during my confession here tonight.

KEMA

Good! You may take the stand and continue your testimony now. (Laughter)

NANA

So, on with the truth. Once my parents had their fill of me and my drug addiction, they decided that I was going to treatment whether I wanted to or not. They said it was final if I was going to stay in their house. Otherwise they would call the authorities and have me involuntarily admitted. I agreed. Told them I would be ready to go and check in the first thing in the morning. They said alright, good night, and went to bed. I couldn't take another attempt at drying out. I didn't want to be away from my friend—drugs—for that long. I could hear my parents voices in my head, and I knew that what they were saying was right, but the drugs spoke so much clearer, wiser, louder, and more demanding. Over and over they argued with the validity of my parents' advice. They told me how foolish their advice was. They told me how hopeless it was for me to even try to come clean. They told me how I was doomed to live life out as an addict and how I had thrown my future and my dreams away. My drug habit actually talked to me, y'all. It did. I swear. It spoke to me. It rationalized to me. It negotiated with me. It lied to me. It defeated me. It destroyed me. My habit now had me—I no longer had it. It had me. It was now the master and I was now the slave. Fifteen. Addicted. Juvenile record. Jailbird. Prostitute. Failing grades. I had no choice but to agree with the my addiction. I was doomed. Hopeless. Lost. Conquered. Of everything I lost, the most important thing drugs took from me was my hope.

VOONA

But here. How did you get here?

KEMA

Oh yeah. I knew they were preparing to take me to the center the next morning. My addiction told me that I shouldn't accept the help. So I took the advice of the addiction. During the middle of the night, I got up climbed out of my window, maneuvered my way down the streets managing to avoid the street lights, then ran as far and as fast as I could. I ran until I just couldn't run any more. I ran and ran. Trying to out run cocaine. Trying to leave marijuana. Trying to escape alcoholism. Trying to out sprint prostitution. I ran. And I ran. And I ran. And I ran. Until I ran into you guys. And then . . . for some strange reason I stopped running. And every since that day, you guys have been my strength and inspiration to stay clean. The rest is history. I've been here with you guys for two years now, and I've never even thought about going back to drugs even though I have had to accept the sad fact that I'm never going back home again.

VOONA

Why not? What did home ever do to you?

NANA

Nothing at all. It's what I allowed drugs to do to my wonderful parents and home through me. See, I can never forget the hurt and disappointment I saw in my parents' eyes and heard in their voices every time they looked at me or spoke to me. I remember the humility and embarrassment I caused them as they sat there in the court and embarrassment I caused them as they sat there in the courtroom and heard the judge sentence me to time for prostitution and street walking. So the night I jumped out of my window, I turned and took one final look at the house and my bedroom window because I knew I'd never see it again in my life. (Pause)

VOONA

Well! I guess now that everybody has confessed that leaves only me holding on to my little bag of secrets. Well you don't have to ask. I'm a big girl. I volunteer to take the stand. Hey, ain't somebody gonna swear me in?

NIKI

Hey, girl do you?

VOONA

You know I do.

NANA

Proceed with your confession please.

VOONA

Thus goes my confession. Pure and simple, I'm here because I have no place else to go.

KEMA

It ain't that pure.

NIKI

And it sho' ain't that simple. Come on, Lucy. You still got some more 'splaining to do. Come on now, 'fess up, 'fess up.

VOONA

Alright. I'm getting there. Give a sister a minute to breath now. I know I'm still on the stand, but y'all are right, this really ain't that easy. Never knew telling the truth could be so hard and intimidating. But here goes. OK. Here's my story. I played cool and quit school to "hangout" with the older girl. I thought that made me look real fly to be hanging and seen with the older girls. You know what I mean. I mean there I was in the seventh grade and I was hanging with the big dog high school chicks. Good for the image, man. Or so I thought. When I grew up and noticed that the older girls had all gone away, I found myself in a sad shape. I was too old to be one of the younger girls and too young to be old. Yet I hadn't accomplished anything with the time that had passed me by. I had no job, no money, no education, no experience, no skills. I mean what was I suppose to do? I had nothing. I didn't have one thing to show for all the years I had wasted.

KEMA

No matter how bad you were hitting it, you always had home, Voona.

VOONA

Home? I ran away from a state facility for girl orphans. I'm not like you and you and you. I NEVER had a home . . . a family . . . and all that other girly-girly stuff kids grow up fighting over today. This (pointing to the streets) ain't new to me. This is as good as anything else I've ever known or had before. The streets are and always have been my home. It's always been me against the whole world. Always! And for some reason . . . I never seem to win either. You know something. Just one time . . . ONE . . . I want to win just ONE TIME! Then maybe this whole fight will seem worthwhile.

KEMA

Parents?

VOONA

Never knew them.

NIKI

Family?

VOONA

One sister some place over in Hattisboro. She got lucky. Some family over there adopted her. Gave her a home. But I can't have no contact with her because I'm a runaway and they say I just might be a negative influence on her. So I can't talk to my only family I got.

NIKI

You hurt much?

VOONA

I don't know. Really don't. Can't even say that I know just what hurt feels like. If hurt makes you feel empty, and left out; and if it won't let you have hope and dares you to have memories then, yeah, yeah, I hurt. But the truth is I been feeling like this so long that I don't know when I'm feeling normal and when I'm hurting. That's scary ain't it? That a 17 year old child has hurt so much that she can't even identify pain no more. Life really ain't been no crystal stairs for me either Langston. I feel you on that one, brother. I know where you coming from. 'Cause it sho' ain't been that way for me either.

KEMA

You could go back to the home you know?

VOONA

Sure I could. Just like any the rest of y'all could get up and go back to where y'all came from too. It's the same thang with me. The only difference is I'm an orphan and y'all ain't.

NIKI

But, Voona, what about your future. Your dreams? Hopes? Desires?

VOONA

They're just like those pains I just told you about. I don't know what those are no more. I'm afraid to dream, cause dreaming is good, but you have to wake up in order to make it come true. And I'm afraid if I wake up, I just might see something I really can't handle. If I hope then I set myself up for disappointment. And if I desire, I set myself up ridicule. So I don't have any of those things in my life. I can't afford them. They cost me too much. And I ain't willing to pay that particular piper.

NIKI

You said you wanted to win just one time, didn't you?

VOONA

Sure. Don't everybody?

NIKI

No. The only people who truly want to win, are those who participate in the race—NOT those who stand on the sideline and watch the race. And right now, Voona, you're only watching.

VOONA

Sure I'm watching. That's a fact. But you know why? Because watching is the only thing that I can do and not fail at. If I try to get back in the race, I'll probably only get knocked down. If I try to run it, I'll probably only trip over another obstacle. So what's so bad about watching other people run their race?

MEKA

Because other people run their races in order to win their prizes. Nobody can win your prize for you, Voona. Nobody can win back your peace and happiness except you. Nothing can make you forget a failure faster than a victory. And nothing can replace fear and hopeless, better than success and faith.

VOONA

Yeah! Yeah! Yeah! I know it all sounds good, but . . .

KEMA

But what? But you would rather go on hurting for the rest of your life? But you are too afraid that if you tried you might succeed, and that you don't know how to handle success? But you are more willing to accept sympathy, pity and sorrow than you are to accept friends and help? No, girl, it's not that it all sounds good, this time it all IS good. The question is what are you going to do with the good that's been brought to you.

NIKI

You ain't gonna answer her?

VOONA

I don't know how. I mean what am I suppose to say? Ain't nobody never said nothing like that to me in my whole life. You . . . you . . .

KEMA

It's called a friend baby. That's all. I'm just your friend, and I need you as much as you need me, but together we all can do this thing.

NIKI

Don't worry about your past girl. We all got one. But whatever the past is, let the past forever be the past. Tomorrow is where we are headed. And we are going to have a bright tomorrow . . . or somebody's gonna have to answer to all of us. And nobody in his right mind would want to have to answer to four ornery, angry females.

VOONA

God! Thank God! There's still hope for me!

NIKI

Much hope my sister. Much hope.

MEKA

Who-a-a! Check out the flames. The fire's getting low.

NANA

Yeah. And the old hawk's starting to kick up again too.

VOONA

Over there (pointing). I saw some wooden crates and old magazines when we came up. We can break them up and keep the fire roasting for a little while longer. Come on let's do it (the quartet retrieves the paper and wood and bring it back to the fire. They prepare it for burning. Place it on the fire and warm themselves as the flames roar once more.)

NANA

Getting late and cold. Think we'd better bed down and try to keep warm 'till morning.

NIKI

You know, I feel almost as if I just met y'all tonight for the very first time. Now I see why you wanted me to tell the truth, the whole truth, and nothing but the truth. It's like . . . I don't know. It's like I'm free.

VOONA

I know. I learned that a long time ago. Hiding lies only make you a better liar and more of a slave to the lies and deception you try to pawn off on others.

NIKI

Hey?

VOONA

Yeah?

NIKI

Sorry I hit you. Really I am.

VOONA

Don't you understand?

NIKI

Understand what?

VOONA

You weren't hitting me.

MEKA

Could have fooled me.

VOONA

(Sarcastically) Not that it hasn't been done before. (Meka smiles and waves her off. The girls all preparing their bedding for the night.) You weren't really hitting me, Niki. And I knew that. You were trying to hit all the people you are angry with. You tried to hit your mother because she abandoned you and your trust. You tried to hit your stepfather for what he'd done to you. You tried to hit everyone who refused to believe you. Don't worry about it. I understand. Oh yeah. I got something for you too.

NIKI

For me? What?

VOONA

(Goes into her bag and pulls out a stuffed bear. Goes over and hands it to Niki) I call him Bonkers because he's so comical. Anytime I fell like I need a friend, a smile, a hug, I go in my bag and pull out old Bonkers and he always know just what it is I need. He's great. You'll enjoy him. I'm sure of it.

NIKI

But he's your friend and companion.

VOONA

So are you. And over time he'll also become ONE OF your best friends too. But he really isn't my best friend any more. You guys are. That's what the truth, the whole truth and nothing but the truth does for you. It allows people to accept you for being just what you are and not what you seem to be.

NIKI

(Goes over and gives VOONA a big hug.) Thanks, Voona. Listen I hate to stay on this so long, but I'm feeling guilty about hitting you. Here, please hit me back. Please. (She closes her eyes and squints face in preparation for the lick. The others stop and watch. Voona draws back, starts to swing, then stops her open palm inches from Niki's face. Then she grabs her and pulls her over to her quickly and plants a big kiss on her cheek. The others burst into laughter. Niki opens her eyes and begins screaming . . .) He's an angel! He's an angel. I whispered in his ear that that was exactly what I wished you would do instead of punching my lights out and it happened. You did it. He's magic.

NANA

Okay girls! I do believe it's bedtime for Bonzo. Got some harsh weather rolling in tonight.

KEMA

How do you know? (The girls are tucking themselves in. The fire continues to burn. Lights are dimming.)

NANA

I don't. It just sounded like the adult thing to say at a time like this. Anyway night John Boy!

NIKI

Night Sue Ellen.

KEMA

Night Ma.

VOONA

Night, Grand Pa. (Winds can be heard howling. Paper blows across stage. Flames are disturbed.) Looks like you were right about the weather tonight, Nana.

NANA

Yep! And I'm right about one other thing too.

KEMA

What's that?

NANA

That we're all good kids. We just need the love of some good people. You know, some people who won't look at us or our pasts so hard and be so eager to judge us by our mistakes.

`KEMA

Yeah right. And when you find some of those people you be sure to let me know because I sure do want to meet just one of them. Alright?

NIKI

Well, I think she's right. OK. True, we did make some big mistakes in the past. I'll give you that one. But who hasn't?

NANA

Yeah. They look at our mistakes and try to crucify us all the days of our lives. But they look at Monica's and make her rich.

VOONA

Monica?

NANA

Lewenski.

KEMA

Oh yeah. You got a point there. I guess making a mistake out here ain't the same as making one in the white house with the President, huh?

VOONA

Obviously not. You see any rich white girls sleeping anywhere near you?

NIKI

On the real, though, I do think you're right about what you just said.

KEMA

What?

NIKI

About if people could just not judge us long enough to get to know us. Listen, there are millions of said stories just like ours and even worse walking around on America's streets everyday. Ours ain't the only ones. But every time we even walk close to some middle or upper class stay at home soccer mom, she clutches her purse, turns her head, shuts off her feelings, and tries so hard not to see us that she nearly goes blind trying to look the other way.

VOONA

Yeah, and the sad thing is that very same middle to upper class stay at home soccer mom may be going home to sleep with the same kind of abuse and deception that pushed us out here in the first place.

KEMA

That's real, man. Like they say, all that glitters ain't gold.

VOONA

You know what our problem is though?

NANA

Talk. We're listening.

VOONA

Outside of us, who else is even crazy enough to think about giving us the time of day let alone another shot at life? Who? Name me one person—if you can. (Silence) See? That's what I thought. Not one. See it's easy for people to SEE you out here on these streets. That don't cost them nothing. No time. No concern. No caring. Nothing. But for them to care about you enough to ask you what happened? Or is there something he or she can do to help get your life back on track. Now that costs them something.

NANA

Yeah. It costs them love and concern. It costs them humanity and unselfishness, not to mention caring.

VOONA

Right. And this is America baby. Ain't nobody got no time to care about you or nobody else as far as that goes. America—the land of the free and the home of the never ending mon-ey. It's the place where the golden rule is not do unto others as you would have them to do unto you, but he who has the gold rules.

NIKI

Hey, but check this out. We beat the odds, baby.

KEMA

How you mean?

NIKI

We took that chance, baby! We took it. We took that chance on one another. And I swear man—it was the best chance I ever took in my entire life.

VOONA

I'm feeling you girl! Ditto that my sister! Ditto!

NANA

Sho' you right, girl.

KEMA

All day long.

VOONA

And on that note, I think I can finally say good night.

NIKI

You ain't never lied, girl. I can feel that old hawk stirring up his nest again.

NANA

Yeah he'll come blowing through here like the west winds in a few.

VOONA

Hey, chill out before y'all talk him up.

KEMA

(Remove a small G.I. Joe-like figurine from her bag and carries him approximate 10' upstage. She holds him up to the heavens, kisses him, then carefully places him on the ground. The others notice her but say nothing as they are practically bedded down now. However, Voona cannot resist the temptation.) OK, Gabriel. This is your time baby. Go do you thing, man!

VOONA

I'm sorry. I'm sorry. But I just can't let this one slide. I gotta do it. I just gotta. Home girl, what you doing?

KEMA

Who me?

VOONA

Yes you!

KEMA

What does it look like? I'm posting Gabriel on guard duty.

NANA

Gay—who?

KEMA

Gabriel. He's like my guardian angel. Every night before I go to sleep I post him. He's my protection.

VOONA

Him? That little guy right there? He's your protection.

KEMA

Well don't go and insult him just because he's small.

VOONA

I'm done. This day is a wrap for me. I've seen it all now. Gabriel standing guard.

NIKI

Hey, look out now. Y'all know I use to be an angel myself back in the day.

VOONA

What-t-t?

NIKI

Yeah. I never told y'all about that?

VOONA

You tripping too hard for me, girl. The hawk must have moved in here, froze your brain, and moved back out before I ever felt him.

NIKI

Scouts' honor.

VOONA

Hey, don't go there on me.

KEMA

I'm with you on that. Let's just take this conversation to the breakfast table with us tomorrow.

NIKI

Agreed.

KEMA

It's done then. Breakfast it is.

NANA

Hey, hold it down. I'm already asleep.

NIKI

Just one person to believe in us just one more time.

KEMA

Yeah. Just one.

NIKI

Anyway, I just want to say thanks to y'all for taking a chance on me.

KEMA

Hey, if you don't stop so much yapping we just might take our chance back . . .

VOONA

Yeah, and give it to Monica or some other deserving intern.

KEMA

Hang in there, Gabriel. Don't let the hawk get to you.

NIKI

Yeah. Night Gabe.

KEMA

Night ladies.

KEMA

Night my sisters.

VOONA

Night all.

(LIGHTS DIM THEN DIMINISH. SPOTLIGHT FALLS ON GABRIEL STANDING GUARD. HE WINKS. LIGHTS. WINDS CAN BE HEARD HOWLING.)

CURTAINS

WHO DID WE KILL THIS TIME?

Cast of Characters

KEMP—A tough street kid of about 17 years of age. The unofficial leader of the group.

DANTAE—Another tough street kid of about 16 or maybe 17. He is also a member of the gang.

COLDBLOODED (CB)—Insensitive and ruthless 18 year old high school dropout and gang member.

KENDRA—A tough and street-hardened 17 year old girl who still has a hidden core of humanity, pure love, and concern for others.

BABY MAE—An innocent and mentally challenged 16 year old girl whose link to reality comes and goes. However, her insight into situations is often far more penetrating and revealing than the insight of any of her other so-called normal friends.

RALPH—An innocent 15 year old black youth who happens to be caught in the wrong place at the wrong time.

COP 1—City policeman.

COP 2—City policeman.

SETTING

LOCATION: A city park.

TIME: The present.

(Stage is set to depict an outdoor park setting. Everything is simple, quiet, and normal in appearance. Enters Ralph, a black youth of about 15 years of age. He is dressed neatly and is wearing expensive sneakers and a new stylish athletic style jacket. He crosses, and finds a bench for himself and his hand-carried radio. Ralph is in a jovial mood and is obviously enjoying listening to his music. He sits, head bobbing and body musically engrossed, and begins to eat his burger and fries. Four youths enter and take notice of Ralph and his attire. Their gestures indicate they like and want what he is wearing. One of the four youths leaves the group and signals that he will circle around behind Ralph and perform a holdup once the others have successfully distracted him. The trio approaches then harmlessly crosses stage. The holdup goes off as planned.

KEMP

(Holding one hand over Ralph's mouth and a knife in the small of his back with the other one.) Shut up! Shut up! Don't open your mouth or it'll be the last thing you'll ever say! You got me? Say? (Ralph shakes his head yes. Kemp nods to his gang to come over and hold Ralph's arms securely.) Kendra (looking around for the police) get his coat. Dantae, you take off his shoes.

DANTE

Yo, dog! Lighten up on the name calling, bro. Sherlock Holmes here gonna know everybody in the family by the time you get through making all these personal introductions and all.

KEMP

Alright! Alright! I hear you, dog! Just ain't got no time for no lecture while I'm talking care of business though. Don't worry about nothing though. I'll be sure to make it all right before we leave here. Not to worry. By the time we get through with him, homie here ain't gonna know nobody in this family, his family or any other family. See what I'm saying? Baby Mae!! (Baby Mae is a young innocent, nervous acting youth who seems to have been drawn into the scene more by peer pressure than by her own reasoning and decision making.)

BABY MAE

What? What? What? Huh? What?

DANTAE

Chill out, Baby Mae!!! Chill out. Calm down. Give the man a chance to tell you what he wants. Stop being so nervous. You making us waste valuable time.

BABY MAE

T-t-t-time? W-w-who? Me? Naw I ain't neither. I ain't made you waste no time. Uhn-Uhn. Uhn-Uhn. (Rocking back and forth as she talks. Her head and eyes constantly move as if she's actively searching for someone or something.) Show ain't. Not me. Uhn-uhn.

COLDBLOODED

Shut up, Baby Mae! You getting on my nerves with all that stuttering and rocking back and forth. Just shut up! Gone, Kemp, dog, tell Baby Mae what you want with her.

BABY MAE

(Suddenly stops rocking and looks at Coldblooded) How-how-how come you talk to me dattar way? A-a-a-ain't done done nothing to cause you (starts back rocking) to talk to me like you doing.

KENDRA

Baby Maw. Listen. In case you didn't notice—me, and you and our friends here—well, we kindda pulling off a robbery right at the moment—and we really ain't got time for all this other stuff right now. OK, Baby Mae? You see what I'm saying?

BABY MAE

(Still talking to Coldblooded as if she never heard Kendra addressing her.) CB, you know you-you-you don't got to yell at me like that. I know y'all say I-I-I-I be—I be slow and . . .

COLDBLOODED

(Interrupting rudely) Naw, Baby Mae, you ain't *even* much slow, girl; you just a plain out *retard*!

BABY MAE

S-s-s-see there! Se-se-see there! You-you-you be talking about me bad some mo' (Pointing to Coldblooded.)

KENDRA

Aw, dog. Come on, man. Why you got to go there? You know how sensitive Baby May is man.

BABY MAE

A-a-a-and I ain't sen-si-less neither (Pouting immaturely as she's angry.)

KENDRA

Naw, Baby Mae. I ain't said nothing about you being *senseless*, Sugar. I said you are *sensitive*.

BABY MAE

(Eagerly yet innocently) What d-d-dat mean?

KENDRA

It means that thing hurt your feelings real easy. Know what I mean? It mean . . .

KEMP

Aye, cut all the crap out man! What y'all think this is? A group therapy session at Children' Hospital or something.

KENDRA

Well, you know what they say . . . if you can't get help at home, please get help somewhere.

BABY MAE

A-a-an-and this *is* somewhere ain't it? He-he-he-he! (Baby Mae laughs very hard at her own joke. She is obviously easily impress by her own sense of humor.)

RALPH

Hey, man, look. Y'all got my shoes and y'all got my jacket. I ain't got nothing else man. I swear it man. I ain't got nothing else. And I sure don't know y'all. Bsides that, if y'all ust take the stuff, I ain't gonna report it no way. Wouldn't do no good. Police would just say it's another mugging, killing in the hood anyhow. C'mon, man, y'all know that's the truth.

COLDBLOODED

What you trying to say, brother?

RALPH

Aye, man. I'm trying to say please, please don't hurt me. Take whatever I got that you want . . . but don't hurt me. It ain't worth it, man. Ain't noting I got worth my life, brother!

KEMP

Dog, man! I just hate to hear a brother beg. Don't y'all?

COLDBLOODED

Shoot yeah. Make him sound like some kind of a wuss or wimp or something along those lines. (Punching Ralph's shoulder as he speaks.) Can you catch what I'm saying, brother?

BABY MAE

H-h-h-hey, hey, w-w-when you . . . h-h-hey wh-wh-when you . . . wh-when you—when you called me . . .

KEMP

SPIT IT OUT, BABY MAE!!! I'm tired of all that confounded stuttering!! Now if you can't talk then you just need to just shut up 'till you can!! Now what do you want? Spit it out!!

BABY MAE

I-I-I-I ((Kemps rolls his eyes in Baby Mae's direction as if warning her again about the stuttering.) I w-w-was g-g-gonna ask you, K-K-Kemp. I-I was gonna a-a-ask you, what you had w-w-wanted with me wh-wh-when you ca-ccalled me a min-min-minute ago. Yeah. Yeah. T-T-That's it. A-a-a minute ago.

KEMP

(Thinks about her question. Then answers.) Oh! Oh yeah! I was gonna tell you to grab his music box. We can take it back with us too.

BABY MAE

O-o-oh the mu-mu-mu . . .

KEMP

Just grab the darn music box and shut up will you?

BABY MAE

O-o-o-okay, Ke-ke-e-mp! I-I-I'll go g-get the bo-bo-boom, boom—the music box, a-a-and take it b-back w-with us. O-o-okay.

COLDBLOODED

Yeah. Get the music box and shut up why don't you? (Whispering to the others after she passes him to get the box.) Dummy! Why is it I always get stuck with the doggone dummies in my group?

KENDRA

Lighten up, CB. Must be your adrenalin, man.

COLDBLOODED

What you talking about?

DANTAE

You're being a little hard on Baby Mae, don't you think?

COLDBLOODED

Hey, it ain't my fault if old girl is one French fry short of a happy meal, is it?

KEMP

Hey, dog, listen man. We ain't got no time to be out ere on this scene yapping about no happy meals and old girl's (nodding in Baby Mae's direction) missing fries—if you get my meaning. (Nodding in Ralph's direction.) Know what I'm saying? We still got some unfinished business here we need to bring to a quick close. Everybody tracking with me? Can I getta amen up in the church house today y'all?

ALL

AMEN!!

COLDBLOODED

Hallelujah!

KENDRA

Glory!!

BABY MAE

(Pointing to and laughing at Kendra.) G-g-glory! He-he-he. G-g-glory!

KEMP

Alright! Alright! Check this. We gotta go on and handle this little situation we got here real quick y'all 'cause I'm pretty sure it probably ain't long fo' them boys in blue come trekking through here on their nightly rounds heading to a dough nut shop or something. Follow me? So let's take care of what we got to take care of people so we can roll on up out of here. (Looking around nervously and anxiously as he talks.)

RALPH

Hey, man (obviously frightened). I-i-if y'all think the cops gonna be coming through here soon, y'all better go ahead and take off, dude. I mean, like I said, brothers—and sisters—y'all ain't got to worry about me saying nothing to the police. I'm just glad y'all decided to let me go and to get out of all of this with my life.

KEMP

(Going over to Ralph who is still being held by the gang members.) Oh yeah, wise guy? Says who?

RALPH

Says who? Com on now, man! Y'all got all my stuff. Here, look in my pockets and you'll see I ain't got nothing but a little bit of change left. Spent all my money on this big mac and them fries, dog. Think I got around 39 cents left to my name. I swear man!

COLDBLOODED

You begging again, brother?

RALPH

Doggone right I'm begging, man. Shoot! You crazy or something? (Notices the menacing look CB shoots his way.) I didn't mean it like that, brother.

COLDBLOODED

(Pulling out a knife and approaching closely) Oh no? Then just how did you mean it?

RALPH

What I mean is I'm an A student, and I have made the honor roll every six weeks I've been in school for the last four years. That's how I got those shoes and that jacket. My parents (the group reacts to the word "parents" and repeats it quietly but mockingly to each other as Ralph continues to explain) bought those things for me—well the shoes for my birthday—yesterday—I-I-I turned fifteen—and the jacket was for my grades—when report cards came out last week. I'm just trying to be somebody, man, and I don' want my efforts to end up like this. Not over a pair of cheap sneakers and a starter jacket. I mean . . . my life is worth more than that man. T-t-that's all I meant by that question.

COLDBLOODED

All that yapping and you ain't said nothing yet as far as I'm concerned. Tell me something, nerddie boy, was that the point you was—oops!! Why just listen to my terrible grammar, won't you?—you were—trying to make just now?

RALPH

Yeah. My point is I plan to go on to college and to do great things for my people in the future. But I'll never get to do any of those things if you kill me over some silly shoes and a jacket. Right? I give you my word, man, not a word to the cops if you just let me live. I promise. What y'all say, man? Huh?

KEMP

You know what I say? Do you? (Approaching Ralph and flashing his long blade as he approaches. Ralph's eyes widen with fearful anticipation.)

RALPH

Hey, man. What you gonna do with that? You gonna let me live, right? Right? Right?

KEMP

Wrong! (Drives the knife into Ralph's stomach then quickly snatches it out. Ralph is still being held up by gang members, but is visibly and slowly collapsing.) Like you said earlier, everybody'll just say it's just another killing in the hood. Ain't no biggie. Just a nobody killing a nobody. That's the way it's gonna read in tomorrow's paper. That's the way it always reads when we kill one another.

RALPH

(Struggling to speak as he looks up from his knees) Brothers . . . sisters . . . ME . . . my life . . . my future . . . for that (pointing to his jacket and sneakers.) For that? (Struggling. Breath fading.) ME . . . for that? (Dies. Gang members congratulate one another and begin rummaging through Ralph's shirt and pants pockets. Kendra picks up one of the sneakers and begins to examine it.)

COLDBLOODED

What size them boats any, Kendra?

KENDRA

Aw-w man!! We can't use these thangs, man! Shoot! This boy got some serious dogs! (Holding up one of the shoe for the others to take closer notice of.) Man, these thangs like big enough to be one of the life boats on the titanic, dog!

BABY MAE

Y-y-you mean, y-y-y-you mean, y'all killed that boy for n-nothing then?

COLDBLOODED

Hey, Baby Mae, don't start your mouth again, okay? Just shut up! Just shut up!! Alright? Shut . . . up!

BABY MAE

I-I-I-I'll shut up i-i-if you want me to shut up, but y-y'all still killed t-t-that poor boy for nothing. We can't w-w-w-wear his coat c-c'cause it's the wrong colors, and the o-oother gangs'll j-j-jump on us for w-wearing their colors . . . and is s-shoes . . . his s-shoes, they too big. S-s-so I still s-say we killed this poor boy for nothing.

KEMP

Ain't nobody asked you nothing, Baby Mae! NOBODY!! So just shut your mouth like I told you!

BABY MAE

O-o-ok then, CB. O-o-ok then. I wo, I wo, I won't talk no mo' then. I-I-I'll just shut up then, a-and I-I won't talk no mo. (Pretends to lock lips and throw away the key.)

KEMP

Good! Now let me figure out what we gonna do with this boy. (Searching for a place about the stage to dump the body. Notices Baby Mae who has gone over to the body and is going through the boy's pockets.) What the heck is she doing now? Baby Mae! Baby Mae! What do you call yourself doing? Huh?

BABY MAE

(Calmly as he continues to search the body.) I-I-I loking for some identi, identi,—i.d.

COLDBLOODED

FOR WHAT???

BABY MAE

'Cause-cause I w-want to know w-who we just killed. T-t-that's why.

KEMP

Baby Mae, what difference does it make to you who he is? Who the heck even cares who he is? He's dead and gone now! And it's just that simple, Baby Mae!

We don't need to know his name and where he lived or anything else about his except where we need to go to dump his body!

BABY MAE

B-b-but, K-K-Kemp, for once d-d-don't we N-N-NEED to know who we just k-killed?

COLDBLOODED

You want to know who we just killed? Huh? Say? Is that what you want to know, you little crazy girl? You want to know who we just killed? Then sit down! I SAID SIT DOWN!! You want to know who we just killed. Okay, wisebutt, then I'll just search him over and over until I find some i.d., so I can personally introduce you to this DEAD guy and then the rest of us can go on and take care of our business! BEFORE we are joined by the boys in blue—BETTER KNOWN AS THE POLICE, MABY MAE!! THE PO-LICE!! AND THEY ARREST PEOPLE FOR DOING WHAT WE JUST DID TO THIS GUY!! Can you understand that, Baby Mae? Huh? Can you?

BABY MAE

Y-y-yeah, CB.

COLDBLOODED

Good! Now don't you move! (Goes over and begins frantically searching the body. Finds i.d. in the victim's pocket.) Here! Here we go. Some i.d. (Returns to Baby Mae.) Satisfied? Oh, of course not because you don't know who he is yet, do you? Well, Madam Baby Mae, I am pleased to present to you (Reading from the boy's i.d. card) Mister Ralph Gon-de (struggling to pronounce Ralph's middle name correctly), Gon-del, Gon . . . whatever! Just call him Ralph G. And the boy lives . . . oop, I need to be sure I'm politically correct here. The boy USE TO LIVE at 1496 Livingstone Parkway. Okay? Okay, Baby Mae? Now that you know who we killed this time, do you feel better about it now? Are you happier? Can you live with yourself better now that you know this . . . this . . . smart aleck's name? Hush?

BABY MAE

N-n-n-no, CB, I can't. I-I-I don't feel no better. I a-a-ain't no more pleased; and a-a-and I ain't n-n-no mo' satisfied neither! (Pouting again.)

COLDBLOODED

(Very angry now.) Well what do you want, Baby Mae? What do you want? A personal introduction and a date with the dead guy? What do you want?

BABY MAE

I just w-w-want t-t-to know w-who we killed this time. T-that's all. I-I mean if we gonna k-k-kill someboy, ain't it a s-s-smart thang to know w-who we killing?

KENDRA

Baby Mae, what up, girl? Where you at tonight? You act like you ain't never been with us when we did this befo'. What's up with you tonight? You nervous or something?

BABY MAE

N-n-naw I ain't nervous . . . or s-something. I j-just want to know w-w-who we k-killed this time. That, that, that's all.

COLDBLOODED

I just told you who this nerd was, Baby Mae!

BABY MAE

B-b-but t-t-that ain't what, t-that ain't w-what I mean though.

COLDBLOODED

Girl, we need to change your name from Baby Mae to Scarecrow 'cause you sho' ain't got no brains at all!

KENDRA

Baby Mae, (going over to sooth and calm her) I know living out here on these street gets hard at times and sometimes we try to make sure we remain human but . . .

BABY MAE

(Pushing her away and becoming adamant.) T-t-this ain't got nothing to do with living on no s-s-streets. Th-th-this ain't got nothing to do w-w-with no h-hard ti-time neither!

KEMP

Then what in the world do this have to do with, girl? Say? Tell me!! 'Cause I'm just about tired of trying to follow this trip you on right right now, Baby Mae!! Go ahead! Shoot straight! Talk to me! Talk to all of us! Tell us what your craziness tonight is all about. 'Cause I seriously ain't tracking you girl!

BABY MAE

O-o-o-okay! O-okay. I-I'll tell you . . . a-all y'all . . . I-I-I'll tell y'all right now. (Baby Mae's affects change as does her posture. Her face becomes strong and firm. She sits upright. She is no longer rocking and her eyes are piercing. She speaks directly into problem of the group—and this time without as much as a hint of a stutter.) You have called me crazy . . . and compared me to a scarecrow that has no brain. I accept that. You have referred to me as a retard. That I also accept. But just a few minutes ago we all participated in the killing of a young black youth whom we did not and to this very moment do not know. O h, we know his name . . . we know his street address . . . we know he claimed to have been an honor student at some local school. We know that the papers will not write much about him in the headlines tomorrow and the evening news will say even less. Nevertheless, we killed him . . . even though we still don't know who he is.

Was this 15 year old black boy the next Martin Luther King, Jr.? Was he the next dreamer of the black race? Or maybe he was destined to follow in the footsteps of Denzel Washington and set Hollywood ablaze for the next forty years? Maybe this dead boy was the next Malcolm X, Nelson Mandela, Tupoc, Michael Jordan, Tiger Woods, or Booker T. Washington. Who was he? Who was he? And better yet . . . who did we just kill?

Did we just kill the first black President of the United States of America? Did we just shoot down a black fighter pilot? Did we just murder the first black man who would have traveled to Mars and back? Did we just stab to death the cure to aid? Did we just destroy the brain of the world's best scientist? Who is that laying over there in a pool of blood paid for with a pair of dirty old sneakers and an over priced athletic jacket? Who did we kill this time?

Was that the first black man in this city who would have owned his own bank? Is he the politician who would have brought jobs in here and helped to get drugs and prostitution out? Who is he? Who did we kill this time? Langston Hughes? A modern day Harriet Tubman? W.E.B. Dubois? Booker T. Washington? George Washington Carver? Thurgood Marshall? Bill Cosby? Magic Johnson? Who did we kill this time?

A doctor? A writer? An architect? A clergy? An educator? An engineer? A musician? A community leader? A father and mentor who would have served as a role model to many black boys and girls who do not have good and responsible parents in their homes—such as ourselves? Who did we kill this time?

And for sneakers and a jacket. Sneakers that are manufactured in South Asia at a cost of less than $4 a pair, then brought into this country and sold for $120 a pair. For a jacket that will be out dated this time next year, and whose colors will only get us killed if we wore it anyway. For these useless and fleeing things, we took this innocent and promising life. But whose life was it? Who was he? Who did we just kill? Oh sure, we know who his i.d. says he is, but which one of us could look into our own little magical crystal ball and see what it is . . . a-a-ah! I must be politically correct!—and see what it WAS that this dead boy would have become in the future? Can you do that Kendra? What about your Coldblooded? Any of the rest of you? Huh? Anybody? All I'm asking you to do is to look over there then look back over here (pointing to her eyes signaling to say it to her eye to eye) and please, some . . . please . . . tell me who did we kill this time. (Returning to her original spot on the floor and return to her old self with each spoken word.) That's all I want to know. I-I j-j-just want to know, who-who did we k-k-k-kill this time. (Resumes rocking as in the opening scene. That's a-a-all I w-w-want to know. D-d-d-do you know, K-K-Kendra? (Pauses. Shakes her head no.) Y-y-you, Dante? (Glances downward. Nods no.) An-n-ny the rest of y'all know? A-a-any y'all really know who we killed this time? Me neither. Me n-n-neither. I just wish we w-w-ould have let him l-live so we could have been saying, l—look who we let live this time. Th-th-that's what I wish.

COP 1

(Rushing in with his partner. Guns drawn.) HOLD IT!! POLICE!!

COP 2

FREEZE!! DON'T MOVE!!

COP 1

DOWN! DOWN! ON THE GROUND I SAID. PUT YOUR HANDS SO WE CAN SEE THEM! (Kicking the gang member's feet apart.) Spread'em buddy!

COP 2

Pat'em down. I'll cover you.

COP 1

Roger. Assume the position. (Cop one is assisting CB to his feet and talking to him as he does so. He continues to assist each gang member up as he prepares to search and secure them.) You look like you should already know it.

COLDBLOODED

Yeah. Yeah. Whatever. (Removes the crime knife from Coldblooded's possession and tosses it at his partner's feet. Continues and pats down all members of the gang except Baby Mae. She has no moved from her original position.)

COP 2

Hey you. Hey!! (Yelling at Ralph's body.)

COP 1

What's up with him? Strung out?

COP 2

(Goes over and begins to inspect the body.) Hey. Hey. (Shakes him) Hey! (Notices the blood on his hand. To the other cop.) Sergeant, this guy is bleeding.

COP 1

He's what? (Notices that Ralph is not wearing any shoes.) This guy's also barefooted.

COP 2

What would you say the temperature is out here tonight, Sarg?

COP 1

Mid 60's. Upper 60's at the highest. Throw in the wind chill and you're back down to mid if not low 60's again.

COP 2

That's about what I figured too, Sarge. That's a little chilly to be outside strolling through the part without shores or a jacket, wouldn't you say?

COP 1

Sure would. (Goes over and make a more care examination of the body. Rolls him over and notices the stab wound. Leaves the body and return to the gang and his partner.) Murder. He's been killed. Stabbed in the stomach.

COP 2

Stabbed? With something like this? (Lightly kicking the knife taken off of Coldblooded.)

COP 1

I'll go one step further and say not with something *like* that, but with that *exact* knife.

COP 2

I can see a slight trace of blood still on it. That'll be all forensics will need to match up the blood on this knife with that of the body.

COP 1

Any you kids want to talk about this now, or would rather wait and so it down at the station? (No response.) His partner goes back over and quickly searches the body for I.D.) Who is he, Hawk?

COP 2

No luck. Can't tell without I.D. and the kid's got no I.D. on him.

BABY MAE

Y-y-y-you can't tell who he is just by looking at his I.D.

COP 2

What?

BABY MAE

Y-y-you can t-tell w-w-who he is j-just by l-looking at his I.D. A-a-all his I.D. t-tells you is h-his n-name and w-where he-he-he lives, t-t-that's a-all. But it c-can't t-tell you w-w-who he is. Ain't, ain't n-nothing b-but the g-g-good Lord c-c-can do that.

COP 2

Well, we'll ask the good Lord that question on the way downtown. Well for your sake you'd better hope the Good Lord says the right thing, because if He doesn't you're in for a long vacation away from these street.

COP 1

Who the devil is she?

COP 2

I don't know. Most likely one of them, but it ain't hard to see she ain't the shiniest marble in the bag.

BABY MAE

I w-w-wish I knew w-who he was though.

COP 2

Why? What difference would that make now?

BABY MAE

N-n-now? N-n-ow? W-w-well none n-now.

DANTAE

(Breaks in quickly out of fear Baby Mae may says something incriminating.) You got no right talking to her. She's retarded. She ain't got no idea what she's saying.

COP 1

Yeah? Well you do. So let's go, buddy. You and your partners got an appointment downtown.

COP 2

We may as well leave her. She ain't gonna be no good to us. A good judge won't even admit her statement as creditable, and a good attorney would make us look like fools for even taking an affidavit from a retard.

COP 1

Yeah. You're right. Watch'em while I go over here and call this in to the precinct.

COP 2

Roger, Sarge.

COP 1

(Moves DC. Communicates with precinct, then returns to the group.) Ambulance is on the way. I gave the location and told them we'd load these guys up and be ready to split this scene just as soon as they got here and took him away. I gave him a description of these two (pointing to CB and Kemp) and he assured me that they already had records and outstanding warrants as long as the Great Wall of China. Based on his memory and my description, Sgt. O'Malley said he was sure both of these bad boys were out on parole and that without worry it would be many moons before they would be out again.

COP 2

Repeaters, huh?

COP 1

Repeaters. (To Baby Mae) You still don't have any idea who he is, do you?

BABY MAE

N-n-naw. Y-you?

COP 1

Sure don't little girl. And that's the sad part. He died before we ever got a chance to see just who this young man really was. You know what I mean? Before he ever got a real chance to live and to show us just who and what he really was or could become in this life. Sad. But it happens all the time. All the time. (To his partner) Let's go. (They start off when Kendra suddenly remembers that the cops said they were not taking Baby Mae with them.

KENDRA

(To the cop.) You said you were leaving her here.

COP 1

Yeah. What about it?

KENDRA

I need a minute to talk to her. Just a minute, that's all. She's like my little sister or something, Officer. I already told you she's retarded. All I need is enough time with her to explain to her what's happening and how to get home. That's all. I just need to be sure she understands that we're alright even though we can't leave here with her. (Cops looks curious.) Hey, what am I going to do, Officer? Run away in cuffs? I'll be right over there for goodness sakes! I just need to tell her how to get home . . . that's all.

COP 2

Give her a minute, Sarge. What could it hurt? The wagon's here. I'll go load these up while you're waiting for her and the ambulance. (Jokingly) You can even start writing up the report on all this excitement up while she's giving the retard directions home then bring her out to the truck when she finishes.

COP 1

You got about two minutes on that bench over there to get everything in you need to tell her, even though I doubt that she'll understand or remember a word of it anyway. By that time the ambulance should be here. Go on over there and talk to your leader, but whatever you do don't make me have to chase after you. Two minutes. Wouldn't waste'em if I were you. (Cop 2 escorts the other gang members away.)

KENDRA

Yeah, yeah, yeah, Mr. Boss man. Whatever. (Officer beckons over to the bench. Baby Mae remains on the bench observing the dead body. Kendra approaches and sits next to her. Her back is to the cop.) Baby Mae, you don't know nothing now you hear? Nothing. You ain't seen nothing. You ain't heard nothing. You don't know nothing. You hear me? Nothing, Baby Mae. We're already in enough trouble . . . and no sense fooling ourselves . . . it's gonna be awhile before any of us is out again. (Pause) It's gonna be a long time before I see you again, Baby Mae. (She hugs Baby Mae. Baby Mae bends over at the waist to allow for the hug, but does not respond emotionally.)

BABY MAE

Well, what I s-s-suppose to do while I d-don't see you, K-Kendra? (Quickly and childishly before Kendra can respond.) You be back tomorrow, won't you?

KENDRA

No, Baby Mae.

BABY MAE

Wednesday?

KENDRA

No, Baby Mae.

BABY MAE

Next week?

KENDRA

No, Baby Mae. No. No. I won't . . . we won't be back for a long time. I think you might want to go back home and be with your mama and family again.

BABY MAE

Y-you g-g-gone call me tomorrow? (Quickly before Kendra can answer.) What's my phone number?

KENDRA

867-4382. Area code 590.

BABY MAE

Y-y-yeah! Yeah! T-f-that's it! Y-y-you g-g-gonna c-call me?

KENDRA

Sure. If I can . . . I will. I promise.

COP 1

Hey, don't get teary eyed now. Let's go.

KENDRA

I'm coming. I know my time's up—Bossman!! I'll see you (pause) sometime in the future, Baby Mae. I hope anyway.

BABY MAE

O-okay. I-I-I still got to f-f-find out w-w-who we just . . . (Two attendants enter. The police officer points to the body. They acknowledge, secure the body and take it away.)

KENDRA

(Quickly interrupting her) YEAH! YEAH! YEAH! I know. And when you find out . . . you let me now so that I never . . . ever . . . do this again.

BABY MAE

O-o-okay. I-I-I'll let you know, Kendra. I-I'll let you know.

KENDRA

(Gives Baby a big hug and kisses her on the cheek. Let's go of her hand very gently and slowly.) I love you, Baby Mae.

BABY MAE

(As if oblivious to Kendra's remark.) M-m-my, my, my m-mama, s-s-she'll be glad to s-see me come home. S-s-she'll be glad.

KENDRA

So will I. You never should have been out here anyway.

BABY MAE

You g-g-gonna call me t-tomorrow, right?

KENDRA

Just as soon as I can, Baby Mae, I will. I promise.

BABY MAE

You know my number? (Quickly) What it is?

KENDRA

867-4382. Area code 590.

BABY MAE

Yeah. Yeah. He! He! T-that's it. T-that's it.

KENDRA

I love you, Baby Mae.

BABY MAE

I love you too, Kendra. I-I l-l-love you too. (Very childishly as if she does not fully understand her words. Cop leads Kendra away.)

(To the audience as she sits on stage with only the dead body and resumes her rocking.) M-m-m-my, my f-friends . . . they all gone. Kendra s-she say for a l-long time. But K-Kendra s-sh-she gonna c-call me tomorrow—tomorrow. (Looks and sees the music box.) O-o-o-oh. The mu-mu-music box. They didn't t-t-take the mu-music box with them. (Looks over and see the jacket and shoes. Goes over and retrieves the items.) C-c-coat. S-s-shoes. Human l-life. A f-future. A past. A p-p-person. A t-thing. Our h-hope. Our pr-pr-problem. Our dreams. Our m-mistakes. I wonder . . . I wonder . . . Just who did we kill—this time. (Lights)

CURTAINS

WHEN MEN DON'T CRY

CAST

Johnny Johnson, Jr. (present)
Johnny Johnson, Jr. (Flashbacks 1, 2 and 3)
Chamber guard
Warden
Chaplain
Mr. Pinder
Johnny's daughter
Johnny's son (present)
Nadine (flashback)
Principal
School security guard
Hank
Student #1
Student #2
Bryce
Aisha
Physician
Angels
Attendant
Female student
Other students as needed

(This is a highly flexible cast which could be reduced by 50% when cast members
are allowed to play more than one role.)

SETTINGS

A prison execution chamber

The family kitchen

A school classroom

A private and cozy location

(Spotlight illuminates an empty gurney sitting center stage seemingly awaiting the start of yet another legal execution. Cast enters from alternating wings as each line is performed.)

CHARACTER 1

How many tears does a silent heart cry?

CHARACTER 2

How many dreams does it cause to die?

CHARACTER 3

What happens to a boy who at a young age bids his innocence good bye?

CHARACTER 4

What happens to a man who does not cry?

CHARACTER 5

What happens to pain that is treated as pride?

CHARACTER 6

What happens to the boy who is kicked and scorned just because he tried?

CHARACTER 7

What happens to the man who feels as if his whole life he's always been denied?

CHARACTER 8

What happens to a man who has never ever cried?

CHARACTER 1

What happens?

CHARACTER 2

What happens?

CHARACTER 3

What happens?

CHARACTER 4

What happens?

CHARACTER 5

What happens?

CHARACTER 6

What happens?

CHARACTER 7

What happens?

CHARACTER 8

What happens?

CHARACTER 9

What happens to the heart of a child who does not cry?

CHARACTER 10

What happens to the vulnerable mind of a boy who can't understand why?

CHARACTER 11

What happens to the un-winged world of a man who will never learn to fly?

CHARACTER 12

What happens to the boy who becomes the man who does not cry?

(Each character exits after asking . . .)

CHARACTER 1

What happens?

CHARACTER 2

What happens?

CHARACTER 3

What happens?

CHARACTER 4

What happens?

CHARACTER 5

What happens?

CHARACTER 6

What happens?

CHARACTER 7

What happens?

CHARACTER 8

What happens?

CHARACTER 9

What happens?

CHARACTER 10

What happens?

CHARACTER 11

What happens?

CHARACTER 12

What happens?

(Gurney remains illuminated briefly following speaker 12's exit.)

(Soft music is played as the prison guard enters to perform a final check of the execution chamber. He does so then returns to the chamber where he beckons to the prison warden who enters displaying a stern countenance. He re-inspects the chamber then nods to the security officer to lead in the other officials. The guard goes over and quietly leads in a youthful prisoner. He is clad in prison garb and is shackled and handcuffed. He offers no resistance as he is lead to the gurney and prepared for execution. Following the preparation, the warden double checks everything then nods to the guard signifying his authority to bring in the prison doctor and chaplain. The officials are ushered in and briefly inspect the execution setting then step into their obvious "official places" and nod to the warden. The warden again nods to the security guard who goes to the chamber door and escorts into the chamber the victim's and prisoner's family members who take their positions on the observation stand. There is a noticeable emotional reaction by members of the prisoner's family as they enter and see him strapped to the gurney prepared for execution. Once they all are in place, the guard returns to his position near the door. All is done in silence minus the appropriate setting music.)

WARDEN

Johnny Thompson, Jr., do you have any last remarks you'd like to make before being executed upon the recommendation of a court of this state based upon your proven guilt for death of 17-year-old Felicia Regina Evans?

JOHNNY THOMPSON, JR.

Yes sir, Warden. I do. (Swallows) Yes sir, I do. Er, Warden, how long do I have to make my last remarks?

WARDEN

Your life is the open book of what you were about, Johnny Jr. There is no need for you to try to get a religious conversion or a death bed forgiveness at this point. I know you have a lot to say, but it's too late now. This is neither the time or place for lengthy talks. At this, the final moments in your life, you've either done the right things in life or you're dying as a result of having made the wrong decisions during your life. Albeit, you've asked for time to make your final remarks, so go on now. Make your speech and hopefully your peace with these people as well because it's the last chance at it you'll ever have. I also hope that by now you have also already made peace with whatever supernatural source rules supreme in your life. Because as I said earlier, this will be the final time on this side you'll have this chance. OK, Thompson, the chambers yours. Makes your remarks then we will proceed with your execution.

JOHNNY THOMPSON, JR.

Execution. Huh! Execution. It sounds like such an unreal term for me to be dealing with at this point in my life. Execution. You know it's defined in the dictionary as putting to death of or carrying out of a legal order. And now here I lay waiting to be executed. And why? Because I'm a sick serial killer? Because I'm an incurable rapist? Because I'm a murder? Because I'm this great big nasty monster society fears? Because I'm something that no one or nothing could have helped . . . tamed . . . changed . . . influenced . . . SAVED? Why? Why, Warden? Why are you about to commence this execution on me? (To security officers) Officers . . . why did y'all have to handcuff me and shackle me and walk me down here to strap me to this gurney just to be killed? Doctor . . . shortly, you who will pronounce me a dead man, a societal problem dealt with and permanently fixed, a menaced finally removed from society. But why does my existence command your presence here tonight?

JOHNNY'S SON

Daddy! Oh, Daddy!!

JOHNNY THOMPSON, JR

Family members . . . both mine and the victim's . . . . why have I brought you all together under these hate-filled and heart wrenching circumstances?

JOHNNY'S DAUGHTER

Daddy!

JOHNNY'S SISTER

Baby, we still love you.

JOHNNY THOMPSON, JR.

And especially my own family—why have I done this to you? Why have I done those things necessary to bring us all together . . . under these horrifying and painful circumstances? Because there is no other way for me . . . or God . . . to let you know, that I am here because nobody saw the need to challenge what I *said* I was and to take me back from the streets and to give me life again. While you're all here to see me die, none of you came to my aid in order to help me live.

WARDEN

Your time is up, Thompson.

MR. PINDER

(Father of the victim. He has come to see this execution and harbors much pain which has been concealed over the years. Nonetheless, unexpectedly it is he who seems most interested in hearing the prisoner's last words) Hey! I mean . . . with all due respect, Mr. Warden, please, could you let him speak just a little longer please?

WARDEN

We operate on a very precise time schedule here, sir. The prisoners are given only a certain amount of time to say their final good byes—and the prisoner has been afforded that time already.

MR. PINDER

My point exactly, Warden. Not enough time to help a poor, crying, hurting kid to live . . . but more than enough time to watch him die.

WARDEN

I'm sorry, sir, but as I said earlier, he's done.

THOMPSON

Can you believe this? Even now, no one wants to hear what I have to say. Just kill me and send me away, but for God's sake, don't listen to what the prisoner has to say!

WARDEN

You've had your time, Thompson, so stop your complaining. We told you exactly what the rules were before we brought you out here.

THOMPSON

Right, Warden. You told me what your rules were but I didn't have anything to say about those either. Remember?

WARDEN

I don't argue with convicted killers, Thompson!

MR. PINDER

I want to hear what he has to say, Warden!! Now I'm a member of the victim's family. I've had to endure this pain I've been carrying around for many years. My family and I drove more than 400 miles to see justice served here tonight . . . but, if you don't mind, (softening), Warden, *please*, I believe there's something he has to say that will ease our pain a lot more than just standing here and seeing him put to death. Would you please . . . just this one time . . . would you please grant this prisoner just a little extra time . . . for the sake of my hurting and confused family.

JOHNNY THOMPSON'S DAUGHTER

Please, Mr. Warden. Please grant my daddy just a few more minutes to be with us. I want to hear his story too. He never told it to me either. Please, Mr.Warden.

CHAPLAIN

On behalf of the prisoner, I join the family in registering this very human request with you, Mr. Warden. Please. Let's hear the last words this young man has to share with the human race. Who knows what gem of wisdom we might take from his final utterances, Warden?

WARDEN

(Reluctantly) As requested, Chaplain. However, I must say this is highly unusual . . . no! Not highly unusual . . . This is TOTALLY different than anything we have ever done in the past . . . .

WARDEN

And out of gratitude, I'm sure I speak for everyone present, these events shall remain confined to this chamber and be remembered as an act of extreme compassion on your part. Thompson, you may continue with your last words now. Tell me, Thompson, tell all of us . . . what is it that you would like for us to know. What is it that you are trying to tell us with your last words. We need to know and only you can tell us. Your time has been extended but it is running out as we speak . . . so you don't have much clock to play with. Go ahead talk to us. Tell us what it is you wish for us to know as you prepare to leave us.

JOHNNY THOMPSON'S DAUGHTER

Tell us, Daddy. I want to know.

JOHNNY THOMPSON'S SON

So do I.

JOHNNY THOMPSON'S SISTER

Me too.

CHAPLAIN

Tell us, Thompson. We're waiting.

(Flashback scene is emerging into view slowly as Johnny begins his explanation.)

JOHNNY THOMPSON, JR.

I never intended to end up like this. Who does? I never wanted anything like this to happen to me. Who does? I always wanted the same things for me that you and every other man wanted to have or happen in his life. I wanted a future . . . a family . . . I wanted success . . . I wanted acceptance . . . but I didn't know how to get those things . . . so I went after the things that I did know how to get. I went after attention . . . . a reputation . . . . an image. It wasn't that that was what I wanted to do or be at that time, it's just that that was all I knew how to be. And so I started working on it early in life.

(FLASHBACK SCENE OPENS IN BLACK. GOSPEL MUSIC CAN BE HEARD COMING FORM THE SMALL RADIO IN THE KITCHEN. NADINE, THE WIFE, IS PREPARING DINNER AND PERFORMING OTHER DOMESTIC CHORES AS WELL. FINALLY SHE FINISHES THE FAMILY'S DINNER AND SITS READING HER NEWSPAPER WHEN HER HUSBAND ENTERS. SHE IS VISIBLY AFRAID OF HER HUSBAND. HE SAYS NOTHING. HE TOSSES HIS COAT ONTO THE KITCHEN TABLE, ROLLS HIS EYES AT NADINE, SLAMS THE RADIO TO OFF, AND GOES OVER TO INSPECT THE FAMILY'S MEAL. HE LIFTS A PIECE OF CHICKEN AND PREPARES TO BITE INTO IT WHEN HE NOTICES THAT THERE IS A SLIGHT BURN ON ONE SIDE OF THE KITCHEN. HE GLARES AT NADINE, FLINGS THE KITCHEN ONTO THE STOVE AND GOES OVER TO HIS JACKET AND REMOVES A SMALL CALIBER PISTOL FROM THE POCKET. HE THEN GOES OVER TO THE TABLE WHERE A TERRIFIED NADINE HAS ALREADY BEGUN TO ATTEMPT TO ESCAPE HIS WRATH. WITHOUT AS MUCH AS A WORD. HE GRABS HER BY THE HAIR AND TOSSES HER ACROSS THE ROOM. HE FOLLOWS HER TO THE OTHER SIDE OF THE KITCHEN, STRADDLES HER AND SLAPS HER HARD ON THE FACE THREE TIMES.)

NADINE

(Johnny's Wife): (Deep, nervous, and rapid breathing) Johnny please. Johnny. No Johnny! Please Johnny. Johnny please! No more, Johnny. Please. Please. Johnny I'm sorry. Johnny, I swear, Johnny! I won't do again. I . . . I . . . I . . . I promise, Johnny. I promise (cough, cough) Johnny. Baby, I'll never burn the chicken again. I promise. JOHNNY NO! JOHNNY! (HARD SLAP IS HEARD. SOUNDS INDICATE LADY WAS KNOCKED OVER FURNITURE.)

JOHNNY JOHNSON, SR

Shut up!! I said shut up, woman. Didn't you hear me?! Shut your mouth right now! Now you shut up or I'll stick the barrel of this gun in your mouth and open up the back of your head right now.

NADINE

Okay, Johnny. Okay, baby. I'm quiet now. Okay? See? I'm quiet, Johnny. See I'm not saying a word. See? Johnny I'm quiet now. You can put the gun away now, Johnny. See . . . See . . . See Johnny. See how quiet I am. See Johnny. I'm just as quiet as can be. (Deep and nervous breathing can be heard)

JOHNNY JOHNSON, SR

You just can't shut up can you? Can you? First you burn up the food and now here you are yapping like a hurt dog or something. (Pistol cocking can be heard.) You just don't believe I mean what I say do you? Huh? You take me for something to play with, don't you? (Yelling) I SAID DON'T YOU?

NADINE

W-W-W-hy no Johnny. No, you know I don't take you for nothing to play with. You know I know you much better than that. It's just that I don't want you to do nothing you'll regret in the future, that's all.

JOHNNY JOHNSON, SR

(SOFTLY AND INQUISITIVELY) What did you just say, woman? What did you just say? Did I hear you threaten me?

NADINE

Threaten you? No Johnny! Of course not!

JOHNNY JOHNSON, SR

Didn't I hear you say something 'bout "regret?" Ain't that what I heard you say? That you gonna make me regret something in the future.

NADINE

N-n-n-no, Johnny. No. What I meant was the children. Angelica and Johnny Jr. I mean, I know you could kill me just like that, (snapping her finger) Johnny. And I know it wouldn't even matter to you . . . . b-b-b-but just think about our children growing up without a mama.

JOHNNY JOHNSON, SR

Well, let me, just tell you this woman. Any woman who can't fry a skillet of chicken without burning a piece of it, ain't much of a mama no how and far as

I'm concerned, sho' ain't much fit to live. (Stands up and puts the gun to her head) Know what I mean?

NADINE

Johnny, come on, Baby. I know you ain't fixing to blow my brains out just 'cause I burned a couple of pieces of chicken. Are you, Johnny? Johnny . . . (begging for her life) . . . it's not like I do this every time I cook, baby. Johnny, please . . . d-d-don't do this to me. Please Johnny. I'm begging you baby. I-I-I'll tell you what. (Johnny Jr. enters and stands in the doorway observing what's going on. Slowly he approaches from behind his father.) You let me up a-a-and I'll go over to that stove and cook you the best c-chicken you ever tasted, Johnny. I promise you I will, Johnny. P-p-please.

JOHNNY JR

(Softly and confused) Daddy . . .

JOHNNY SR

Get out of here, Johnny Jr. Get now. You hear me?

JOHNNY JR

Daddy (goes over closer) . . . What are you doing, Daddy?

JOHNNY SR

I told you to get out of here Johnny Jr., and I don't plan on telling you twice either. Now GIT!!

JOHNNY JR

Or what, Daddy? (Daddy's eyes roll towards son. Gun is still at mother's temple.) Or what? Or you'll make me stand here and watch you savagely kill my mama? Or maybe you'll decided to make her watch you pistol whip me. Or maybe you'll kill me to get back at her from burning your favorite piece of chicken. Leave or what, Daddy? Leave or what? (Father suddenly jumps up and grabs Jr. in the collar and places the gun to his head.)

JOHNNY SR

Why you little punk! Didn't I tell you to leave! Didn't I? Didn't I try to save you from this? (Screaming in his son's face.) Didn't I?

JOHNNY JR

(Calmly and emotionless.) You never answered my question, Daddy. Leave . . . or . . . what?

JOHNNY JR

O-o-oh. So you suppose to be a man now, huh? HUH? (Slapping his face several times as he talks to his son) Mr. Big Stuff, huh? Ain't scared of me no more, huh?

NADINE

Johnny don't do him like that. Please! He's just a little boy. (Quickly and erratically points gun at her as she tries to approach. She immediately stops in her tracks and tries to explain.) No! No! No! Johnny. I was only trying to get to Jr. so that I could comfort him. I just want to comfort my baby, that's all.

JOHNNY SR

Sit down! Sit down right now or I'll kill you and this boy right now! SIT
DOWN!! NOW!! (Laughs. Then to his son.) You a sissy or something, boy?
Yo' mama say she just want to comfort you. You need comforting, Jr.: Huh?
Come on talk to me, son. You need comforting? (Mockingly) By yo' MAMA?
(Observing at his son's face and noticing a tear streaming from the corner of his
eye) What is that? What. is that on your face, boy? WHAT IS THAT I SEE ON
YOUR FACE JOHNNY JR?

NADINE

Baby please.

JOHNNY SR

SHUT YOUR MOUTH, WOMAN. NOW WHAT IN HECK IS THAT I
SEE RUNNING DOWN THE SIDE OF YOUR FACE, JOHNNY, JR???!!!
WHAT IS IT?

JOHNNY JR

Nothing, Daddy. Nothing.

JOHNNY SR

Man! Nothing? (Highly vexed)

NADINE

Johnny, please, don't do him like that. He's only a boy.

JOHNNY SR

(SCREAMING) I TOLD YOU TO SHUT YOUR FACE UP WOMAN. NOW YOU OPEN YOU R MOUTH AGAIN AND I JUST MIGHT TAKE IT OUT ON (pointing the gun threateningly toward junior) PRETTY BOY FLOYD OVER HERE. (To his son) That's a tear I see on your face, ain't it, boy? You're crying. Ain't you? You're crying real tears. Tears boy! My boy is crying real tears. Well haven't I told you a thousand times that real mean don't cry? Haven't I? (Growing angrier and louder as he talks) Haven't I told you that a thousand times that I don't cry . . . my daddy didn't cry . . . and his daddy didn't cry . . . . and his daddy didn't cry. We don't cry. Not the men in this house. WE DON'T CRY. (Shaking the boy violently) What kind of sissy are you anyway . . . to let the world see you cry? We hurt . . . but we don't cry. We get lonely . . . but we don't cry . . . we need help . . . . but we don't cry . . . . we get depressed but we don't cry . . . we have bad days and hard times but we don't cry! (He is so engrossed in his dialogue that he does not see his wife coming behind him with an object in hand) We are men! MEN! MEN! And like I've always told you, real men never let the world see them sweat. Real men never let the world know how they feel or what they need. They just keep right on going like there ain't a problem in the world they can't defeat all by themselves, but real men . . . and especially my son . . . REAL MEN . . . DON'T CRY! (His wife rushes over to his blindside and strikes him over his head with the object. He collapses to the floor. She collapses to her knees in tears. Jr. picks up the gun and hurries over to embrace his mother.)

JOHNNY JR

It's okay, Mama. It's okay.

NADINE

I know it is, baby. I know. And it's okay if you want to cry too.

JOHNNY JR

No, mama, I don't. I never want to cry again. I want to be a man. And my daddy says . . . real men don't cry. No, Mama . . . No . . . I don't want to cry. Real men don't cry. (Mama's sobs get louder. She and son remain embraced in the center of the floor. Dad is unconscious on the floor. Music comes up. Lights. Scene reverts back to the execution chamber.)

MR. PINDER

Johnny Thompson, are you telling us that you murdered my daughter because you saw your father beat up on your mother? Is that what you're trying to get up to believe with your last words?

JOHNNY JR

What I'm really trying to get you all to believe is that it's hard for a young man to model manhood if he has never had a model in his home to compare himself to. Boys are funny. They talk a good talk. But deep down inside they all know they walk a poor walk. And it's because we're trying to ask them to become something they have never seen . . . or experienced. We want luck . . . and time . . . and height and weight, and . . . heavy voices and mustaches to turn these susceptible, vulnerable, neglected and abused PITIFUL boys into nurturing, responsible, productive, motivated, fathers, husbands, citizens and leaders. But where are their models. (Pause) I exploded and committed a murder . . . because I never knew just how badly I needed help. I never knew just how badly I needed to cry. The man in my house told me that real men don't cry. And inspite of everything else he was . . . I believed him . . . and shaped my life and my behavior around his words. For some strange reason, I really believed that real men don't cry. And so here I am. Because I didn't know how to cry. Even when I was offered an invitation by other men to cry . . . I refused to . . . because my daddy said real men don't cry . . .

FLASHBACK #2: (Teacher enters a classroom that is in a state of total disruption.)

TEACHER

Students! Students! Boys and girls! Hey, son, sit down. Jonathan, Jr., take a seat!

BRYCE

I got your seat alright, you old hag! You better get up off me up in here. (Throws paper at teacher) Talking about sit down. Shhhhh. You know like I know, *you'll* sit down and right quick like too. (Pulls out a cigarette while eyeballing the teacher. Sticks it in his mouth and announces defiantly) The brother needs a light!

HANK

I got some fire, dog. (Lights the cigarette) You got another smoke, man? (Takes one.) Cool. Cool. (Approaches a female classmate) Dang girl! Mama you sho' nuff looking extra fly and sexy in dem low riding jeans you rocking today, girl. Man shoot! You like . . . WHAM! BAM . . . Can I *pleas-s-sse* do it *again* ma'am?

ASHIA

So was that a real question or was that like one of those rhetorical questions that don't require a response.

HANK

Smart too, huh? I like that. I do. I like that. I can deal with a smart lady as long as she ain't too smart. Too much. Feel me?

ASHIA

(flirting) No, but I get the idea that exactly what you want to do to me.

HANK

Hey, That's truth. For real. Ain't trying to act like that ain't real talk. I'm a guy. What you expect? So what's up with me and you hooking up after school today?

ASHIA

Whereever and whatever you want to be up, baby? (Takes the lighter out of his hand and lights his cigarette) So what you go in mind? What's its gonna be?

HANK

What's it gonna be? Me and you, girl, all evening long, Baby. You up with that?

AISHA

(Very flirtatiously) Don't trip boy. You ever known me not to be? You just make sure you don't let your mouth write a check (looks at his butt then slides lighter into his back pocket) other parts of your body can't cash.

HANK

See . . . (removing a wad of cash from his pocket and flaunting it.) That's why I always deal strictly *in* cash, baby and not checks and promissory notes. Anything I tell you, you can go to the bank on it, mama. I figured it's always better to deal strictly with weak, dead presidents than a strong, living promissory note. (Peels off a dollar bill and hands it to her. She takes it, smiles, examines it, hands it back to Hank who neatly folds it and stuffs it in her bra.) I'll be around the back of the building near the science lab right after the last bell. You know our spot. Hey! Don't be late.

AISHA

Not for all the tea in China, baby. You just make sure you're there—on time! (She kisses him on the lips and brushes her body up against him firmly as she passes to move about the classroom.)

TEACHER

Students will you all please return to order? Will you please sit down? Will you please stop acting like animals in here? This is absolutely pathetic! Students . . . .

STUDENTS

(Mockingly) Students . . . . students . . . . students . . . .

HANK

Hey, yo old woman, why don't you go sit yo' old ignorant behind down someplace? 'Cause today is one of them days when we don't want to hear nothing you got to say no how.

MALE STUDENT

(From across the room.): Talk to her, dog! Woof! Woof!

HANK

That's what I'm talking about (giving high five). Shoot! She MUST don't know who she talking to. Shoot! She'll mess around and I'll be done turned this out up in here. Shh-h-h! Old timer just don't know! I'm the HNIC up in here! I call the shots up in this house.

TEACHER

Students listen! This kind of behavior just cannot be tolerated in this classroom nor in any learning environment. I'm sorry but some of you will have to be written up and suspended for your behavior today.

MALE STUDENT

Word dog!! I believe that sister just spoke the word with the magic power. She said something 'bout *suspension* and you *know* my probation officer ain't even hearing that game. Guess that's myclue to sit down and chill out for a minute 'cause I'll tell you, I show ain't 'bout chilling in no detention center nowhere no more. (Closely admiring the figures of two passing coeds.) Especially when a brother can be up in here every day scoping out the fly honeys in their skin tight jeans.

JOHNNY JR

So? Don't nobody care nothing about no suspension! Suspend me! See if I care! Ain't no wimp. Go ahead. Suspend me. I need a vacation anyhow. Matter of fact . . . I think you do too, you old hag . . . . (Starts to throw items at teacher. Others join in.)

TEACHER

(Teacher is yelling to the top of his voice to regain control. No effect. Pandemonium. Wadded paper is flying. Students are yelling, dancing, jumping desks and are generally out of control. Teacher makes it to the PA system and calls for help.) Teacher needs immediate assistance in Room 158 . . . Code Blue . . . again, teacher requires *IMMEDIATE* assistance in room 158 . . . Code Blue. (Security officers and principal arrive almost instantly and enters the classroom.)

PRINCIPAL

Looks like you're having a bit of a discipline problem here, Ms. Clemons. (Kids are still disorderly. Paper is flying and kids are dancing and chair-hopping. Both security guard move around among the students and finally get them into their seats. They resist but eventually comply.)

TEACHER

Somewhat, sir. But they're not always like this you understand. Usually I maintain very good discipline in my class but today for some reason everything just got completely out of hand. I'm very sorry, Mr. Freeman, Sir.

PRINCIPAL

Hey!! Sit down, son.

STUDENT

Shoot man! Look at all the rest of these fools up in here. Why you got to come up here and front on me like I'm the long ranger up in here or something.

PRINCIPAL

(Goes over to student face to face) Listen, Tonto. 'Cause you sho' ain't no Lone Ranger. How would like it if I sent you home along with the rest of these Jerry Springer Show guests for a few days? Huh? (Pause) That's what I thought. Now sit your butt down and take out your book, some paper and a pencil and get to work. (Strikes desk with his stick and yells authoritatively) Do it NOW!! (Directing his attention to other students) Hey, you too! And the same thing goes for you too, son.

STUDENT

SON? (Belligerently)

PRINCIPAL

Did you have a sex change operation, Hudson?

STUDENT

Sex change? (Laughter) Naw I ain't went out like that now. Ain't had no sex change operation.

PRINCIPAL

Good! Then sit down (emphasize) SON! Now! (Everybody slowly fines a seat and sits except Johnny Jr. Principal goes over and confronts Johnny face to face. It is obvious this is not their first confrontation nor out of character behavior for Johnny.) Johnson, what is it with you, Son? You have a hearing problem? Or maybe you just don't understand English very well. Or better yet, maybe you just don't intend on doing what I tell you to.

JOHNNY JR

(Sarcastically) Yes sir, you right . . . yes sir you right . . . and yes sir you right! Now! Next question. Anyhow, what's it to you . . . (sarcastically) Mr. Principal. All you want to do is walk around here and carry a big stick and intimidate us into acting like your own little private tin soldiers. (IN A COMMAND VOICE) SOLDIERS!! ATTEN—TION!!! SI-I-I-T DOWN!! ST-A-A-N-D UP!! TU-R-R-N AROUND. CLOS-S-S-E YOUR MOUTH!! Ain't that it, Mr. Principal? Ain't that what you want? Your very own little corps of student marines? Huh? Well, guess what General Principal. Johnny Johnson, Jr. ain't now or ain't gonna ever be anybody's little private puppet. Yours or nobody's else. So you better wake up bright and early on this sunshiny day and smell the coffee, Sir . . . Johnny Johnson, Jr is a real man . . . and he ain't about to be punked out by you or nobody else. So just back off!

PRINCIPAL

Johnny what is it, son? What in the world is it that has you so mad with the world that you can't even see when people are bending over backward to help you? What is it? Why are you so anti-people? Anti-help? Anti everything that would and could help you if you would just let it. What's the problem, Son? (Emphatically) What's the problem?

JOHNNY JR

Ain't got no problem! And if I did have a problem, I sure wouldn't need your help to solve. I'm a man, Principal Tarver. (Screaming) A MAN! And if I had a problem, I would solve it on my own. I wouldn't need any help. I wouldn't need any counseling. I wouldn't need anything from anybody except myself. 'Cause I'm a man, Mr. Freeman . . . and where I come from . . . men . . . REAL MEN . . . (softly and reflectively) . . . real men don't cry.

PRINCIPAL

Cry . . . cry . . . who mentioned crying, Johnson. Did I? Did Officer Smith? Or your teacher? Which one of your peers mentioned crying? Who? (Pause. Then sympathetically) Is that what you're doing right now, Johnson? In your own little way . . . unknown even to yourself . . . are you crying right now, Johnson?

JOHNNY JR

(Visibly upset) Man you crazy! You don't see nobody crying, do you? You see any tears running down my face? You see my nose running? You see me whipping my eyes? You hear me sniffing and carrying on? All-ite then!! You don't see nobody crying, so just get right straight on up off that trip and just gone right on up out of here. (Turning and walking cross stage. Mumbling as he moves away.) That's what I'm talking about!!

PRINCIPAL

You're only a child, son. No matter your hurt . . . your disappointment . . . your frustrations . . . your losses . . . your consequences . . . your failures . . . you're only a child. And crying is a natural part of being a child. (Pause) I tell you what. Officer Smith, bring him to my office. Ms. Clemems, you may continue with class. And Ms. Clemens?

TEACHER

Yes sir?

PRINCIPAL

Try to maintain better control of your students and classroom situations from now on or you'll be next one in conference with me in my office. Is that clear, Ms. Clemens?

TEACHER

Yes sir. I'm very sorry about this, sir.

PRINCIPAL

Carry on, Mr. Clemens. (Motions for the security officer to bring the student to his office and exits.

(Security guard motions to Johnson to follow him to the office. Johnson begins talking out aloud in he class as he gathers his belongings and slowly making his way across and off stage.)

JOHNSON

So what's up, dog? Know what I'm saying? Like why the general wants to see me in his "chambers"? (Laughingly) So he can talk to me and watch me cry? Oh boo-hoo-hoo, Gen—er—al All-ite. Satisfied? That's all you get man. 'Cause like I told you. Ain't no shame in my game. But there ain't no tears in my game either. My pops always told me crying was for sissies, wimps, and women. Real men—he told me—real men they don't ever cry. (Exit)

STUDENT 1

I wonder (under her breath to the student sitting next to her/him). If he really believes that, then why does he always have to go around saying it? Know what I mean?

STUDENT 2

'Cause he doesn't really believe it. He just uses it to cover up a lot of his hurt and anger. Someday though . . . just like everybody else . . . SOMEDAY . . . he'll cry— even if it has to kill him to do it . . . He . . . will . . . cry.

TEACHER

Sh-h-h-h!! (LIGHTS. Action reverts to execution chamber)

JOHNNY JOHNSON, JR

I guess I could blame everything on my father, my past, the fact that I grew up in the ghetto. Or maybe even the fact that I never finished high school or learned any good or marketable skills. But deep down inside I know . . . I know . . . I'm here right now because of something bigger and greater than that any of those excuses.

MR. PINDER

And why is that, Johnson? Why are you here tonight? Strapped to gurney with needles piercing your veins, family members looking on, media hawks waiting just outside the door, and tears in your family members hearts and eyes? Why are you here?

JOHNNY JOHNSON, JR

Anger made me believe the words my father had forced in my mind and beaten into my heart. I didn't really believe his words. It's just that I was so mad at him for being such a poor man that I didn't want to give him the pleasure of seeing me cry anyway. And so I hid my hurt. I hid my pain. I hid my emotions. I hid my shame. I hid me. Because my hurt . . . my pain . . . my emotions . . . my shame . . . ME . . . were all wrapped up in the tears I refused to cry. The tears I fought back. The tears I dared not let him see. The tears that I thought would make me a sissy to shed.

MR. PINDER

So how does that get you here, Johnson?

JOHNNY JOHNSON, JR

Because I focused on the circumstances and they consumed me. They ate me alive. Then finally, later on in life, I found myself needing to cry, wanting to cry, trying to cry . . . but unable to cry because I just didn't know how to cry. And so all of this anger, frustration, disappointment, hurt just stayed pinned up inside. Boiling like a pot of hot water on a red hot stove. It just kept boiling and boiling and boiling. Soon, I wasn't able to control it anymore.

MR. PINDER

And?

JOHNNY JOHNSON, JR

And that was the night I killed your daughter. (Pause) I never meant to. I never wanted to. I never intended to. I mean . . . really . . . . I didn't even . . . . well, I didn't even know what I was doing. One minute I was talking to the lady I love more than anybody else in the world (flashback. No sound. Male and female on stage acting the roles of Johnson's speech.) and then all of a sudden I was chocking her because she kidded me that she thought she had seen tears running down my face after we'd shared a private moment. I didn't mean to. I really didn't. I didn't mean to kill her. I loved her, but I just didn't want her to see me cry. I was just trying to be what my daddy said was a real man. At least . . . that's what my daddy had told me about being a man.

MR. PINDER

And then what, Johnson?

JOHNNY JOHNSON, JR

Sir, then . . . for the first time in a long time . . . . I cried. I cried. I just held her in my arms and cried . . . and cried. I couldn't help it. I couldn't stop. I cried . . . . I cried.

MR. PINDER

And then?

JOHNNY JOHNSON, JR

Then, Sir, for the first time in my natural life . . . I felt like a real man. (Quickly) Oh! Not because I had killed someone, and especially someone I loved so much, but because . . . because . . . because I had cried. And for the first time ever in my life, I knew that real men DO cry. I never meant to disrespect my teachers, Warden. I never meant to give the principal a hard time. I never wanted to drop out of school. I never meant to hurt ANYBODY, let alone kill the person I love most . . . and most surely, I never wanted to end up in jail, in court, on death row, and now on this gurney . . . . strapped down and punched in like a rabid dog waiting helplessly to be put of his miseries . . . but, where else and how else could I end up if I didn't learn to cry?

WARDEN

Johnson, we are very happy to know that you have learned so much during your time here on death row, but it all too late and for nothing. Just look at those people out there. Go ahead. Look at them. Look at the hurt in your son's eyes. Sense the pain your sister is feeling with every beat of her heart. Hear the disgust and disappointment in the voice of the victim's family. Just look at the collective pain that's standing over there waiting and watching you now.

JOHNNY JOHNSON, JR

I know, Warden. And if I could change this thing I would. But it's too late for me now. Too late. But it's not too late for all the other young boys out there.

WARDEN

What would you have us say to all those boys, Johnson? And why should they listen to us?

JOHNNY JOHNSON, JR

You should tell them that real men DO cry. Real men HAVE TO cry. Real men don't mind crying. And they'll listen. You won't have to justify why they should listen. They're out there just waiting for someone to tell them it's alright to cry.

MR. PINDER

Johnson, do you believe . . .

JOHNNY JOHNSON, JR

(Quickly interrupting Pinder's speech.) I know. I've been there. I know what I'm talking about. They're out there. Go save somebody's son.

MR. PINDER

How do we teach them to cry Johnson? Real tears?

JOHNNY JOHNSON, SR

No, sir. Teach them that they can cry by any means necessary.

MR. PINDER

By any means . . . . What the heck does that mean?

JOHNNY JOHNSON, JR

It means any thing they have to do to release their anger, to control their rage, to subdue their violent tendencies . . . . teach them to do it. If it's walking away from a fight . . . . if it's painting on a easel . . . if it dancing, singing or whatever . . . . just get the anger out. Vent it. Cry it out. But don't let it linger. It poisons the soul, corrupts the mind, and settles in the heart. And a man with a poisoned soul, a corrupt mind, and an impure heart is far more dangerous than a man who just doesn't cry. (Pause) Warden . . .

WARDEN

Yes, Johnson.

JOHNSON

I've made my peace with my Master, and now I've had my last words. (Pause) Let's do it. (The family reacts in silence to Johnson's request. Silence follows. The warden nods. The execution is begun silently. Johnny Johnson, Jr's breathing becomes labored. His eyes remain open as his head falls lifelessly to the side and his gaze is fixed upon his family. The sounds of his final breaths are heard via the microphone positioned directly above his head.)

JOHNSON'S SON

Daddy . . . Daddy (No answer).

(Silence and a pause. The physician approaches and examines him quickly and coldly announces)

PHYSICIAN

Time of death 12:24.

WARDEN

May God bless his soul.

MR. PINDER

(To Johnson's son) It's okay if you cry, son. He was your daddy no matter what crime he committed. And in my heart and soul, I truly believe he was a good man who simply made some bad choices.

JOHNSON'S SON

No sir. I ain't gonna cry. I'm gonna be strong. Just like my daddy was. I ain't gonna cry.

MR. PINDER

You can, you know. You'd feel a lot better if you just went on and got it all out of your system right here and now.

JOHNSON'S SON

(Becoming teary and emotional.) How you know how I'll feel? It's because of you and your family that my family was ever tried for this crime. If it hadn't been for y'all I would still have a daddy. I would still have a daddy. A daddy. (Breaks down in tears. The man holds him against his chest.)

MR. PINDER

No son, it's because of his daddy and his daddy's daddy that he's dead. Bringing a criminal to justice is not against the law. Killing people is.

JOHNSON'S SON

(Turns and looks at his daddy's body. Tearfully . . .) Mr. Warden.

WARDEN

Yes, son?

JOHNSON'S SON

Could you please wipe that tear (pointing to a tear on hs father's face) off my daddy's face? (Warden does so. To Mr. Pinder.) Thanks. I feel better.

MR. PINDER

So do I.

JOHNSON'S SON

You know, for the first time, I guess my dad was really wrong, huh?

MR. PINDER

Wrong about what, son?

JOHNSON'S SON

About real men.

MR. PINDER

Real men?

JOHNSON'S SON

Yes sir, I see now that real mean DO cry. It's just so sad he never learned to cry before now. (PAUSE) But you know what?

MR. PINDER

What son?

JOHNSON'S SON

In a strange kind of way, I feel good for him though.

MR. PINDER

I know. (Wiping his eyes) In a strange kind of way I feel better now myself. (Wipe his eyes.) Come on, son, I'll walk back outside with you. I think in our own way, we've all cried enough for one day. Come on. Let's go. (They all leave. The boy and man get to the door stop and look back at the body and simultaneously wipe tears from their eyes. The man puts his arm around the boy's shoulder. All exit. The body remains center stage on the gurney. As in the opening scene the cast returns as each line is delivered.)

CHARACTER 1

How many tears does a silent heart cry?

CHARACTER 2

How many dreams does it cause to die?

CHARACTER 3

What happens to a boy who at a young age bids his innocence good bye?

CHARACTER 4

What happens to a man who does not cry?

CHARACTER 5

What happens to pain that is treated as pride?

CHARACTER 6

What happens to the boy who is kicked and scorned just because he tried?

CHARACTER 7

What happens to the man who feels as if his whole life he's always been denied?

CHARACTER 8

What happens to a man who has never ever cried?

CHARACTER 1

What happens?

CHARACTER 2

What happens?

CHARACTER 3

What happens?

CHARACTER 4

What happens?

CHARACTER 5

What happens?

CHARACTER 6

What happens?

CHARACTER 7

What happens?

CHARACTER 8

What happens?

CHARACTER 9

What happens to the heart of a child who does not cry?

CHARACTER 10

What happens to the vulnerable mind of a boy who can't understand why?

CHARACTER 11

What happens to the un-winged world of a man who will never learn to fly?

CHARACTER 12

What happens to the boy who becomes the man who does not cry?

ALL

(Pointing to Johnny's body.) This is what happens to the man who does not cry!

(Music comes up. All exit. Angels enter. Remove the gurney straps and escorts Johnny Johnson's spirit away. Attendant enters and begins pushing the gurney off stage. Stops. Removes a handkerchief from his pocket. Wipes tears from Johnny's eyes. Returns the handkerchief to his pocket, covers the body completely with a sheet and slowly pushes Johnny Johnson off stage. LIGHTS)

FINAL CURTAIN

MERRY CHRISTMAS WITH ALL MY HEART

ACT I

(Scene opens in the bedroom of Tabitha. Music is blaring and Tabitha and her friends are enjoying the moment. The bedroom is typical in style and fashion to the average teenager's bedroom. The music continues to blare as the girls, who are scanning articles and pictures of their favorite celebrities, screams can suddenly be heard above it when a popular Christmas musical hit can be heard coming over the radio. The girls race to each find themselves a mock microphone and begin to pantomime the words of the song.)

DJ1

And this is it ladies and gentlemen. Your number one request for station WQEY . . .

DJ2

The official station of all the George Washington Carver High School green and gold WILDCATS . . .

DJ1

Right you are, brother. Wildcatland WQEY is now coming at you loud and strong from its 70,000 watt station in beautiful and historic downtown Wadley,

Georgia with the soulful and sexy voice of none other than the queen Diva herself . . .

DJ2

Mariah Carey

DJ1

Singing her timeless Christmas hit . . .

DJ2

All I Want For Christmas

DJ1 AND DJ2

IS YOU.

VANNA

(After the song has ended.) Whee-e-e. Man! That was like the most fun I've had in a month!

TABITHA

For real! I *love* that song, man! I love it! I love it! I love it!! Guess I'm just a Mariah fan period. I like everything she sings. She's like my own personal Diva, you know. (Starts to sing Mariah Carey's rendition and is BADLY off beat, out of tune, and has no dancing rhythm.)

RITA

Uh-uh-uh-uh-uh. Wh-o-o-a-a-a! Hold up, girl! Hold up! TIME OUT!!

TABITHA

(Innocently) Is there a problem?

RITA

Problem? Yes! For sure! You . . . and your singing. No-o-o, sister. Listening to Mariah is alright for you. But trying to sing like Mariah. Well in my humble opinion, that's *not* ok for you. You just ease up on the singing and we'll tolerate the rest. Come on now. E-e-e-ease up. Easy. Easy. (Trying to pry the make believe mic out of her friend's hand.) Tabitha. Let go of the mic. Put the mic down on the bed and slowly step away from it Tabitha. Put the mic down. It is what's best for all living things, Tabitha. You have to do it for all humanity, Tab. Put the mic down. Now. You will only be arrested if you *don't* put it down.

TABITHA

You can clown around about my singing if you want to, Rita, but girl you know that song is the bomb at Christmas time. And Mariah Carey? Child please. Now you know that sister can blow like no other.

VANNA

Yeah . . . that's right. And nobody in this room's arguing about whether or not *Mariah Carey* can chirp like a bird. Baby, it's *your* chirping that's causing all this concern . . . if you know where I'm coming from.

TABITHA

No you didn't. I know you didn't just go there on me.

RITA

Child please. Don't be fronting like you all that surprised and stuff 'cause with those notes you were just hitting . . . er . . . missing, somebody had to go there on you.

VANNA

Yeah and in a hurry too, girl, 'cause you wouldda outright destroyed that poor woman's song if somebody hadn't stopped you.

TABITHA

(Returning to her magazine and appearing indifferent toward the remarks.) Well I don't care what y'all say. One thing I know for sure is this is one sister who can san-n-ng . . . and I hope y'all took notice that I didn't say sing either. I said I'm one sister who knows she can sa-a-ang . . . and I know that too, so it won't be necessary for any of y'all to comment on that little piece of truth I just shared with y'all. Shoot I know I can sa-ang . . . I've been sanging every since I was two years old . . . matter of fact, I think my mama said, I started sanging before that. Now here y'all come up here fronting on me talking 'bout some "'cause you wouldda straight missed up that poor woman's song if somebody hadn't stopped you." Girl shoot, y'all must be crazy. (Starts humming/singing again.)

RITA

(Prayfully) Father, grant me this ONE prayer for Christmas and that would be that You please send this child a SINGING VOICE this year . . . because the one she's got now . . . well you hear it, Lord And because You do, I don't think I have to say *any* more.

TABITHA

(Bouncing up and down on her bed as if she hasn't a care in the world.) Alright! Alright! So much for the voice. What I really want to know is are you just going to keep us in the dark forever, Vanna? (Stops bouncing long enough to cast a serious glance in Vanna's direction.) Or are you going to come clean with us about you and Mr. Wonderful?

VANNA

AAAWWW!! I don't believe you, Tab!! What's up with that? I already told you. There is nothing going on between Rayburn and me. Okay? Okay? Okay?

RITA

(Reclining lazily across a chair) Okay. (Pauses and clears her throat.) I hear you girlfriend. It's just that that ain't the word that's been buzzing the halls at good old GWCHS lately.

TABITHA

Well, Rita, you know those halls now. Everything's buzzing around in them . . . including walked two legged buzzards—with backpacks and Air Jordans on.

VANNA

Oh-oh-oh. Child, speaking of buzzards y'all, guess who called himself interested in me?

TABITHA

Ou-ou-ou. Sounds like some more good gossip 'bout to be birthed in here to me. That's what we're here for sisters. Good old fashioned juicy gossip. Go ahead now. Talk to us. Tell all, baby. Tell all!

RITA

I know that's right. You know good old fashioned quality gossip is getting so hard to come by now a day. It's as if young people today text and email so much they've forgotten the age old techniques to creating and spreading good quality and unfounded—and probably untrue—cynical gossip and rumors. Ladies, I declare, where has this skill gone? Was it taken out of our schools along with the right to prayer? Ridiculous! Anyway, you were saying. Go ahead. You know we're listening, girl. Speak now or forever . . .

TABITHA AND RITA

HOLD YOUR PEACE!!

TABITHA

No can do my sister. This gossip I'm about to let loose on y'all is too good—did you hear me? I said TOO GOOD for me to be holding on to. Y'all ready for this?

RITA

Give it to us even if we're not.

VANNA

Honey, the little buzzard who got his tail feathers in an uproar over yours truly is none other than that little short Fredderick Laneski!!

TABITHA AND RITA

O-o-o-o. My! My! Vanna!

VANNA

Don't Vanna me. Y'all said you were ready for it.

RITA

Yeah. But we were only ready for something *reasonable!* Frederick Laneski's not reasonable. At least not for you he's not!

TABITHA

Fredderick Laneski??

VANNA

Alright already! Y'all make it sound like he's some kind of disease or something.

TABITHA

That's exactly what that little nerdy boy is. I swear it. Frederick Laneski is either a disease or he a something. I don't know which one he is, but I do know that he's one or the other! Girl, come on! Get real! Who are y'all suppose to be? The odd couple? I thought you had some gossip. That's not gossip. That's a threat! Frederick? Vanna, the little geek is no more than three and half feet tall. And that's when he's wearing platform shoes! Girl, you need to forget about that one—and quick too!

RITA

Oh man! Speaking of forget! I totally forgot to do any of my Christmas shopping so far and Christmas is only one week away. I can't believe I still haven't bought anyone anything yet. Let alone bought anyone anything, I haven't even made out a list yet. Guess my memory is about as short as Vanna's crush, hush?

VANNA

Jokes, jokes, jokes. But I bet the joke won't be on me when you wake up Christmas morning and there are loads of gifts beneath your Christmas tree, but none of them from you to anyone—because you forget. So, short memory one, just when do you plan on making out your list, Rita, when Santa's on his way down the chimney . . . or up the walkway, or where ever he comes from these days?

RITA

I don't know. I don't know when I was going to make out a list this year. For some reason, it just hasn't hit me yet, you know?

VANNA

(Going over to her and looking confused) What hasn't hit you yet?

TABITHA

What is there to hit? It's Christmas, girl, and the only thing you need to worry about hitting is the mall.

VANNA

Girl don't even trip about it. This year is the same as every year. You know the routine; just go pick up some cologne for Dad, socks for brothers, makeup for Mama and a toy for Timmy and just call it a day. Don't complicate your life with the simple stuff girls, too much living left to do and too many more important things left to focus on. Take it from me, socks, makeup, cologne, toy and call it a day.

TABITHA

Well not quite a day. I mean after all the malls are just filled with all kinds of interesting sights at Christmas time girls. Some are them are tall . . . some are short . . . some look good . . . some smell good. You know, the best thing about Christmas shopping at the mall? It's the gifts you can find for yourself after you finish shopping for others.

VANNA

Now, honey, that's worth putting up the Christmas tree for.

RITA

No! No! Y'all are missing the whole idea. That's not it for me anymore. I mean I just . . . I just don't see Christmas that way anymore. I mean . . .

VANNA

Girl please, what do you mean?

RITA

See, it's . . . I don't know—just hard to explain I guess. I don't know.

VANNA

And it sure doesn't sound like you do either.

RITA

I guess I'm trying to say, just for once I want to be a part of something bigger than just decorating and gift buying at Christmas. I guess I'm getting bigger and older now and I would really like to know what Christmas is REALLY all about. Y'all know what I'm saying?

VANNA AND TABITA

HECK NO.

RITA

(Tries to speak but can't find any words. Takes a deep breath) Oh boy!! This is much harder to explain than I ever imagined. I don't know. I just get this feeling that something special will happen this year and before Christmas is over, maybe all of us will have a better understanding of what Christmas is really all about. (phone rings . . . she calls to her mother offstage.) I've got it, Mom. Excuse me, ladies.

TABITHA

Is it just me or is the sister tripping?

VANNA

Knowing you AND her, it's probably a little bit of both. But personally I think the poor child has gotten a little too closely associated with those vultures in the hall at school.

RITA

Vanna! Tabitha!! It's HOPE! (They race to the phone and take turns yelling at the receiver) Hey girl!!

VANNA

HOPE!! What's up?

TABITHA

We're just here chilling. What's up over your way?

VANNA

Heard any good gossip lately, girl?

TABITHA

If you haven't, don't worry about it. We got more than enough to share with you.

RITA

Now can I talk? Do y'all mind? Since this call was for *me* and all? May I have your permission to talk on *my own* phone now? Thank you very much. (Into the phone) So, what's the scoop girl?

HOPE

No real happenings. Just chilling. Thought I'd call and check y'all out for a minute.

RITA

What's up? Is everything good with you? You sound a little down in the dumps for some reason.

HOPE

Well, to be honest, I am a little down, but it's nothing big. Everything's cool.

RITA

Hey. My girl's down. Say no more. The posse's on its way over there to handle whatever the problem right now.

HOPE

Hey, y'all ain't got to do all of that.

RITA

That's where you're wrong once again, sister. You're one of the posse. Don't fret it one bit. It's all cool. We're on our way out the door and over to your house right now. Be there before you even know it. See you in a few.

HOPE

Rita, really, you don't have to . . . hello . . . hello . . . hello.

TABITHA

What's up.

RITA

Something's up with Hope. She sounds a little bit down and depressed. (Getting her coat and hat) I told her we were on our way over to her house right now to cheer her up. If we leave now, we should make it to the corner just in time to catch the next bus. Alright posse! Saddle up! Time to ride out!! (They get their hats/coats/gloves, put them on and exit.)

SCENE II

(Scene opens with youth of approximately 15-16 years of age on stage stage. She is somber in mood and appearance. Christmas music can be heard in the background. No motion on stage for approximately 30 seconds. Youth's head tilts slowly upward. Her eyes scan R-L. Dart back and forth then retraces scan. She is obviously abnormally attentive to something in her surroundings. Visible/audible sigh then returns to a mood of deep depression. Pipes, her younger brother by a few years, enters suddenly. He is an inconsequential kid with an air of irrepressible joviality about himself. Pipes moves about the stage looking for nothing in particular, then acknowledges HOPE's presence.)

PIPES

Hi Hope.

HOPE

(Hope is lethargic and slow to respond.) Morning.

PIPES

Hee-ey!! That sounds funny, doesn't it? Hi Hope. (Musically) Hi Hope. Hi Hope. How are you today? (Pretending to have a microphone and places his imagined microphone in front of Hope's face as he continues singing.) Hi

Hope. Hi Hope. And what did you just say? (Laughing at his own humor. Hope shows no response.) What's up, Hope? You don't look so good this morning. (Spots a deck of cards. Goes over and removes them.) Wanna play? Rummy . . . blackjack . . . . spades . . . . hearts . . . . (sarcastically) old maids.(Hope nods no) Why not? It's not like you're really doing anything right now. (Notices her depressed mood. More seriously.) Say? What's with you this morning, Hope? What's the matter? What's the problem, Hope? What's going on with you?

HOPE

(Raising her eyes and head as if she doesn't believe her ears.) What's the problem? What's the matter? What's going on with me? Hmmp!!! (Visibly upset) I really don't believe you, Pipes!!! I just can't bring myself to believe you just asked me such a stupid question!! What's the matter? What do you think is the matter, Pipes? Say? What do you think? What do you think could possibly be the matter with poor little hopeless Hope?

PIPES

Hope, I really didn't mean to . . .

HOPE

(Interrupting) Oh shut up, Pipes, will you? With a sibling like you who the heck would ever need a single enemy. (Pitifully) Just . . . go away . . . a-a-and leave me alone, will you? I just feel like I need to be by myself for a while. Okay?

PIPES

You sure, Hope?

HOPE

Yeah. Yeah. I'm sure. Just for a little while, Pipes. Okay?

PIPES

(Christmas music is playing softly as Pipes turns to walk away.) You know I'm here if you need to talk, Hope.

HOPE

(Snapping) NO!! (Calming) No. Pipes. I don't want to . . . well I don't need to . . . to talk.

PIPES

Sure Hope. Whatever you say. See ya' later. (Starts off again.)

HOPE

Pipes! You're the best little brother a girl could ever have. You're not just my little brother, you're also my very best friend too, Pipes. If it weren't for you, I don't know how I would have made it through this whole adoption ordeal. It amazes me at how you're able to do it so easily yourself. But you're doing a great job. I'm just glad you and I were fortunate enough to have been adopted into the same family. But right now, it's just that I need some time to myself. OK?

PIPES

I hear what you're saying, Hope. But you know what? Siblings and friends always talk about what's going on with them—even in adoption homes. It's part of being a family, Hope. (Pause)At least that's what I always thought family and best friends did. I'll give you your time and space, Hope, but if you need me, you know how to call me. Later. (Starts off.)

HOPE

PIPES!!! (He stops and turns to face her) Don't you dare leave this house without giving me a monster hug. (He does not move despite her opened-arms invitation.) Please Pipes. Please. I need it. I really do. More than you could ever know. Please. (Pipes crosses and hugs her. He loosens his embrace and strokes her hair gently.)

PIPES

Hope . . . you really okay?

HOPE

Not really.

PIPES

Then why don't you . . .

HOPE

(Placing her finger over Pipes' lips to stop his speech.) Don't worry about it. We'll talk later. I promise.

PIPES

Promise?

HOPE

Promise. (Pipes smiles at her and prepares to exit R. At the door, he stops, looks back, winks and gives Hope a thumbs up gesture. Hope returns the gesture with a labored smile. Pipes exits. Music starts. Hope slowly crosses DR then freely wanders about the stage then finally over to a chair where she flops down in disgust. Suddenly and without warning.) I hate you, CHRISTMAS!! I hate you!! I do! Do you have any idea what you do to poor little kids like me? Do you know what it's like to be poor, and the child of poor parents who work their butts off all year long just so we can eat and sleep and have SOME of the things that all of the others RICH children have?? Do you?? Do you? Do you know how much it hurts to have to go and walk around the mall—FLAT BUSTED—(turning her pants pockets inside out) . . . ten, nine, eight, seven, six, five, four, three, two and even one shopping day left 'till the sing biggest day of giving in whole world. (She does not see Pipes who has quietly re-entered the room. Pipes reminds quite and still near the door.) Do you know? Do you? Can you feel the hopelessness of a poor child who wants to give something very special to someone he or she loves dearly, but cannot afford it? Can you imagine the disappointment of a son who is unable to buy the simple neck tie he wants his father to have or the daughter who can't buy that simple bottle of perfume? Do you know what it's like to walk through a crowd with everyone singing beautiful Christmas carols and carrying TONS of department store bags that are literally bursting open with the special and expensive gifts they will present to their loved ones . . . and make them so happy on Christmas morning? (Sobering somewhat) Then, you must also know what it feels like not to be able to do or to give at Christmas, because you . . . you don't have anything to give. Yuletide? Season of joy? Hmmp!! You just don't know what you do to some of us, Christmas. (Wipes a tear from her eye.) You just don't know.

PIPES

(His voice shocks her) I don't know if Christmas is responsible for that or if you are responsible for all of that yourself, Hope.

HOPE

PIPES!! I thought you were gone. You said you were . . .

PIPES

I know. And I did leave, but it was freezing outside and so I thought I'd better come back and let you know that there's at least a full inch of ice on the walkway and front steps . . . just in case you were planning to go some place.

HOPE

Well . . . thanks, Pipes (moves away from him), but I wish you would have let me know that you were coming back. I mean, I did tell you I needed some time to myself, didn't I?

PIPES

But you don't, Hope. What you need is time with others who are so much less fortunate than yourself. Then you will be able to see just how little the fragrances, shirts and ties and other material things really matter.

HOPE

I don't get what you're saying, Pipes.

PIPES

Sure you do. Remember what you said about those parents who work themselves to the bone just so that kids . . . like you and me . . . can have what they never did?

HOPE

Yeah.

PIPES

How can you ever repay THAT, Hope? That's what's really important, Hope, and that's what Christmas is all about.

HOPE

Oh come on, Pipes. Lighten up, man. No child could EVER repay his parents for everything they have given and sacrificed into his or her life.

PIPES

Maybe you can . . . maybe you can't. But nothing ever comes as close as giving someone you love a special gift from your heart at Christmas time.

HOPE

Come again, my brother. You lost me at that last intersection you just crossed.

PIPES

Hope . . . ties, makeup, clothes and all of that stuff isn't what means the most to someone that you love with all your heart. It's not the material things that matter to them. It's the special things that no one else can give them . . . share with them . . . promise them . . . or reward them with . . . except their very own little unique and special . . . YOU. That's what means the most to parents and loved ones, Hope. And on this Christmas you can finally present such a gift to those whom you love too. I'm sure they would be the first to let you know that no one has ever or will ever present them a more lovable, meaningful or memorable gift.

HOPE

Pipes, you're completely confusing me.

PIPES

Where's my heavier jacket. I think I left it over here yesterday. (Sees it.) Oh, there it is. Think about it, Hope. I'm sure it'll all make sense by the time you sleep on it for a while. Love you, Hope. See you tomorrow. And be sure you tread on the those steps and that sidewalk with extra care, you hear? (Exits.)

SCENE III

HOPE

(Music plays as Hope walks about the stage conversing with herself.) It's not so much that I hate Christmas. It's just that I hate being poor *at* Christmas. I mean, just for once in my life I would love to just walk into any store in the mall and just say, "Wrap it up. I'll take it. Oh, don't worry about the price. Money is no object. And besides. I know it's just what she wants." Boy wouldn't that be a miracle at Christmas? To finally be able to give someone special just what it is they really want and need from me this Christmas. Boy! What an unbelievable and perfect Christmas gift that would be! But who knows? Maybe someday . . . *DEFINITELY* someday . . . I'll be able to do just that. I know I will. I know I will. I will . . . I will. (Hope sits on the couch and stares off into space) I will . . . I will. (The sound of the door bell ringing startles her.) OH!! The door!! The door!! Oh boy. I guess I must have been thinking a little too hard about this Christmas thing and all. The door. The door. (Enter the three girlfriends with whom she'd spoken earlier.)

VANNA

Honey fear not! For behold we come to take you to the mall and to shoppeth away all they frustration. Getteth thou coat so we can goeth.

HOPE

Hey, girl.

VANNA

Watcheth thy tongue you heathen! We knoweth no one who is called girl! We are royal and are called wise women from . . .

HOPE

I now. I know. Let me guess. From the east.

RITA

Dead on time, sister. The east side of 4th Street, but that's close enough for us, Honey. After all, we never did say how far east anyway did we? (Laughter)

TABITHA

(Taking Hope's hat and coat and quickly draping them on her.) Come on, girl!! Move it!! Move it!! Come on will you? You move slower than my grandma.

HOPE

What's with the big rush and all? Where are we going, to a fire or somewhere?

VANNA

Not exactly. But we are going to the next hottest spot in town. You know, where all the in guys . . . and chicks . . . are. We're going to the mall for about three or four hours.

RITA

Yeah girl. We're going to do about thirty minutes worth of shopping for the family . . . you know a tie, nail polish, socks, undies . . . same old same old. Then we'll spend the next three to a half hours REALLY shopping, if you know what I mean.

TABITHA

Yeah. For big bulging muscles.

VANNA

And pretty smiles.

TABITHA

And nice bodies.

RITA

O-o-o-oh-h-h!! C'mon child. Let's GO. The longer I stand here and talk about it, the more the idea of squeezing through over crowded mall and carrying stuffed bags filled with insignificant items appeals to me.

VANNA

I'm with you on that one!!! Tonto, get on your horse 'cause Lone Ranger is riding off into the sunset (Mimics riding her horse to the door then stops.) Well, posse, what you waiting for? There ain't no gold but there's a whole lot of pleasure in dem dare malls and um a' aiming at getting my fair share. Y'all come on now. Giddy up boy!! Giddy up!! (Enters Pipe nearly colliding with the 'horse riding' Vanna)

PIPES

Who in the world was that cowgirl, Sheriff? (Laughter)

TABITHA

That was one ready to go Christmas shopping woman.

PIPES

You can say that again. So, is that what you girls are about to do . . . go shopping?

TABITHA

Yeah. Just as soon as Grandma gets the molasses out of her body and decides to step it up so that we can get there before closing time.

HOPE

Listen, girls, I'm really not in the mall nor Christmas spirit. Okay? So why don't I just let you guys go ahead and enjoy yourselves. I'll talk with you when you get back, alright?

RITA

Of course not, Hope!! That's like a totally stupid idea. We're a team. Now you just get up and come on and let's go and enjoy the Christmas season together . . . you know . . . like the posse we are.

ALL

Yeah girl. Come on. What's up with all that pity?

HOPE

No. I'm not going to the mall.

RITA

But I though that was why you wanted us to come over, so we could all go shopping together . . . and just hang out.

TABITHA

Yeah. You know. Chill.

HOPE

Thanks posse. But . . . (crosses downstage) . . . well . . . (obvious difficulty with words) . . . I really called you here because I just needed someone to talk with (music) . . . not TO, but *with*. I just thought that maybe since we are a posse you guys would be the best ones in the world to understand what it is I'm feeling right now. I thought you'd be able to understand what I was seeing. I thought you could understand my thoughts. (Pause) I didn't need to shop. I didn't and I don't need the mall. I just needed a friend. That's all. A friend. Sorry I've spoiled the mood. I really didn't mean to. It's just that I'm not, you know . . . well, my family just doesn't have the money we need to buy the gifts we want to give so that we can be sure everybody gets something meaningful and something they want. The money's just not here. Besides, I live in a single parent home with two other sisters and brothers . . .

(sorrowfully) . . . and I can't buy them anything for Christmas. I mean, can't you see where I am? Can't you feel me? Can't you hear my heart? You guys are going to the mall to pick up some "insignificant" items. I can't even do that!! I can't pick up ANYTHING. I'm broke, Vanna. I'm busted, Rita. I'm disgusted, Tabitha. And all at Christmas time. Do you know how that makes me feel?

VANNA

Hope, girl, we're your posse! You're one of us. If we have . . . you have. We'll help you get your family something very special for Christmas.

TABITHA

You know it, Hope. Now stop this moping and (cowboy accent) let's get down to dat dare mall, partner.

VANNA

Don't worry about anything, Hope. We've got you covered. This will be the posse's gift to you. (Goes over and hugs Hope.) It's okay, Hope. Just remember God is good all the time and all the time God is good. So don't focus so hard on what you don't have, just be grateful for the things that you do have. You're still a lot better off than many people you know.

PIPES

There are many special and valuable things you could give to your family, Hope, that no one else can give but you . . . and you can afford them all.

HOPE

(Irritated) What on earth are you talking about, Pipes? You know better than they do what I mean when I say (EMPHATICALLY) WE ARE POOR PEOPLE!!

PIPES

(Calm) I know that, Hope. I've always known you were poor. But I've also always known that you are bigger than money. You are more powerful than sales at the mall. Your worth can never be wrapped up in a box. And your heart is too big and kind to ever be limited to just giving at Christmas. Like I told you earlier, everything I've said to you will make more sense after you've slept on it for a while. Trust me. It will. Girls, Hope really needs some time to herself to . . . sleep. Come on, if we hurry we can catch the next bus to the mall. See you when I get back, partner. (Girls wave and the group starts off R. Pipes stops, looks back.) Hope . . . just sleep. That's all you've gotta do. Just sleep. (Exits. Hope is visibly upset and depressed. Tosses her hat, coat, newspaper, etc . . . Glances at the couch. Does not move. Glances again. Goes over and reluctantly sits. Music. She reclines to a comfortable position and finally dozes off. Christmas angels appear and dance about the stage. They awaken her and she dances with them. Telepathically they communicate to Hope the true meaning of Christmas. The enlightenment is obvious. Hope's understanding is now opened and elevated. She is returned to the couch and completes her nap. The angles exit.)

ACT II

(Girls are re-entering onto the lower stage carrying the tons of packages they just purchased at the mall.)

VANNA

Child . . . child . . . child . . . . child . . . child!!! Honey, I say did ANYBODY see that fine-e-e-e looking brother standing at the cologne counter in Macy's? Honey did ANYBODY else see him except me and the Christmas ANGELS, child? Whew! Girl I'll tell y'all the truth. When I saw that tall, dark and handsome brother in those two sizes too small but fitting tight in all the right places Calvin Kline jeans, I think my whole nose just went on strike and just stopped working right there on the spot.

TABITHA

Listen, Sister Girl! Would you ever go in a fast food restaurant hungry and not notice the hamburgers?

VANNA

NO.

TABITH

Would you ever go in a jewelry shop and not look at the diamonds?

VANNA

Of course not.

TABITH

Would you ever go in the meat market and not look at the prime rib or the t-bones?

VANNA

For sure not.

TABITHA

Then why do you think we'd go in a mall and not check out the most valuable merchandise? You sound like you're trying to call us slow or something.

VANNA

(Pauses for a second. Then gets it.) Oh yeah!! Yeah. My bad. I guess forgot.

RITA

Forgot? Lord have mercy. How in the world can you forget something like that? (Emphatically and dramatically) Oh great and awesome powers of the universe I implore you to please help my poor homie, 'cause you know . . . sometimes she's with us, sometimes she's ahead of us . . . but most of the time . . .

ALL

She's just a little behind us. (Laughter)

TABITHA

(Pulling an unwrapped gift out of the bag and showing it off.) Hey! Check it out!! Cool, huh?

RITA

No cooler now than it was when you bought it in the mall.

VANNA

Rita, what's with you? I mean, you just weren't you old *flirtatious* self at the mall today and now you're acting and sounding all grumpy. What's up, sis? You uptight about something?

RITA

(Hesitates then pushes all of the shopping bags away. Finally . . .) Yeah. I guess I am and there's really no need to lie about it.

TABITHA

(Still somewhat jovial and bouncing on the bed as she speaks) OK. Go ahead. Spill your guts.

RITA

Spill my guts?

TABITHA

Yeah. Sure. Spill your guts. Talk. Get it out. Whatever the magic word is—just start doing it.

VANNA

(There's a long silent pause. The anxious girls grown impatient. Then . . .) HELLO!!! EARTH TO RITA!! EARTH TO RITA!! WE MERE MORTALS ARE WAITING FOR YOUR SHIP TO LAUNCH! 5 . . . 4 . . . 3 . . . 2 . . . 1 . . . . BLASTOFF! DO WE HAVE A SUCCESSFUL LIFTOFF? EARTH TO RITA PLEASE CONFIRM LIFTOFF . . . 'CAUSE WE'RE ALL SITTING HERE WAITING ON YOU, BOO!! GEEPERS, IS IT REALLY THAT HARD TO JUST TALK TO US?? WE'RE YOUR HOMIES!!

RITA

Naw . . . come on now, come on now. You know it's not hard for me to talk with you guys. And I'm not way out in deep space or anything like that.

VANNA

You couldda fooled me on that one!

RITA

I'm still here with y'all. It's just that I keep thinking about Hope. You know. I could feel what she was saying. I could actually understand it. Maybe even a whole lot better than any of you can. I mean . . . well, I just wish she wouldn't let things like that get her down. You know what I mean?

VANNA

Sure we do, G. I mean we're all down with my girl, but we can't help it if she doesn't want to go malling with the crew at Christmas time.

TABITHA

That's right.

VANNA

If you're so concerned, Rita, why didn't you say all of this *before* we went to the mall?

RITA

Timing. She needed her space and time to think and be alone and I didn't want to ruin that for her. (Pause) Hey, don't let me be a party pooper!! Y'all go ahead and gift wrap everything; I think I'll give old girl a call and see how she's perking over there. (Goes over and dials the phone. Pipes answers. The trio talks. The others continue to wrap gifts. Then with a combination of excitement Rita runs over to the others and announce . . .) You're never going to believe it!

ALL

(Very dry and sarcastically) Sure we will. We'll believe it. Try us.

RITA

Awww!! You three are sickening but anyway . . . I just talked with Pipes and Hopes and you wouldn't believe how happy Hope sounded. She almost blew me away over there on the phone. She wants us to come by right now.

ALL

Now?

RITA

Now!! Now!!! Now!!! Come on let's go!! (Pulling the others up) Said she had something very exciting . . . very . . . different . . . . very . . . .

TABITHA

Don't worry about it. We're coming. Right behind you!!

(They all grab their hats and coats and head out quickly to Hope's house. Exit. Lights.)

SCENE II

(The trio enters Hope's house, but Hope's voice can be heard long before they enter the door. Hope is gleefully and enthusiastically shouting instructions to Pipe as they put the finishing decorations on the Christmas tree. The remaining of the living room has already been transformed into a beautifully decorated Christmas visual. Hope is no longer depressed. Curtains draw open slowly as Hope shouts instructions to Pipe who is standing in a chair placing the star atop the tree.)

HOPE

Almost! Almost! (Pipes places the star atop the tree) Good! Perfect! You did it Pipes! Now that really looks like Christmas!! Whadda ya think, Pipes?

PIPES

(Turns and admires their work.) That's cool! That'll work. (Pauses glances at Hope then in a serious sounding voice . . .) Hey Hope! It's good to have you back, girl!

HOPE

Back? I never been anywhere?

PIPES

Well . . . in a way you did. I mean when you were depressed and all . . . you . . .

HOPE

(Waving her hand) AA-h-h forget it! I was just having a bad day, that's all. Feeling kind of sorry for myself, I guess. Sorry I put y'all through all that.

PIPES

Hey! What are friends for? Right? (There's a knock at the door. The three friends enter before Hope can say come in.)

RITA

Fear not, Sister Girl! It's just us royal women from the east again . . .

VANNA

Same old address too, east side of 4th Street.

RITA

For real, Honey . . . in the house!! (Stops and looks around. Appears shocked) UNNN! Unnn! Unnn! Check out the *scenery* in here!!! Out with it, girl!! What happened in here since we left?

VANNA

And what's up with all the gifts, Hope? (In an accusing tone) You went shopping and didn't even tell us!!

RITA

Oh man, Hope, now that's really low. We're suppose to be your home girls. We wouldn't go shopping and not tell you.

HOPE

And I didn't go shopping and not tell you either? That's why I asked you to come over here today. (The girls are all looking puzzled.)

VANNA

So what's in all those boxes? (Goes over to examine some of the boxes.)

PIPES

Nothing. All of them are empty.

VANNA

EMPTY?!!! Is that true Hope? Are you putting up all this decoration and wrapping *empty boxes* to give to people for Christmas?

TABITHA

(Interjecting quickly) Now Hope . . . no offense, sister girl . . . but if you answer that question with a yes . . . (shaking her head violently)then we've got a much bigger problem than we originally thought.

HOPE

But that's just it.

VANNA

What's it?

HOPE

They're not really *empty*. There's something in every one of them. You just can't see it . . . or feel it . . . or . . . you know . . . it's not something physical.

TABITHA

So-o-o (trying to figure this out in her head) . . . LET ME GET THIS RIGHT NOW . . . you're going to give somebody something for Christmas that they can't see or feel . . . or something that's not . . . as you put it . . . *physical*?

HOPE

(Enthusiastically) Right!! You're finally getting it, Tab!

TABITHA

Uhm-huh! Hometeam, I have heard enough. Girls, I there's a slight problem in this house . . . and I think it's name is Hope. But don't worry, it's nothing the old posse can't fix in a hurry though! HUDDLE UP!! (Raising her hand like the center on a football team) I think it's time to discuss the team's next play.

RITA

Chill!! Chill!! I know all of this sounds and looks crazy, but the truth is this (trying to explain) crazy stuff . . . all makes perfectly good sense to me.

TABITHA

(Falling back in a chair and holding her head) O-o-oh great wise men from the East!! Now there are TWO!

VANNA

With the same problem! What is this epidemic that's infesting our posse?

PIPES

Rita's right, girls. I thought all of this was silly too until I really thought about it, and now Hope's gifts make more sense to me than anything we bought at the mall today.

RITA

Listen, suppose . . . just suppose . . . we couldn't have gone to the mall today.

PIPES

And suppose you wanted to buy something for someone that you really loved but just didn't have the money.

RITA

How else would you let that person know how you were feeling about them deep down in your heart? I mean if you can't give a sweater, or cologne, or other things from the mall . . . if you could buy nothing at all because you were too poor . . . on Christmas day how would you let people know that you still loved and appreciate them? You see?

HOPE

And that's exactly what I'm doing. I'm giving something special to people who are very special to me. I'm giving what cannot be sold or bought. I'm giving what no one else can ever give for me. I'm giving a special piece of me. (Silence. Then . . .) Pipes, give Rita, Vanna and Tabitha those boxes we put aside for them. (Pipes quickly retrieves the boxes, returns and distributes them as told.) I saved these for you all. I thought you might want to share a special gift with someone too.

VANNA

But I don't know how to do this, Hope. I mean, I'm use to going to the mall and you know . . . wham! bam! thank you ma'am! I'm done with Christmas shopping. Now let me go . . . *shopping*!

PIPES

(Casually waves off the last remark and begins to explain.) Don't worry about it. I'll show you. I have a couple of boxes to fill with special gifts too. Come on. I'll show you how to do it. It's fun. You'll see. (They exit)

HOPE

Oh, this is going to be the greatest Christmas I've ever had in my entire life! It's so good to finally know what Christmas is really all about. (Music. A Christmas angel enters and dances with Hope again. The duo finishes the dance and the angel exits just as the others are entering.)

TABITHA

(Hope is still staring at the door through which the angel exited.) Hope! Hope! HOPE!!

HOPE

(Jumps) Oh! Oh! What?

RITA

We're done. What's the matter? You look as if you just saw a ghost.

HOPE

Well it wasn't exactly a ghost (as if in a trance, but it was the closest thing to it I've ever seen.

PIPES

This was really fun, Hope (placing the gifts around the tree).

VANNA

It was more than fun. It taught us a lot about the real meaning of Christmas.

TABITHA

Yeah, I can't wait until Christmas morning to present mine.

RITA

I can't either. (Goes over to Hope) I knew the meaning of Christmas was changing deep down inside for me too, Hope. I just didn't know how. Now I do. I feel so much better now.

VANNA

I think we all do.

PIPES

Hey, how about a little Christmas music before all y'all go and get teary eyed on me.

RITA

I heard that, G. Turn out the tunes and let's see what piping, PIPES.

(Pipes goes over and turns on the radio. The DJ is announcing . . .) Once again we're coming at you loud and strong from WUVS station 101.1 on your radio dial where all the Carver Cats tune in daily to hear the latest from the very best the music world has to offer. And speaking of the very best, ladies and gentlemen, once again here's Maria Carey with the old Wildcat Christmas favorite . . . All I WANT FOR CHRISTMAS IS YOU!!! (The girls look at each other in shock. Skirmish around to find make shift microphones and begin pantomiming to the song. Curtains. Music gradually fades.)

ACT III

Curtains re-open to cast members comfortably seated on stage. (A) cast member approaches the center stage and begins the following speeches:

CAST MEMBER 1

Act III of this play is no act at all. Rather, it is both the perfect opportunity and the perfect time for each of us to present to someone very special in our life, a unique and precious Christmas gift that we wish them to have and that only we can give them.

CAST MEMBER 2

These are all special gifts that we are presenting out of our hearts and not out of the lines of a theatrical script. We make these offerings tonight of our own personal volitions and desires and with no enticement, encouragement, or compelling from anyone other than ourselves and our hearts.

CAST MEMBER 3

We make these presentations to the individuals chosen because of their significance to us and in our lives. Ironically, in all the years we have been around them, we have habitually failed to publicly reward their diligence, dedication, love, and emotional resilience and support.

CAST MEMBER 4

But tonight is their big night as we will make our heartfelt presentations to individuals whom we personally believe to be some of the most deserving of praise and recognition individuals in the world. Ladies and gentlemen, our special presentations.

This play has been created, written and is presented in a unique format. The final act of this play is no act at all. It is the realizations of Hope's enlightenment. In Act III of this play each cast member comes center stage, requests the presence of a special individual to join him/her on stage, removes his/her special gift from beneath the tree, has the recipient open it and reads aloud to the audience his/her unique Christmas presentation to that individual. This makes this play unique as it never lends itself to the same ending no matter how often it is performed. Likewise, it permits every cast member, regardless of differences or rationales an equal opportunity to present his/her most personal and memorable gift to anyone in the world s/he wishes without an associated monetary cost. Written specifically for a group of young kids, below are some of the gifts they presented during the one and only performance of this play. Note the absence of gifts to fathers. That is because all cast members were from single parent homes. Cast members are reminded that the following presentations are only samples and can but do not have to be considered as a part of their presentations. The beauty and power of this script is that it permits the cast to actively participate in the writing of its ending with each production of it and that it provides a public venue whereby thanks and admiration may be acknowledged, presented and received.

CURTAINS

MOM, I SEARCHED AND THOUGHT AND SEARCHED AND THOUGHT SOME MORE WHEN I WAS ASKED WHAT UNIQUE GIFT I WOULD LIKE TO PRESENT TO YOU TODAY. REALLY, I DIDN'T KNOW WHAT TO GIVE. AND SO, I ASKED MYSELF WHAT IS IT THAT I WOULD LIKE FOR YOU TO HAVE THAT COULD LAST YOU A LIFETIME, AND THAT ONLY I COULD GIVE IT TO YOU. AFTER THINKING AND SEARCHING AND THINKING AND SEARCHING, I DECIDED TO GIVE YOU THIS "GUARANTEE OF ETERNAL LOVE." AND IT READS AS FOLLOWS:

MOM, I'LL ALWAYS LOVE YOU, NO MATTER WHAT COMES OUR WAY.

I WILL BELIEVE IN YOU ALWAYS AND GOVERN MY LIFE BY THE THINGS YOU DO AND SAY.

I WILL NEVER ALLOW ANYTHING TO DISRUPT, DIMINISH, OR DESTROY MY FAITH IN YOU,

BECAUSE YOU'RE NOT ONLY MY MOTHER; YOU'RE THE KEEPER OF MY HEART TOO.

YOU'RE MY COMPASSION AND STRENGTH AND WISDOM AND GRACE,

YOU'RE MY LANTERN DURING DARK TIMES AND MY GUIDE IN THIS HUMAN RAT RACE.

YOU KEEP ME FOCUSED AND PRAYED UP AND WILL NEVER LET ME QUIT

AND FOR ALL OF THIS AND MORE, THIS DAY, I COMMIT

TO LOVE YOU DEARLY AND ETERNALLY WITH ALL MY HEART AND ALL THAT I AM AND SHALL EVER BE,

THIS COVENANT I GLADLY ENTER INTO TO BE KEPT IN MY HEART ETERNALLY.

I, _____, PRESENT THIS GUARANTEE OF ETERNAL LOVE TO MY MOTHER, _____, ON THIS ____ DAY OF _____ IN THE YEAR OF OUR LORD _____.

GOD BLESS YOU, MOM AND I LOVE YOU WITH ALL MY HEART.

SIGNED _____

MOTHER IS A STRANGE TERM

IT DOESN'T ALWAYS MEAN THE ONLE WHO GIVES BIRTH.

SOMETIMES IT MEANS THE ONE WHO LISTENS, THE ONE WHO TALKS, THE ONE WHO CARES, THE ONE WHO GUIDES, THE ONE WHO LOVES, THE ONE WHO TEACHERS OTHERS HOW TO LOVE.

IN MY LIFE, YOU ARE THAT PERSON. THOUGH NOT BY BIRTH, GOD HAS STILL GIVEN ME THE MOST WONDERFUL MOTHER I COULD EVER HAVE KNOWN. IF I HAD BUT ONE WISH TO BE GRANTED BY THE ALMIGHTY ONE, IT WOULD BE THAT I TURN OUT TO BE HALF THE PERSON THAT YOU ARE.

THANK YOU FOR ALL YOU'VE DONE OVER THE YEARS FOR SOMEONE WHOM YOU NEVER BIRTHED. BUT, THEN TOO, THAT'S JUST YOU ISN'T IT? HAD IT NOT BEEN ME, YOU WOULD HAVE FOUND ANOTHER CHILD FROM SOMEWHERE TO LOVE JUST AS YOU DID ME. IT'S BECAUSE OF YOUR ABILITY TO LOVE SO PURELY AND DEEPLY THAT I IN TURN LOVE YOU THE SAME WAY.

THANK YOU . . . THAT'S WHAT I WANT TO PUBLICLY GIVE TO YOU TONIGHT AND THIS CHRISTMAS SEASON . . . MY MOST HEART FELT THANKS . . . FOR YOUR PRESENCE, INFLUENCE AND UNCONDITIONAL LOVE IN MY LIFE.

THANK YOU . . . I LOVE YOU . . . AND MERRY CHRISTMAS FROM MY HEART.

MOM,

YOU'RE THERE FOR ME AS EACH NEW DAY BEGINS
YOU'RE THERE FOR ME AS EACH OLD DAY ENDS
YOU'RE THERE FOR ME WHEN I HURT AND DARE NOT CRY
YOU'RE RIGHT THERE EACH TIME I SMILE, EACH TIME I SIGH.

YOUR LISTENING EAR HAS NEVER EVER BEEN FOUND TURNED
AWAY
YOUR KIND AND LOVING WORDS ARE MY STRENGTH TO MAKE
IT THROUGH ANOTHER DAY
YOUR TENDER TOUCH IS MY REASSURANCE THAT ALL WILL BE
WELL
YOUR EVERLASTING FAITH DEMONSTRATES TO ME THAT I TOO
CAN PREVAIL

AND SO TONIGHT I GIVE YOU . . . MY HONOR AND ADMIRATION.
FOR I KNOW OF NO ONE ELSE IN THE WORLD WHO COULD DO
ALL THE WONDERFUL THINGS THAT YOU DO . . . DAY IN AND
DAY OUT . . . AND ALWAYS . . . WITHOUT ONE COMPLAINT OR
EXPECTATION IN RETURN.

I TRULY THANK GOD THAT GOD CHOSE YOU TO BE MY MOTHER.
GOD BLESS YOU. I LOVE YOU AND CAN ONLY PRAY THAT OTHERS
WILL BE BLESSED WITH A MOTHER AS WONDERFUL AS YOU.

MOM,

THERE ARE SO MANY DIFFERENT GIFTS I COULD HAVE CHOSEN TO GIVE YOU THIS TIME OF YEAR THAT I NEARLY LOST MYSELF TRYING TO THINK OF WHICH ONE TO CHOOSE. SUDDENLY, I REMEMBERED SOMETHING I HAD BEEN TOLD MANY TIMES BEFORE AND SOMETHING THAT YOUR VERY ACTIONS PROVE TO ME EACH DAY. AND THAT IS, THAT THE MOST PRECIOUS THING IN THE WORLD TO GOOD, KIND, CARING AND LOVING PARENTS IS THEIR CHILDREN.

AND SO THIS CHRISTMAS, I HAVE CHOSEN TO GIVE YOU NOT CLOTHES, FRAGRANCES, MAKE-UP OR ANYTHING LIKE THAT. INSTEAD I HAVE CHOSEN TO PRESENT TO YOU . . . THAT WHICH IS MOST PRECIOUS TO ME . . . AND THAT IS MY HEART. THIS CHRISTMAS I AM PRESENTING TO YOU MY HEART AND ASKING YOU TO BECOME THE PERMANENT KEEPER OF IT.

FOR ALL THAT A PERSON IS COMES OUT OF HIS HEART. AND SINCE I KNOW THAT IT IS YOU WHO ARE RESPONSIBLE FOR SO MUCH OF WHAT IS IN MY HEART, I'M SIMPLY ASKING YOU TO SAFEGUARD IT WITH YOUR LOVE, PROTECT IT WITH YOUR PRUDENCE OF WISDOM, AND FOSTER IT WITH THE STRENGTH OF YOUR LOVE.

THE HEART IS CONSIDERED OUR MOST VITAL ORGAN. WITHOUT IT, SURELY THERE WOULD BE NO US. YOU ARE CONSIDERED THE MOST VITAL PERSON IN MY LIFE. WITHOUT YOU THERE WOULD BE NO ME. I CAN THINK OF NO ONE ELSE IN THE WORLD WHOM I WOULD PREFER TO SAFEGUARD THAT WHICH KEEPS ME ALIVE EACH DAY.

BUT YOU . . . I OFFER IT TO. AND NOT JUST BECAUSE I TRUST YOU WITH IT. BUT MORE IMPORTANTLY, BECAUSE I LOVE YOU WITH IT. TAKE CARE OF MY HEART, MOM . . . BECAUSE A BIG PEACE OF YOU IS IN IT. I LOVE YOU, MOM . . . WITH ALL MY HEART.